HOW I PAID TRIBUTE TO MICHAEL JACKSON

The story of Michael Forever The Tribute Concert.

By
Andy Picheta

For the fans of Michael: You were right

PREFACE

The legal battle between a major financier of Michael Forever and Chris Hunt and Michael Henry ended this week, and at the time of writing both sides now await judgment. The two producers of the show were accused by QuickDraw, an entertainment investment fund, of Breach of Trust, Dishonest Assistance, and Knowing Receipt. Chris Hunt's company, Iambic Media, was accused of Breach of Copyright for making TV programmes of Michael Forever from materials belonging to QuickDraw. Judgment is expected in a few weeks.

Once the result of QuickDraw v GLE LLP, Hunt and Henry is handed down, two more separate actions against the UK founders of Global Live Events are expected to commence. Warner Chappell will be looking for judgment that the injunction they slapped on the live TV transmission was justified, and film financiers Octopus will be vigorously seeking an explanation of how some of their money, from a development fund administered by the pair, got swallowed up by the concert.

And so the saga of this tribute concert to the King of Pop rumbles through the courts, a trail of accusation and recrimination, a husk of a dream crushed under the weight of legal submissions and evidence bundles. However it ends, it won't be pretty. Here's the story of how it started.

I hope you understand, and smile now and again.
Andy Picheta, London, May 2012

Introduction
"It doesn't matter who's wrong or who's right"

Even if you can't see it, you can always tell when the shit is hitting the fan. My name is Andy Picheta and I own a rather nice hotel in the Highlands of Scotland. For a brief moment in the middle of 2011 however, I found myself deep within the hellstorm of intrigue, lies, deceit, hate and vitriol that is a sad part of the true legacy of Michael Jackson. Sitting here now, looking out over the November blaze of colour in the forests that surround my Scottish highland hotel, watching eagles lazily circle over fields, I feel I have emerged, scathed but unbowed, from some medieval siege of blood. As I survey the carnage that surrounds and is *Michael Forever* – the craters of legal disputes, the rubble of broken promises and unpaid bills, the glinting studs here and there of a few perfect blooms, the gems of memorable, unrepeatable and in some cases amazing performances – I can think only to write it all down, to try and make some sense of the stream of middle earth fire that even now cascades around the event and threatens to consume everything in its path.

It's a cathartic exercise for me, of course, but I also think the MJ fans deserve to know what went on. Some fans came to the show, despite the waves of hate that surrounded it, and had a great time, saw some great and some not-so-great performances of Michael's music, and went home happy. That was the mission, to put on an entertainment, and in part, in that respect, *Michael Forever* succeeded. Other fans felt let down, disappointed and even betrayed, although this last emotion belongs more fairly to the hundreds who worked on the show and, like me, remain unpaid. They too, should know what went down, why it failed, and who failed them.

It is only from the relative safety of my ten acres of Scotland, protected by two ageing Highland cows and a drive that will shortly be impassable through snow, that I can begin to unravel the maelstrom of a very surreal time. For me it was a revisiting of a previous career, a re-finding of a sudden spurt of raw power and energy that seemed to surprise no one but myself. It was one hundred and twenty days of pulling, dragging, kicking and, by sheer will and determination, eventually midwifing the birth of a scrapping, bawling, brawling, scrawling bastard of an aberration that perhaps should never have been allowed to live at all.

It seems quite dreamlike now, of course, and were it not for the emails from the unpaid, the phone-calls from the concerned, and the letters from the angry, I could almost write the whole thing off as a figment of my still febrile imagination. But the emails are there, from February 2011 to now, making up 53% of all the emails that Google expects me to ever receive in my lifetime. I should re-read them all to delve back into the detail of what happened. But there are so many – 17,012 in fact – that I'll probably just use them as a resource, dip in and out, to highlight and underscore. I'll include a few that waypoint the way. Any typos in them are not mine, unless of course I wrote the email. If I read them all again I'll probably burst into tears for what might have been.

Sadly, the option to sift and choose was not available during the run up to the show. I'm sure there are powerful email sorting programs with clickey buttons to aid all manner of sorting and clicking and highlighting, but for me, computer born and raised with MS-DOS and a blinking green cursor, such buttons are never highlighted enough. So the deluge of messages in the run up to the show merely showed up the limitations of email as a communications tool. At least to me. When there are hundreds coming in every day, twenty or thirty an hour, the volume of the flood often buries the important. The email you need has dropped down to page three of the inbox before you've even seen it, hidden by layers of stuff and Groupon vouchers.

"I sent you an email!" was an oft-heard cry on the phone – well so did three hundred others on that day. Sorry. Must have missed it. Unfortunately, some of those missed in this way were important – an urgent meeting, a conference call in one hour, a time sensitive demand for payment – all of them buried in an avalanche of "forwards" and "copies" and "fyi"s. Ten minutes spent formulating a considered reply to one email meant half a dozen messages arriving whilst doing so – one or more of them sometimes making the considered reply being drafted redundant. Blimey – what a way to work!

So what was a highland hotelier doing on a, perhaps "The", Michael Jackson tribute concert? How did twelve bedrooms in the Cairngorm Mountains become a master suite at the Intercontinental Hotel in London? Why Michael Jackson? Why Cardiff? Why me? And why did it all go so terribly wrong? The road to hell is paved with good intentions; none piled more high than the corpses around *Michael Forever*. The answers to what happened lie in the characters I met along the way, and the way they interplay and overlap, and in some cases underplay and interlap. Some are key and others incidental, some are funny and others mean, some did their best and others took the piss, and together they form as good a narrative path as any.

So here it is, laid before you as I experienced it. It's by no means the whole story, but it is mine. The timeline is sometimes bent, characters combined, or abridged, and this story is far from the total truth. It's my recollection; flawed and incomplete but worth telling. How it will end I cannot know; this tale is still stuttering to its conclusion of either the realisation of a worthy tribute, or an unwatched non-film in the trim bin of history.

CHAPTER 1.
CHRIS

Foolish of me, I couldn't see
The forest for the trees

With perseverance, the snail reached the ark. It is pertinent to what happened on *Michael Forever* to go back to the beginning. It may amuse you too. So I'll start with how I met Chris Hunt, and why. But first, a peep into the world of hospitality.

I bought a hotel in 2007, seeking a re-balancing of the self away from the uncertainty of producing shows for TV, away from the fast lane, the cut-and-thrust of Soho media life, to a more tranquil, measured way of being. I had been through much, lived a lot, and was ready for a little bit of peace and quiet. I wanted a life of a landowner with a big house, a well-stocked bar and fine wine cellar, all funded (because I sure couldn't afford it) by like-minded guests paying a fortune to momentarily glimpse and experience what I had. Unfortunately I could only afford such a lordly paradise in the Highlands of Scotland, where land is cheap and bucks get lots of bang. It was all going swimmingly too, a parade of lords and Dukes and bankers and wankers, until the banks fell over and suddenly nobody had any money.

The high end customers disappeared, replaced by low end bargain hunters with top end expectations but zero understanding of what they were getting. Our carefully crafted menus for instance, full of amazing local produce, were rejected for items from our new and hastily constructed bistro offerings such as burgers and fries or, worse still, for take-in fish and chips from the local chippy (brought in by the guests I add, not served by us as our own), that stank out the rooms and left stale cooking oil aromas drifting around the hall. This I found particularly galling, as I'd invested a lot of time and money to make sure that our public areas never, ever, smelled of stale cooking. This one area of focus went further than any other to distinguish us from other Scottish hotels. The guests however, distinguished themselves only by how much they annoyed me. One extended family of pasty vegetarians, on receiving a specially crafted feast of roasted vegetables, smoked paprika nut rissoles and vibrant red pepper and tomato salads, complained that the food was "too orange". When asked what they wanted, they chorused "macaroni cheese". When they got exactly that, they still complained, from the checked-out safety of TripAdvisor, that "we had to make our own menus up". My preferred vegetarian option – "don't come" – was dismissed out of hand by The Better (Rebecca, my long-suffering better half).

We invested many tens of thousands in renovation, redecoration and improvement. We replaced clashing tartan carpets – two different plaids, neither complimenting the other, with new oak floors (complaint: not Scottish enough). We built a huge terrace, complete with flaming torches that were hardly ever lit (too windy), canvas sun awnings that were torn to shreds in gales (in July), and outdoor furniture that rotted in the perpetual rain (in June, July and August). Every bedroom got a make-over, every public room a restyling away from tired tartan and dreadful doilies toward something modern, chic and stylish. It was worth doing for the pre-crash, pre-credit crunch guests, because we could point at the sculpted bay trees and charge accordingly. (Until the first -20 frost killed them. Then we had to discount for a lack of bay trees, sculpted or not.)

Not all of those high-end guests, of course, were full of the joys of staying at the hotel, ready to shower thanks and compliments for their good fortune. Some were pretty obnoxious. I remember one shooting party, with us for the grouse in late August, as a particularly nasty bunch of tossers. He was a hedge fund manager, up with his three Harrovian sons and some "friends" he was no doubt trying to impress. They began in the bar, complaining that the ice cubes weren't round enough, moved to the restaurant moaning that the wine was rubbish and not red enough (excuse me, but there ain't nothing wrong with a Clos de Beze Geverey Chambertin, on my list at the time at £150 for the 2003 – a bargain), and the food pretentious crap and portions too small or too big, or too cold or too hot. Then they returned to the bar to drink a barrel of Stella, which the young Harrovians later vomited back into their bed sheets. Their three day stay ended with an argument over the bill. They objected most to the £45 charge for the bottle of sloe gin they'd ordered with their picnic lunch.

"It's only about six quid in the shops," they moaned, quoting a price from 1982 when they last had hair and abs. Now call me short-fused, but this argument, that something is "cheaper in the shops", drives me round the twist.

Well bugger off out of my hotel, drive the 28 miles to the nearest sloe gin shop, buy the gin, drive down the road to the glassware store and buy something to drink it out of, then eventually turn up to your twenty-five grand a day, four grand an hour, grouse shoot three hours late, you sneery, wanky conceited, arrogant, odious poo person. That'll cost you, in fuel and missed grouse shooting, around eleven thousand pounds. Instead and for your own convenience you've asked me to drive to the gin shop, get you the gin, get some sparkling crystal ware and linen napkins, place them in a very posh wicker picnic basket, and then sort out the rubbish on your return. Forty-five quid for that kind of service doesn't seem that pricey to me, in fact I've just saved you £10,955, but what do I know?

Perhaps they would have paid for the gin if I hadn't put "Vomit cleaning charge £50" against the two rooms occupied by the offspring. They couldn't argue with that one.

The upgrading of the hotel was however, a waste of money for the Aberdonian benefit-scroungers that came post-credit crunch. They made the shooting party with the Sloe vomit seem positively angelic. One happy group, from Glasgow rather than the Granite City (but sharing attitude and outlook), presented a sub species of human entirely unknown to me before starting this hotel lark.

Father, daughter, wife and husband, together with small baby-sized sprog, turned up just after Christmas. The ground was covered by two feet of snow. Front and rear drives had been plowed and gritted, but the temperature was dropping down to around minus eighteen at night, so the salt was ineffective, and our roadways were covered by sheet ice. Vehicular access to the hotel was impossible, even by towing up the hill with our 4x4 Beast, as we called our Nissan Pathfinder.

One of them, I can't remember which but I think it was the young husband, walked into reception and told us his Vauxhall Stigmata was stuck down by the road. I drove down in the Beast, spent ten freezing minutes waiting while they searched for their tow hook and then tried to haul them up. The ice defeated the traction and the spinning wheels scattered the applied grit. Giving up, I directed them along the main road to the village hall car park. I had cleared this of snow the previous day, and was unofficially using it as the hotel overspill car park.

Once they had parked I loaded them and their bags into the Beast and returned to the hotel. Without the weight of the

Vauxhall we made it up the hill without difficulty. Assuring them that the shuttle service was available on demand, I settled them into their two superior rooms and went off to do something else.

Soon the bell on the front desk was rung, quite vigorously. Some guests are quite timid with this device, embarrassed to be summoning service they would gently tinkle it, half hoping nobody will hear. Others give it a good thrashing, full of either bonhomie or anger – you could never tell from the ring but from the facial expression that greeted you on emerging from 'the back of stairs'. This lot were neither angry nor bonhomious. They brusquely informed me that they wanted to invite his son, who lived locally, for a family meal at the hotel. The father, grey hair but black eyebrows which appeared several seconds before he did, required my assistance in preparing this event. The son, he explained, had married an Indian woman, and her parents were in the area too. Would it be possible, he asked, for the meal to be served in two separate rooms, because he did not wish to sit at the same table as the Indians. Charming bloke.

And would it be possible, he went on to enquire, if this meal could cost less than ten pounds per person? Charming Scottish bloke. His scrawny, life battered wife stood silently by, half a step behind him. His daughter, harsh yet quite pretty (pretty harsh?) minded the sprog and her husband was nowhere to be seen. Maybe he was part Indian too? I declined his suggestions as politely as I could, and he went away, no doubt to research the other segregated dining options available in the area for under a tenner.

Later, they needed to get to their car to drive to a nearby restaurant. Slightly annoyed at ferrying my own guests so they could spend money at a restaurant other than mine, I nevertheless bit my tongue and shipped them down to the village. My annoyance increased however, when three hours later they wanted shipping back. I had just sat down to supper, but I pulled on boots and headed down to get them. I bundled them in and drove back, as fast as I could and mindful of my cooling dinner.

A day or so on, and they were checking out. (They'd had the family lunch, but without the son or the Indian side of the family.) The daughter questioned the service charge. They wanted the bill split three ways (Three? Was the sprog paying separately?) Eyebrows wanted a discount, because his car was not available to him outside the hotel. She wanted money off because the warm milk freely provided for the child was too warm. He was very upset because my driving was reckless, and there had been a skid at one point during one shuttle. The toast was cold. There was too much snow. The room was too hot. They continued to trot out spurious nonsense in an obviously rehearsed and pre-planned way. I began to visualise them in their rooms, or perhaps driving really slowly in their Vauxhall Chlamydia, preparing for this moment with lists and diary entries and photo evidence. Unfortunately for them it wasn't working. I saw no reason to discount them anything, and Eyebrows got angrier and angrier. The daughter, a heartless thin slab of female right off the old block, steamed in too, citing motherhood and outrage in equal measure. The wife was silent, and seemed to shrink as Father's voice rose. The young husband busied himself with the bawling product of his loins, and contributed nothing but steaming embarrassment and perhaps a growing fear of what he had married into.

The row brought The Better out from the kitchen, where

she spends days baking the most amazing cakes you will ever taste. She quietly led me away, and then took Eyebrows into the bar. She offered him eighty five pounds off the bill, so getting rid of them from our reception area and the hotel. They marched down the icy drive, struggling with suitcases and bairn and carrycot and anger. A fresh fall of snow had blocked them in at the village hall, and they had to dig out their car by hand. I had driven down to watch all this, and when I had my full of their discomfort I executed a perfect 180° handbrake turn, returned to the hotel, and took the £85 using his credit card details supplied on check in.

Unsavouries like these and the constant moaning ("Breakfast is supposed to be at eight, and it's now three minutes past and I've nae had any"), made me quickly see that hoteliering at the lower end of the market was no fun at all. So I amused myself by reprinting the breakfast menus, replacing "full Scottish" with "full English" and scoffing silently as the Glaswegians either spat the words out between clenched teeth or, more commonly, listed each item they wanted on their plate individually, rather than speak the filthy name of the country just to the south and which has owned their miserable tartan arses since bailing them out in 1707.

"D'yae nae have any potato scones?"

"No I fucking don't. I refuse to slap some disgusting starchy cardboard on your plate of bacon, egg, sausage, black pudding mushroom and tomato, just as I refuse to rename the dish "Scottish" by so doing. So piss off."

I thought of mining the car park to blow them up on the way in, and tripwires from the chandeliers to garrotte them on the way out, of harvesting their credit card details without ever letting them come, of fining them for being low-lifes. Not that I could ever complete any such plan, as I was forever getting interrupted by some Scottish idiot wanting a room for 58p. It once took three days to hang a barometer, which immediately set itself to stormy and stayed there. I was in danger of becoming Basil Fawlty, but with guns.

So when friend and long-time employer Chris Hunt rang me in early 2011, telling me that he may have a Michael Jackson concert and would I be interested in getting involved, it didn't take me long (about a nano-second actually) to say yes. I had no idea what I was letting myself in for, but even if I had, that "yes" would have still shot from my mouth like the well-aimed globulet of hope it was.

My last effort with Chris had been on *King Lear* in 2008. Ian MacKellen's considered interpretation, helmed by the irascible Trevor Nunn for the RSC and lauded by the critics, went before the cameras at Pinewood Studios in January. Chris, together with Richard Price, was producer and also, together with Trevor Nunn, director of the TV. This uncomfortable triumvirate became increasingly bitter during the shoot, as Trevor resented Richard for supporting Chris as co-director, seeing no need for any assistance with transposing "his" stage play to the screen. Chris in turn seethed at Trevor who did nothing to hide his anger and contempt, and Richard became increasingly frustrated with Trevor for failing to see the existing structure in a positive way.

As line producer I did what I always do, which is make the thing happen. Pushing shit uphill seems to be my specialty, and although a miserable time was had by all, I still got to direct the sword fight scene, because both Trevor and Chris were unavailable and – I like to think and perhaps kid myself – both knew I'd make a quick and efficient job of it.

I first came across Trevor Nunn when producing *Cats* for

Andrew Lloyd Webber. ALW had just parted company with his long term business partner Patrick McKenna, and was determined to prove he could do the business himself. Andrew agreed to employ me on *Cats* because he had heard good things about me from his manager of the moment John Reid, who famously managed Elton John, but had also managed Michael Flatley, whose show *Lord of the Dance* I had filmed. If this paragraph reads a bit like a treatment for a TV show called *Connections*, where the gestation of some popular programme is shown to link to many others through names and characters common to all, it's because that's what the business is: who you know, what you've done, and who knows you for doing it.

Andrew did a quick deal with PolyGram for a *Cats* DVD, and then found himself facing opprobrious opposition from the show's director, Trevor Nunn and designer, John Napier. An added complication was the animated movie deal with Paramount that Andrew's Hollywood producer, Gary Lucchesi, had negotiated a couple of years previously. Choreographer Gillian Lynne was the only member of the creative team to actively support the filming, leading Trevor to bemoan that *Cats* would be "turned into a fucking dance show". At an incredibly acrimonious meeting in the bright luxury of the Really Useful Group's conservatory meeting room, Trevor insisted the timing was wrong, Napier banged his chest intoning "nonsense, nonsense" to the rhythm of his blows, and Gary Lucchesi looked paler and paler as he vainly searched for somewhere to hide. The luvvies were getting the upper hand and Gillian was close to tears. It fell to me, as Andrew had absented himself and no other executives of the Really Useful Group seemed to be available, to push the thing through, insist it was what Andrew wanted, and give Gary some backbone to stop him caving. He rallied, we won the day, and the thing got made, how and when Andrew wanted. Cart of ordure delivered to pinnacle as required. Please sign here for one quite well executed dance show. (Come on Trev, although Shakespeare may be in everything, not everything is always Shakespeare.) *Cats* sold over five million videos around the world, gave Andrew belief in the medium, and gave me three years of gainful employment at the Really Useful Group, producing Lloyd Webber's birthday celebration for ITV (Andrew and 5000 of his closest friends at the Royal Albert Hall) and *Joseph and the Amazing Technicolor School Play* (or something).

It was whilst in pre-production for the latter show that I took a call from someone wanting to produce a video version of *Oklahoma!* Since *Cats* there had been several of these, and the conversation usually went like this:

"Hi, you produced *Cats* which sold millions of units and I'd like to talk to you about filming my musical, *Victorian Earthenware Pottery* which has had rave reviews and has sold out the Stourbridge Playhouse for nearly six days."

"Yes, *Cats* was very successful but also very expensive to produce to the level required to generate such success. The budget was considerable."

Over three million quid actually – a lot of it because having shot the thing in a theatre, Andrew decided it would be better if it didn't *look* like it was in a theatre. It was a very clever decision and one that undoubtedly contributed to the feeling of the story unfolding within a special feline space, and thereby helped the success of the piece commercially, because the audience believed it and bought into the construct. For me, at the time, it meant two months running between virtually every post-production house in Soho, painting out everything that looked "theatre" – lights, edge of set, dozing stage managers, and so on. Frame by frame.

This was in the mid-nineties, when computer graphics equipment had one twentieth of the power available today. But back to the calls:

"Ah, well we hope you can help us with *Vee-Eee-Pee*, as we like to call it. We have a budget of fifty eight pounds. Could you do something at that level?"

"At that level I can hang up. Goodbye."

"It's somebody called Chris Hunt," said my assistant one sunny afternoon, "he wants to talk to you about filming a musical."

I took the call, weary by now and looking to be quite inventive in my description of what, exactly, I could achieve for the paltry sum they believed would bring them world domination of the musical video market.

"My name is Chris Hunt, you produced *Cats* which was very successful and I want to talk to you about filming *Oklahoma!*"

"Yes, *Cats* was very successful but also very expensive to produce to the level required to generate such success. The budget was considerable. What level of budget do you have?"

"Well, I have three million pounds, possibly three point two. Could you do something at that level?"

"When can we meet?"

Oklahoma! was enjoying a very successful run at the National Theatre. It starred pre-Wolverine Hugh Jackman, and was directed by none other than Trevor Nunn. The film producer finding the money was Richard Price. The film producer looking to help Trevor co-direct a multi camera show was Chris Hunt, and the guy who had actually produced and directed multi camera shows before was me. I alerted Chris to my previous dealings with Trevor, where I had pushed Cats into production despite his concerns, and learned that Trevor bore me no ill will for so doing. His royalty from the video sales would in any case have assuaged his upset, although it's never about the money for those who have lots.

Sky Movies funded most of *Oklahoma!*, and the film still plays on their channels at Christmas. Chris and I got on, Chris and Trevor got on, and Richard found some money a couple of years later to do *Merchant of Venice* with the same team. This time however, some cracks between Chris and Trevor started to appear early on.

The interplay between the two men is interesting for any number of reasons, and very relevant to this story. Trevor Nunn was and is one of Britain's most successful theatre directors, known measure for measure for Shakespeare and musicals. He brings a huge and focused intellect to the work at hand, dissecting, digging, exploring the text, drilling down to the syllables themselves, then dragging the meanings into the open, placing everything within the narrative stream, and pouring it into his vessels – the actors. Some directors work with the actors and others on the creative team (designers, choreographers etc.) in a collaborative way, exploring and arriving at a sense of the thing together, as equals on a journey of discovery. Trevor Nunn is not one of these, not as far as the bulk of the cast is concerned. His encyclopaedic knowledge, vast intellect and huge commercial success have combined to create a massive self-belief and confidence that brooks very little debate. If some argument does arise, the view which prevails is always Trevor's.

Some actors enjoy his softly spoken direction of steel. Others less so. I witnessed an extraordinary explosion by one of the leading cast of *Merchant of Venice*, about a week into the shoot.

"You fucking martinet, how fucking DARE you treat me

like some stage school child!" he screamed, much to the bemusement of the film crew and embarrassment of the rest of the cast. Trevor, tight lipped, turned and walked off the set. The actors found a sudden and deep fascination with buttons and other costume accessories, the crew polished bits of cameras that needed no polishing, and the floor manager looked at me beseechingly. I suggested an early break for lunch. I thought Trevor would be angry at such a blatant contempt for the director, but he was quite sanguine about it:

"It's been a long time coming, and David has many issues with the role," he said calmly when I asked him about it later. I don't think he was being forgiving though, but once again supremely and untouchably confident in what he was doing.

Other glimpses into the cast's opinion of their director included snide asides, tongues poked out at Trevor's back, and much bitchiness in those two repositories of a thespian's angst: the make-up and wardrobe rooms. The stars however, Ian MacKellen, Henry Goodman, Hugh Jackman – all deliver amazing performances in Trevor Nunn-directed plays. It's the second row that tends to moan, it's the B team that has the issues, and it's mediocrity that Trevor struggles with, and I think that's what he saw in Chris – a mediocre film-maker somehow elevated to a position where he could see himself as Trevor's intellectual and creative equal, much to Trevor's bemusement and later anger. So that's Trevor Nunn – man of genius, talent and no compromise, driven and single-minded as to outcome. To me he's always been charming. Returning from lunch one day to the Shaftsbury Avenue base of *Michael Forever*, I bumped into him outside the Haymarket Theatre where he was director in residence. Dressed in his usual denim shirt and jeans, he was effusive, friendly and full of the joys of working with Ralph

Fiennes. This warm greeting ignored his massive falling out with Richard Price and Chris Hunt over the aftermath of *King Lear* and Richard's insistence on giving Chris the co-directing credit he wanted so much, and which Trevor passionately believed to be undeserved.

To get three hours of Shakespeare filmed in three weeks is a tall order indeed. Working six day weeks – that's ten minutes a day. Not quite soap speed but certainly double the norm for TV drama. The task is made somewhat easier by taking an existing production from the stage. The cast is well versed and using four or more cameras can really speed things up – two-way dialogue for instance, can often be covered in one take instead of four. Of course there are huge compromises to be made in the lighting of a scene, the blocking has to be spot on, and the size of the performance needs a fine balance (there's no point half raising an eyebrow in a wide shot, or, worse, gesticulating like an E-munching raver in a big close up).

Three hours of musical is even harder to achieve in such a short time. *Singing in the Rain*, for instance, took six months to shoot. Complex action involving dozens of cast members is what makes a big musical number (*Jellicle Cats, Farmer and the Cowman, Song of the King*) very impressive on the stage, but very time-consuming to film. Loading in dozens of cameras will get the coverage, but invariably there will be elements of choreography – important to the story – that are missed, or unlit, or early, or late, or miss-cued and so in the wrong place. In a proscenium arch theatre, everything plays to the front, which is great on stage but quite dull on film, so an element of re-choreographing is needed, to better use the space, to create lines of action that don't all run up and down stage. Capturing a big dance number on film takes time, because it takes time to get the camera in the right place.

The second biggest issue is with the singing. It's one of the biggest technical annoyances in a musical, when the actors, happily chatting away, advancing the story, making narrative, suddenly stop all that and burst into song. Bastards. It means the sound department has to put away their microphones, stop recording, and switch on the playback. The actors meanwhile, have to mime to the vocals they recorded some three weeks previously in a recording studio. Here's the thing about miming: It's a skill. Some can do it spot on. Some anticipate the music and do it early, some wait to hear the music and do it late. Some do a bit of all three, sometimes during the same song.

Here's the other thing about miming: Don't mime. The whole shape and form of the body is just wrong if a person mimes. You have to belt it out for real, breathe for real, time it for real, to have any chance of looking real when singing – especially in a close up.

Physics comes into it too. The actors, needing to hear the music and themselves clearly, cannot have in-ear monitoring, because the earpieces would show, and so detract from the carefully built edifice of false reality the audience needs to buy into. The playback to which they mime/sing comes from monitors (speakers), which have to be out of the shot, say 15 metres away (50 feet in real money). Sound travels at 343 metres per second, so it takes 1/25th of a second to get from monitor to actor. That's one frame of film difference, and one frame out of sync. There might be three or four actors all at different distances from the monitors. Now add back in all that anticipation and/or reaction, and the result is that the mouth movements (picture) can be anything up to 4 or 5 frames out of sync, in either direction, with the audio.

The same is true for dancers, who somehow contrive never

to be in sync. The tightest performance live will be found wanting on camera, because the relationship between action, audio and audience is so very different when filtered through a camera lens and onto a screen. Actually, it's the absence of filtering, the absence of the brain interpreting what it sees, joining the gaps and smoothing the edges, that means greater care has to be taken when presenting something for film. The best example of how it can all go horribly wrong on film (at least at the beginning) comes from Michael Flatley's Irish danc-o-rama *Lord of the Dance*. A key part of the impact of this show, and *Riverdance* before it, came from pre-recording the tap dancing, and making the sound of the taps an integral part of the audio design. The sound of forty pairs of feet, dancing away on a specially constructed hollow stage, was recorded one damp Dublin Tuesday at Windmill Lane Studios. The cast were tired, having been out celebrating a birthday the night before. Michael was his usual demanding, unforgiving self, pushing for perfection, relentless and driven. It was not a happy day for those involved, and indeed two male members left the troupe the day after the sessions. The remainder muddled through, depressed, hung-over and unmotivated by anything other than fear of their leader's drive. These were young kids, many still doing A-levels, all of them amateur Irish dancers riding the massive wave of craic that was flowing out of Eire at the time. They were not hardened pros, and the show was better for it. But on those dance record days, the performances were definitely muted.

We filmed *Lord of the Dance* on its opening night at The Point in Dublin. The success of *Riverdance*, and Michael's popularity, meant the new show was a huge success. A capacity crowd roared with approval as Michael and the troupe delivered some stunning dancing held together by a narrative of some good meets evil in a vague Celtic myth kind of nonsense. It didn't matter – everyone loved it. And the dancers? They loved it too, jumping, leaping, flying and dancing their hearts out. They jumped twice as high as at Windmill Lane. They tapped twice as fast as at Windmill Lane. They spun quicker, flipped better and performed completely out of sync with the pre-recorded taps. It didn't matter in the hall; the lighting, the amplified music and effects, the excitement of performer and audience, the very physiology of sight itself all led to nobody noticing the taps were out of synchronisation. The camera images however, told a different story to the soundtrack. After the filming I spent two weeks in a dark room in North London painstakingly matching taps to dancers' feet. It wasn't much of a deal in the big numbers, but when it was a soloist or dancing pair, it had to be right. The director of course, had used many close ups of those magical feet, which meant finding a tap that corresponded to the image of toe or heel hitting the stage and sliding its position on the soundtrack, by fractions of a frame, until it lined up with the picture. Michael Flatley can tap 38 times a second. The camera only runs at 25 frames a second. That means there's 13 taps happening that the camera cannot see. Nor can the human eye. Only flies and humming birds can see movement that brief. Maybe he was dancing for them. Lord of the Fly Dance? You see, filming dance ain't just a question of pointing some cameras at the stage.

Back to *Oklahoma!* This is where Chris Hunt came in and set out his stall, convincing Richard Price and Trevor that he held the magic recipe to resolve the sync issues that had plagued them on their television adaptation of *Porgy and Bess*. Had he come from a music video background, had he lived, breathed and in some cases deconstructed the whole concept of playback, he would not have needed to hire me. As a documentary film maker, he presented the key to the kingdom to Richard, and looked to me to open the lock.

The prize for Chris was a co-directing credit with Trevor for the TV presentation of *Oklahoma!* A credit which caused some difficulty, because Chris wanted equal billing and Trevor felt the contribution was junior. I couldn't remember the exact nature of the directing credits on *Oklahoma!* so I looked them up on Internet Movie Database (IMDB.com) Here, in this depository of all things film-making that started off in a Cardiff bedsit, Trevor has the sole director's credit, and Chris, Richard Price and I are credited as producers. From memory however, the credit on the screen was "Directed by Trevor Nunn with Chris Hunt". Lawyers and agents spent weeks on that little preposition, which appears to have been airbrushed away, along with Chris' credit, in the IMDB history.

* * *

A year or so later and I'm asked to re-join the party to film *Merchant of Venice*. Chris was again co-producer with Richard Price, who in turn was instrumental in finding the money; most of it came from a millionaire furniture salesman and private jet lease agent in Florida whose wife was an avid Shylock fan. Producing aside, after getting the co-directing credit on *Oklahoma!*, Chris was keen to step up again on *MoV*.

Trevor however, having seen multi-camera once, felt he could manage perfectly well thank you. Without choreographers and dancing in the way, without issues of song and dance sync to hamper the edges of his expertise, he believed the totality of the interpretation was his, and he certainly didn't need a producer directing the Bard with him! A grudging "well you can help, I suppose," was as far as he embraced Chris, and a furious row erupted over the directing credit. Chris certainly put in the legwork, attending rehearsals (Trevor: "What are you doing here?") making copious notes in school notebooks (Trevor: "There's no point writing THAT down!") liaising with the production designer over which wall should float (Trevor: "It doesn't need to be THAT one") and ostensibly choosing key film crew but ending up using Richard Price's choices. On a hiding to nothing from day one, Chris did what he always does, which is persevere, not give up, press on and eventually reach the ark.

Merchant of Venice was not a happy production. Like *Oklahoma!* it brought together elements of the A Team (Trevor Nunn) with a group whose minds and skillsets were not used to operating at the highest level. One of the first tasks I undertook on *Oklahoma!* was to patiently explain to Richard and Chris that none of the cast were going to work for three weeks at a rate of two hundred pounds a week, just because that's what they were paid in the theatre, and Maureen Lipman and Hugh Jackman needed a bit more than the two thousand pounds on the table to seriously consider doing the film. This was an early indicator of Richard and Chris' peculiar approach to the relationship between value and delivery. Neither seemed to understand that the better someone is the more they get paid. Nor did they seem to get the difference between employment and risk/reward, or the crucial contribution that creative people make to the whole, a contribution that goes beyond employment and into the realms of authorship. Their offer to the cast, of what they got for doing the show, ignored the Equity agreements in place for the filming of theatre, and had little grasp of the different rights an actor created when allowing their performance to be televised.

A creative endeavour you see, creates an intellectual

property. Most actors are paid very little for performing on stage, because they can do other stuff during the day, because their performance is ephemeral and has no existence outside of the moment, and because theatre producers drive hard bargains. As soon as that performance is recorded however, it exists forever, and can make money forever. It becomes an asset. The actors' union Equity has negotiated low rates to encourage live performance, and low(ish) rates to encourage filming. Using the film however, requires payments for each kind of use; television, satellite, DVD and so on. Each source of revenue for the film producer is shared with the actor. Richard's central tenet however, seemed to be that he was doing someone a favour if he employed them, and a further favour if he paid them for it. Chris seemed in part to share this attitude. It was a way of thinking that was to have huge consequences on *Michael Forever*.

Chris Hunt was born in Bristol, worked for many years as a staff director on The South Bank Show, and left ITV in the nineties to set up Iambic Productions – in Bristol where he has always lived. From there he did some worthy and not so worthy documentaries. Chris knows a lot of people, is well known in the classical music world, and is like a dog with a bone when it comes to a project. He will not stop, he will not take "no" for an answer, he will duck and dive and worry and gnaw at a thing until he gets what he wants. He is a heavy battleship that plows on, and on, and on. He is however, very Bristol. Slightly provincial, two hours from the capital, and saddled with a staff in which every mile of that distance tells in approach, attitude and mind set. I've seen a few of Chris' documentaries, and they are okay, workmanlike, Ronseal like, but like a Chinese meal, quickly forgettable.

* * *

His biggest stroke of luck came in the late nineties. City investors approached opera impresario Alan Sievewright, who had worked with Chris on a Maria Callas documentary, looking to deliver visual recordings of classical music online. Sievewright in turn approached Chris and, as creative director and CEO respectively, they launched Online Classics PLC. This floated on the London Alternative Investment Market (AIM), at the height of the dotcom boom. Its 20p shares immediately started trading at £1.40, and peaked a few months later at over £2. Chris had five million shares.

The share issue (IPO – Initial Public Offering) had delivered £2 million cash into the fledgling company's bank account and made Chris a multi-millionaire overnight. He set about building the Online Classics website and acquiring rights to programmes. His biggest acquisition was the Reiner Moritz Associates (RMA) library, thousands of hours of classical programmes going back to the seventies. You know the sort of thing – dark, wobbly BBC presentations of wenches warbling Wagner, Leipzig Symphonia offerings of Schubert shot on Soviet era film stock and so on. It didn't matter. This was the cutting edge of internet financial market hysteria, where sellers of knicker elastic added millions to their company values by adding "online" to their company titles.

I don't for a minute under-estimate the graft, perseverance and effort needed to pitch and present to the money, even when they are falling over themselves to part with it. It takes guts, stamina and chutzpah to turn maybe into yes, and Chris was and is loaded with all three. But I'm sure even he would admit that during the dot com boom he was in the right place at the right time.

After the video library, the second biggest spend was on a

launch concert for the TV channel. TV Channel? Chris had quickly figured out that there wasn't the bandwidth available to actually deliver programmes on the web, classical or otherwise, so he leased a transponder on the Astra satellite, announced Digital Classics TV, and decided on a prestigious multi artist gala event to launch it. He asked me to produce it while he went off to fight radio station Classic FM, who were convinced he was stealing their idea.

We settled on the courtyard at Somerset House as the venue, and a Friday in late June as the date. I christened it *Midsummer Classics* "until somebody came up with a better title" (no-one did), promised Chris it would cost "around 250" (shorthand for two hundred and fifty thousand English pounds – blasé I know) and began work. From the outset, we knew the purpose was twofold – to provide some hours of programming that could be packaged and repackaged on the channel, and to actually launch the channel, with column inches and celebrity gossip, royalty and red carpet posing. The first required some talent to do some performing. Chris thought an eclectic approach, where classical meets popular musical, would serve best, so I got hold of Michael Ball and Maria Friedman and musical director Simon Lee, left the classical stuff in the hands of Alan Sievewright, and went looking for the celebrity and the royalty. I hired some PR totty whose claim to fame was having once (or once having – you choose) slept with Prince Andrew (there must be dozens of such blondes dotted around the London PR skyline). We were guided to her by Zoe Twophones (not her real name of course, but a director on Chris' board whose claim to fame was having once slept with Boris Becker, and for carrying two mobiles at a time when just one was still the preserve of the rich and media'd hoi polloi).

Getting celebrity was and is quite easy. Give 'em a free ticket and the promise of a red carpet and they'll bundle out of limos as happy as lemmings over a cliff. Royalty is harder to get. Royalty will only turn out, formally that is, all tiaras and twinkle and handshakes down the line and "what do you do's?" for charity. And not just any charity, but their charity. This is where Zoe and PR totty (PRotty for short) came into their own. Zoe was mates with Jemima, who has loads of charities, one of which had a minor royal as patron. I felt the show needed something more high profile than Jem's offering, and went in search of something a little more mainstream than the Okehampton and Amritsar Benevolent Society. I quickly found myself lost and confused in the bizarre world of the voluntary sector. When you or I give money to charity, we bask in the warm glow of our altruism. We get a fuzzy, feel-good feeling that encompasses our giving, the donation and the good we believe it will do. I made the mistake of thinking that was how charities were too, warm, fuzzy, feel-good organisations that bottled our goodwill and sent it on to those less fortunate. Wrong. The charities operate as businesses, as hard-nosed and rational and results driven as any other. To them, our donations are a part of their revenue stream, and in some cases not a major part of that stream either. Bequests for instance, old ladies leaving their entire estates to some cat charity, in some cases form a far bigger part of the income. The charities will take the money because we give it. They'll use it dispassionately, spending on students in branded vests to pester you on the street, or TV, cinema and radio ads, or to line the pockets of East African dictators so that at least some of the aid gets through. Charities are as tough as old boots, and it's a mistake to think they're soft just because we're soft for giving them money.

You don't just "get" a charity for your event. Offering to give them a hundred grand does not give you any access, any right of association, nor indeed any guarantee that their royal will turn up. It doesn't even get you lunch. The arrogance at the big charities was staggering. Off I went, into the meetings, armed with a guileless charm that was met with stony indifference.

"Why should we allow…" (pause to shuffle some papers) "…Online Classical Television, to um, associate with us?"

"Because we want to do some good, we believe in your work and want to support it. Our event will give you not only hard cash, but publicity too."

"That's all very well, but we need to be sure your event fits our profile, falls in with our overall strategy. Could you tell us, perhaps, how Classic Online proposes to do that?"

"I just want to rent your royal and give you money."

"Well, I'm afraid that is not, in itself, reason enough."

"I'll give you a hundred grand."

"Hmm, thank you so much for the offer, and of course all donations are most gratefully received as they allow Save the Children/Oxfam/Christian Aid/RSPCA to continue our most valuable work. For that level of contribution however, we will assign you to our Small to Medium Donations Team, based not here in our head office in Knightsbridge but on an industrial estate outside Swansea. Would you like their phone number?"

After a few meetings like these I began to despair of ever getting a royal. I knew the Queen was out, as was Anne, Charles and the other first rankers. I was never so naïve as to aim that high, I just wanted somebody to put the "Royal" into our event. PRotty flatly refused to sleep with Prince Andrew again, Boris Becker was not royal at all, and then by chance I found The Blue Cross, a well-established animal charity with the same minor royal patron as Jemima's Okehampton thing. Twenty thousand to them and a posh invitation to one of the palaces secured Princess somebody or other, and our Royal was on. This of course meant that *Midsummer Classics* was now a Royal Gala, and as such more red carpet was ordered, the celebs now rolled in, and all the performers wanted more cash, more stage time, more frocks, more make-up, more everything.

On the production front things were not progressing so smoothly, and the initial simple idea was growing like a lung cancer into a 100-a-day man. Organisers of a Royal Gala cannot allow the royal to get cold or wet, nor discomforted in any way, not even for a second, which meant the original Somerset House courtyard plan (the first time it was to be used for a musical performance), of stage and seating and a light show on the walls, now required beefing up with a rainproof awning, and heating, and yet more red carpet, and increased security together with the closure of Aldwych and most of the surrounding streets. The quote was substantial, at over £300,000, and pushed the cost to over half a million pounds. The alternative was to insure against rain on our late June date. The premium demanded was £295,000, so only five grand cheaper than building the roof. I insisted the whole thing should never, ever cost more than £350,000 in total, awning or no awning, and booked the Royal Albert Hall, as it was a) a world class venue and b) had a roof. Its capacity of five thousand, two hundred and fifty seats was eight times more than we were going to have at Somerset House. The stage was four times the size, needed a set and a ton of lighting, and everything was more expensive, bigger, costlier. Concerned at the escalation of the event, I suggested to Chris that he may want to re-consider the whole thing. We'd only spent around £55,000 at this point, so a retreat and rethink would not be financially onerous. Chris was adamant however, that we continue.

We sold very few tickets. PRotty and Zoe may have had intimate knowledge of royals and red carpets, but were no help in getting bums on seats. We had very little marketing budget, so in the end we papered the hall. There was mayhem outside, as last minute radio announcements on Classic FM delivered thousands, and inside the three hour show overran by an hour and a half. I don't remember many celebs turning up; Dawn French came, with hubbie Lennie in tow, and Jem of course. There must have been others, but they are all drowned in the quicksand of time.

To show what good PR folk they were, PRotty and co provided us with a clippings book showing all the column inches their efforts had created. There weren't many, aside of a page in Tatler. The final cost: a shade over half a million quid. The final result: nearly five hours of programming which was sliced and diced every which way and provided the mainstay of the channel's output for a year. It's still available on DVD, it was sold here and there to places like Latvia and East Timor for not very much, and so it probably ended up costing five, maybe ten thousand an hour to the channel. This is about the same as that wobbly Wagner from the Boredom Series of 1978. So costs justified? – Just about. A resounding success? – Definitely not.

And the weather? The evening of the concert was the hottest day of the year, a balmy, muggy night more akin, in late June, to the Mediterranean than London. So we could have done it at Somerset House after all, and for a fraction of the price. Ho hum.

* * *

A few weeks on from the Royal Albert hall gig, I get a call

from a worried Chris. His film of Gounod's opera *Romeo et Juliette*, directed by the charming and elfin Barbara Willis Sweet, in production on location in a balcony-rich castle in the outer reaches of the Czech Republic, was running into trouble. Starring opera singing husband and wife team Roberto Alagna and Angela Gheorghiu, the project was being financed with a myriad of sources including Canadian Film Funding, British TV sales, Czech Republic tax breaks, and Canal Plus. This last investor, France's premier satellite broadcaster, was in on the deal because Gounod was French, as were the librettists and thereby the opera. It no doubt appealed to the French execs to present Shakespeare's love tragedy as a Gallic tale. The Canadians too, were in to embrace French Canadians with what they saw as an excellent multi-cultural presentation. "It's English, but in French! Great, we'll take three please!"

On the set in the castle, Chris' choice of producer was struggling with the production. Her experience was miles from the filming location she was in charge of, and her office was a kilometre away from the location. Neither mobiles nor walkie talkies worked well enough to provide communication to the set, where the heads of department had decided, French, English, American, German and Czech, and in the absence of any authority, that they were making a feature film. Unfortunately Chris had raised only enough money for a three week, multi-camera re-working of an existing production, along the lines of *Oklahoma!* Doubly unfortunately, there was no existing production so everything had to be designed, built and rehearsed, from scratch. The movie mentality meant that the cameraman refused to shoot a second camera. The operatic stars, used to performing in the evenings, refused to accept early morning calls for make-up and wardrobe. The extras bitched, the sound department moaned, and poor Barbara, through no fault of her own, had in the first week – one third of the time available – shot less than twenty minutes of the three hour production.

I arrived on the Saturday, watched an afternoon of progress so slow that made paint drying seem like something Lewis Hamilton does, and called a crisis meeting that evening. I told the cameraman that if he didn't save time and shoot with two cameras I'd sack him and get someone who would. I helped Barbara reschedule the remaining time, cajoled Angela to come in two hours earlier for make-up, got the Czech army to run a field telephone down to the set from the production office so someone could be heard shouting, and very publicly bollocked the costume designer for being late on set the following morning. I wasn't proud of doing so, because his attitude only mirrored everyone else's, but I needed a scapegoat, and he was universally hated amongst the crew. A cheap shot, but it worked; the crew started pulling together, and the film finished on time.

Shortly after arriving in Back-of-Bratislava or wherever, I had offered Chris the opportunity to pull out, costing the abandonment at around £400,000. Again however, Chris was determined to finish the film. Later, the Canadian funding dropped out, because it was either not French enough or too English, and Channel 4 reduced their contribution, leaving Digital Classics to fund the £500,000 shortfall on the film. Hopefully, eventually the film recouped its costs, but I doubt anyone made any money. The once cash rich company was beginning to feel the chill wind of the arse-end of cashflow.

As the century and millennium came to an end, so did the good times for Chris. As a company director he was never allowed to sell his shares, so his multi millions were only ever paper wealth. When the dot coms crashed, and many lost millions, Online Classics went from over £2 a share to under 2p a share. Thank God it was only paper. But, unlike most casualties of the time, this company did not fold. Chris refinanced, did some deals, got more cash, renamed it DCD Media and went on a buying spree, creating a company that today includes Done and Dusted, September Films and a host of other well-known production companies, distributors and film libraries. DCD is a medium sized indie in the world of the super indies that now control TV production in the UK. Chris' tenacity made the owners of the companies he acquired wealthy men and women, but his reward was to be ousted from the Chief executive position and sent packing, defenestered as financial jargon has it (thrown out of the window), with only Iambic Productions as his consolation prize, released back to him as part of his severance deal. He knuckled down, made some more worthy documentaries, mainly about ABBA, and one day took the call that was indirectly going to lead to *Michael Forever*.

* * *

Rene Jamieson is a well-known talent booker who has, for years, worked with UK chat host Graham Norton. Her address book has absolutely everyone in it, including Chris, with whom she has worked in the past. She had also found some of the acts for *Midsummer Classics*. She also knew Michael Jackson, who liked her enough to send helicopters to LA to bring her to parties at Neverland.

Sometime after journalist Martin Bashir's nasty documentary on Michael had aired in the UK, Rene was approached to find a documentary maker who could make a more sympathetic film about Michael, to balance the very negative portrait Bashir had created. The approach had come from people known to be friends of the star, and Rene believed that ultimately it had come from the man himself. Michael of course had filmed Bashir filming him, and released a film showing the Brit journo in a very negative light indeed. Rene's mission however, appeared to be a separate part of the Jackson fightback, a film about the music and the talent.

The Bashir documentary is excruciating to watch. Michael appears other-worldly, trusting and open, while Bashir seems the essence of dirt digging and salacious mendacity. As Michael talks of his sleep-overs and slumber parties, it is Bashir that seems to get the hard-on, as his subject innocently hangs himself in front of the prurient journo, who pushes and questions in a way that anyone less trusting would immediately find suspicious. Jermaine's ghost writer puts it very well in his book *Michael - Through a Brother's Eyes:*

"Michael's true character was torn up by a warped edit...This wasn't a world exclusive: it was a hatchet piece that could boast about its access, not its truth."

The effect of the broadcast on Michael was devastating. Rightly, he felt betrayed, but more seriously the documentary handed ammunition to the prosecutor who, in a long campaign more reminiscent of a medieval witch-hunt than modern day democratic legal process, had been investigating the singer since the early nineties.

That Michael needed a TV riposte was clear, and his own anti-Bashir programme, crafted from the material his people had filmed, went some way to providing it. What is unclear is whether the quiet suggestions for the music based piece came from him, his circle, or Rene herself. Rene was known as someone Michael had met. She also knew David Gest, whose history with Michael is well known. When she approached Chris about making the documentary, his key and early question would have been about access to Michael, as that would have been the broadcasters' first question to him.

Enough must have been said about the shape of the film to encourage ITV to commission it. Whether access to Michael was promised, suggested or mooted is a matter that will undoubtedly have as many shades as people you ask. For ITV it wasn't a deal breaker, probably because they felt another pro Michael Jackson film, with or without the participation of the star, was needed to balance the Bashir hatchet job they had screened earlier in the year. Chris' milieu of music documentaries was well suited to the task. Forget the allegations of child abuse, the weirdness, the sleep-overs, the (shock horror) glasses of wine. Focus on the music, the talent, the genius.

Next stop LA, and interviews with brother Jermaine and soul legends Smokey Robinson and Gladys Knight. While Rene delivered Lisa Minnelli (via David Gest) and worked on getting to the King of Pop, Chris went off to meet La Toya. With her was manager, friend and guru Jeffré Phillips, who promised much, and swiftly delivered an interview with Katherine Jackson, Michael's mother.

For Chris, sitting in LA waiting to see Michael was frustrating, and Rene seemed no closer to securing the seemingly all-important interview. He confided his concerns to Jeffré, who had already delivered on one promise (Katherine), and who now promised to deliver on another, assuring Chris that he could get to Michael. Jeffré's sudden involvement in the project infuriated Rene. She saw him as a threat not only to her role on a film she felt she had co-created, but also a threat to securing the contribution from Michael. In her mind, Jeffré's involvement would muddy the waters and cause confusion, with the same request peddled and presented by different sources. So Rene left the project, falling out with Chris over his refusal to give her a co-producer credit on the film, a refusal prompted in part by his new-found belief in his new best friend, the new best booker in town – Jeffré Phillips.

Michael had no involvement in the resulting documentary, *The Michael Jackson Story*. His appearance is limited to archive, and that archive is in turn limited by what little is available to be cleared for broadcast. The ownership of the songs, pictures and videos of Michael Jackson was a complicated matter in 2003. One party, Sony Music say, would give permission to use a video clip, only for another to deny the same use because they held either a separate right, or in some cases believed they owned the same one. Chris' approach was to use the material and wait to be sued. It was a tactic that had worked more often than not, especially in classical music world where money for lawyers is more scarce. He had also got into trouble with Abba for similar perceived transgressions. A nasty letter, a difficult phone call, eventually all smoothed away by the promise not to do it again and the payment of a few thousand pounds to the aggrieved party.

The night before *The Michael Jackson Story* was due to air on ITV, two senior executives from the TV channel were enjoying a post-football match pint in their local pub. Their attention was drawn to Sky News on the television above the bar. Aerial shots of American police cars tearing up a narrow drive, lights flashing and sirens wailing, appeared on the screen. The scrolling caption sent the two execs scrambling for their phones: "Neverland raided by police. Michael Jackson arrested on child molestation charges", read the moving headline. The broadcast was pulled. Michael was in big trouble. Chris' luck might have finally deserted him.

CHAPTER 2.
JEFFRÉ

You sit around in the strangest place
So take off the mask
So I can see your face

Jeffré Phillips is a clever man. He is urbane, charming, intelligent and very, very slippery. He is so slippery he gives Teflon the feel of a Vapona sticky flytrap. Should the men who make non-stick things (pan makers, space vehicle designers, perpetual motion machinists and the like) ever get hold of Jeffré they'll bottle him and call him SuperTeflon. Except nobody can ever get hold of Jeffré, because he's just too damned slippery.

Chris met Jeffré again in LA in September of 2010. Michael's death had given new life to *The Michael Jackson Story*, because unlike the breaking news of his trial, which had led to the show being pulled from broadcast, the breaking news of his death meant everyone with a transmitter needed a Michael Jackson piece, and Chris' was uncontroversial, workmanlike and, with a bit of last minute editing, up to the minute.

This September meeting with Jeffré was the inception of *Michael Forever*, and the sperm was most definitely Jeffré's. I learnt this in an unusual way.

I was walking my dogs up a hill behind the hotel, where the view promised a view of more hills, trifle-layered into the far distance and emphasising the vast openness of highland Scotland, when my phone rang. Bizarrely it was a call from Chris' phone but not from Chris. Up a hill is one of the few places in the highlands where you can actually get a mobile phone signal, but that's not the bizarre. It was a pocket call, and his phone had decided to ring me just as he was in a meeting discussing a Michael Jackson concert with someone. I thought at first he was talking about the documentary, but it soon became clear that this discussion was about something more.

Pocket calls are never distinct – you get words, phrases if you are lucky, but everything is muffled, like listening through a wall or, indeed from a pocket. Chris' phone, a Blackberry, would phone me quite often, you know, to keep me informed, tell me the latest news, and just generally catch up and chew the cud. It was happening often enough for me to want to steal his phone for a moment and insert a new contact called Aardvark or something, just so there'd be someone ahead of me in the contacts list to take all these calls! But on this occasion I was glad I hadn't, because the call I was listening in on, not with much success, was very interesting. I gathered that Chris was going to find some money, and the guy he was talking to (Jeffré?) was going to deliver the Jacksons, and both would combine in a massive tribute concert.

That September meeting in LA between Chris and Jeffré not only laid the seed for the event that would be *Michael Forever*, but also prepared the fault lines that would ultimately lead to the whole edifice collapsing on itself. Chris was somewhat in awe of Jeffré. Jeffré was capable of charming a corpse not only back to life, but of getting it to put on make-up and dance a jig on its own grave. Jeffré was so smooth that Mr Smooth would feel decidedly rough when standing next to him. And Chris, although urbane, was no match for the Silver Surf of Jeffré's dialogue. That Jeffré had singularly failed to deliver Michael for the documentary, despite promising to do so, did not dampen Chris' ardour when Jeffré presented his big idea. He, Jeffré, would deliver the Jacksons and a host of A-List stars. He, Jeffré, would build a tribute to Michael, a show that would reach out to the huge fan base, a show that would sell out in seconds, that would play in stadia and run in cinemas and on DVD and the web and on phones and inside refrigerators and in every other which way, all around the world. Jeffré would create an event that would be so huge that it would outsell *This Is It* ($400 million). He, Jeffré, friend of the family, colleague of Michael, who loved Michael so much he'd spent over a week in Michael's house, immediately after his death, guarding it from 'bad people', would pay tribute to the King of Pop. And he would make Chris his partner in this enterprise. For this to happen, all Chris had to do was find the money. Jeffré of course was the lead figure, he was the one who would gather stars and talent and Jacksons, and so it was only right that he, Jeffré, had 80% of the action. Finding the money, he told Chris, would be a breeze. The words Michael Jackson Tribute would open coffers across the world as wealthy investors saw the gleam of dollar signs and would be so keen to pile in they'd trip over themselves to sign up. Chris pointed out that events such as these are always talent led. "Don't worry," smiled Jeffré, "I've got all the contacts and I can get the stars. But let's keep my involvement quiet, just for now."

* * *

And so it came to pass. Later in the autumn Chris rang me to talk about a number of projects he had bubbling away in his post DCD pot – riding shotgun on a feature film he was putting some money into, a documentary with Melvyn Bragg that needed a Scottish connection, a bit of this, a bit of that and, a slim possibility this, a Michael Jackson tribute concert, to take place in America but broadcast onto screens in stadia around the world. I worked hard to feign surprise about the latter, not able or willing to admit to my eavesdropping, even though his Blackberry had called me rather than me actively hacking into his phone.

I was also quite surprised at the Melvyn Bragg thing.

"I need a Scottish production company, so do you want to be Iambic Scotland?" asked Chris

I smiled at the question, and said of course. To me it was not a big deal, to help out a friend in this way. The Better pointed out however, wiser than I in so many ways, that Chris was gaining our combined production credits, and the weight they carried within the industry.

Apparently and over lunch, Melvyn told Chris about a project which the BBC wanted, but they would only finance it if it came into the network as a Scottish commission. The BBC, you see, ever mindful of accusations of being the London Broadcasting Corporation rather than one serving and engaging the whole of Britain, has for years encouraged regional programme makers by allocating funds specifically for non-London production companies. Especially sensitive was and is the question of the BBC in Scotland, a place which the Corporation treats as a "region", yet everyone there (except me) believes to be a country. The long and short of this emphasis on regionality meant Melvyn's project (the recent one on class) required a Scottish production company to pitch the idea to BBC Scotland in order to get the funds to make it. As I lived in Scotland, Chris reasoned that I could be his Scottish division, hereby making the project qualify as Scottish and getting him, Chris, a chance to work with Melvyn again. Unfortunately, Mark Bell, Head of Factual at the BBC, didn't quite see it that way. He accused Chris of making up a tenuous link with some hotel in the Highlands in order to circumvent the BBC's strict rules on programme regionality. He then commissioned the series anyway, through Melvyn's London production company, thus ignoring those same rules of regionality, but in a different way.

This setback to his northern ambitions notwithstanding, Chris and I toddled off to Glasgow one wintry December day to meet the commissioner there, Sam Anthony, and see if there was some business to be done. For those of you not blessed by being in the molten hot core of UK TV production, I should point out there is a great danger of confusing two different but similar sounding job titles. There are BBC commissionaires, who open the door to the building for you, take your name and issue a pass, and BBC commissioners, who open the door to getting a programme made, take your company name and issue you with a set of guidelines. They sound the same, but are totally different. So we're in Glasgow, looking to see if there's some film to be exposed, some tape to be burned, some programmes to be made. Seems not. Chris spent the entire meeting berating the BBC exec about the perfidy of Mark Bell, the dreadful lack of communication between corporation and independent producer, and the inability to get meetings with commissioners at the BBC (in a meeting with a BBC commissioner). Eventually and politely we were asked to leave, and told to come back with any programme ideas we wanted taken forward.

"These idiots are quite astonishing in their idiocy," he said, as we drove around Glasgow vainly looking for a decent restaurant. I felt that an opportunity had been wasted, but I had to agree that pitching programme ideas to the man whose career highlight was associate producer on the first (and thankfully only) series of *How Clean is Your House USA*, could be a tad frustrating.

Christmas rolled by, and then January. The hotel was under five feet of snow, yet a few brave guests still made it to our door. The previous winter had seriously caught us out. Our steep drive was no match for low profile city tyres and wide profile city drivers. We spent most of the bad weather either ferrying guests to the village hall where they could park, or towing them up the hill to the hotel. None of them had prepared their cars for snow, and the requisite tow hooks, if existing at all, were invariably under all the baggage in the boot and had to be fished out in the dark, cold and wet. I took to telling them to find the tow hook before setting off, but few bothered to heed the advice. So here it is, in black and white: When embarking on a long car journey in the winter, get the tow hook out of the boot. It's usually in with the spare tire, in the tool kit pouch. There. To avoid a repeat of Tow Hook Hell, for the coming winter I ordered a pallet load of gritting salt and waited for it to arrive. Unfortunately the snow came before the salt, so the delivery truck couldn't get to the hotel and offloaded down by the road, leaving me with a ton of salt and an icy, slippery drive that required some salt on it before even our four wheel drive would consider climbing back up.

In early February Chris was back in touch.

"We need to convince La Toya and the Jacksons that this concert is real, so could you send your credits over to Jeffré Phillips? He's building a website for them to look at. It's not a public website, just for La Toya." Now call me confused, but I didn't see why my credits, pretty full of event programming and concert filming though they are, would make a deal of difference when racked against the supposed acres of contacts and well-advertised presence of Jeffré Phillips. And why was Jeffré building a website to impress La Toya, who he managed?

Chris continued: "I've found some investors who are interested, but this is very much Jeffré's show. He is calling the shots. And oh, I've booked the Millennium Stadium in Cardiff.

For this production to qualify for UK tax relief it needs to be in the UK, and Wembley is not available. We're going for August bank holiday Saturday, Michael's birthday. Well, two days from his birthday. Jeffré has a company called Ja-Tail – take a look."

So I did. And here's what I found:

> *JA-TAIL Beverage Company (JBC) was established in May 2006. Our first product line was called "Star Ice" in which we manufactured and distributed with Star Beverage, PTY out of Australia. "Star Ice", came (sic) in 4 different flavors, Green Apple, Raspberry, Passion Fruit and Cranberry. JA-TAIL Beverage Company was the first beverage company to import a flavored malt beverage into America from Australia. "Star Ice" was distributed in the following US states; Pennsylvania, Connecticut, Louisiana, Minnesota, Arkansas, California, Nevada, Massachusetts and New Jersey. It could also be found in over 50 7-Eleven stores and in Costa Rica, Honduras and Sri Lanka. "Star Ice" sold more than 26,000 cases and more than 650,000 bottles from June 2006 to December 2007 with very little, to no, marketing and promotion.*
>
> *"Star Ice" quickly became one the favorite party drinks in Hollywood with such celebrities drinking it as; Kathy Najimy (Numb3rs), Geena Davis (The Long Kiss Goodnight), Jennifer Gareis (The Bold and The Beautiful), James Pickens (Grey Antimony), Isaiah Washington (Grey Antimony), Terri Polo (Meet The Parents), Allison Janey (Hairspray), Jennifer Morrison (House), Anthony Michael Hall (The Dark Knight), Paula Abdul (American Idol), Antonio Sabato (General Hospital), Isla Fisher (Wedding Crashers), Jay Leno (Tonight Show), Pamela Anderson (Baywatch) and Wolfgang Puck (Famous Chef) just to name a few.*

Now I have nothing against Allison Janey, or James Pickens, or even Kathy Najimy, but I do wonder how their acting skills, as evinced by their credits which Jeffré helpfully lists, equip them to endorse a sweet beverage Jeffré is importing from Australia. I've not seen anything from Antonio Sabato indicating "I grew as an actor on *General Hospital*. Although the show helped shape me as a fully rounded human being, it was Star Ice that really gave me the push I needed. What a drink! It's just totally awesome and I hear Wolfgang Puck is a big fan too!" Or Wolfgang admitting he was in a deep, dark pit of Teutonic despair, his cooking confidence a distant memory, even his schnitzel tasteless and rubbery, until Star Ice lifted his culinary talent to a whole new level: "I drink it, I marinate with it, I baste with it. My body sculpt jets in my shower jet nothing else. Thanks you Star Ice and thanks you Jeffré. You put the "he" back into chef!"

I highlight this not only from a sense of mischief, but also to share my genuine puzzlement that arose when landing on the home page of Ja-Tail. All the tags one would usually associate with a media company were there – Events, Music, Publishing, Films, TV, Development, Concerts – every branch of entertainment was covered. And at the end, a rather incongruous, what am I doing here? "beverage" tag. I had to go straight there, and I had to reproduce what I found for you here. Gosh but this LA media world is an exciting one. Ja-Tail makes you wanna get down to your local Honduran 7-11 just to pick up a six pack of Star Ice, knock it back and get on with your career as a soap actor. I mean if La Toya drinks it... and Terri Polo from *Meet the Parents*... it's gotta be great, no?

I once stocked a malted fruit beverage in my bar. I bought

two crates after enjoying it at a food & drinks trade fair. Those things are great – you get loads of free samples and my advice is to leave the car at home. The alcohol flows and by late lunchtime a malted fruit beverage is the ideal thing to help recover a little, to build a second wind and get back into all that wine and beer from Moldova. And the girls serving these drinks, all high heels and tiny tasting cups, are so achingly pretty it takes someone stronger than me to walk away from such fine malted temptation.

The cases sat in my bar for a year. I sold one bottle. Eventually the rest were condemned as out of date by an Environmental Health inspector and I was fined fifty pounds. So I shipped them to Honduras.

I checked back onto the Ja-Tail site the other day, just to refresh my memory of it. I found no mention of the Michael Jackson concert, no mention of *Michael Forever*. No sign of Jeffré's involvement in the Cardiff event, nor that he had 80% of Global Live Events LLP, the promoter of the show. But that is no surprise, and true to form. Jeffré's lack of presence in the run up is one of the reasons the show was a failure. His lack of presence in the aftermath, at the time of writing, points perhaps to darker undercurrents, but that is far in the future in my narrative.

Very early on, Jeffré had intimated to Chris that his involvement should be kept "under wraps". Jeffré's reasoning was that if the Jackson brothers found out he was behind the event they would never sign up to it. They, the Jacksons, would figure that La Toya stood to gain far more than they by signing to a show headed by her manager, and dividing the spoils of Michael's legacy by the rest of his family had already been a painful, fraught and long drawn out affair. None of this dampened the Jacksons' appetite for more infighting one bit.

Jermaine Jackson was particularly keen to maintain what he saw as his position of senior brother and family patriarch. Any Michael tribute had to be with him at the helm. After all, he had nearly staged just such an event – nearly twice. Unfortunately, he had also announced a line-up that included every major act on the planet, and thrown in the President of the United States and Nelson Mandela for good measure. None of them, not the artists or presidents, had been asked prior to being announced. All of them quickly distanced themselves from Jermaine, and all of them joined the other Jacksons in loudly declaring they would have nothing to do with any event involving Jermaine Jackson.

"How is Jeffré going to attract the talent if he can't be seen to be a part of the show?" I asked, only to be told not to worry. Jeffré has teams of people plugged right into the epicentre of the LA music business. Jeffré was on. Jeffré would deliver.

Not finding any clue on his website to Jeffré's past record of delivering anything other than malted beverages, nor anything on the wider web either, I struggled to understand how he would come up trumps. Chris explained that Jeffré was a "fixer". He produced A-List stars at Russian oligarch daughters' birthday parties. Want Beyoncé to sing Happy Birthday to little Miss Abramovich? – No problem. Like the idea of Lady Gaga doing a twenty minute set for Sheik Shimmery in the Dubai desert? – Call Jeffré. And the first time you use Jeffré, you don't pay a fixer fee. Jeffré of course probably still snags twenty per cent from the multi-million dollar artist bill, but he waives his own, special arrangement fee direct from the oligarch. And after the singers have smiled and sang and danced a dance, and the oligarchs and petrol dollar billionaires and heads of state are happiness personified, when they come back for more, it's a million bucks to Jeffré. I hope Gaddafi paid in advance! (Not that I have any knowledge of the now dead Libyan leader using Jeffré's services. I'm just surmising that if he had, if say, Diana Ross had tripped down to Tripoli to personally deliver a rendition of *Chain Reaction* to the reactionary's favourite grandson, it would have likely been Jeffré that had set the thing up.)

This kind of activity leads to a very impressive contacts book. He'll have the artists' private mobile numbers, email addresses and a direct route to them all. But it's all very, very non-broadcast, out of the public eye, middle of the desert stuff. Completely deniable, with audiences of a few hundred people so wealthy they have no time for celebrity. These personal appearances are not handled by lawyers, or agents or even managers. Artists are quite happy to do these private personal appearances because there's no trace after they've gone, and because agents aren't involved they get to keep more of the money. The press doesn't know about them, because the stars' public relations machines don't roll into action to publicise them, record companies aren't involved, and the private clients have enough clout and money to keep the media well away from the event itself, even if the media were interested. "Adele sings for Indian steel magnate" is not much of a story, even if it were true.

A major public appearance however, and the creation of a raft of performance and media rights that go with it, is another matter entirely. The agents and lawyers will swing into action to do the deals. The Artists, Promoters, record companies and the PR departments of all three will usually want to shout about their involvement, these days tweeting, blogging and Facebooking for all they are worth, selling albums and DVDs and merchandising off the back of special appearances at V Festival or Glastonbury or the switching on of Christmas lights in Tulsa, or Cleethorpes, or any other public interface they find themselves at. Unusually, with *Michael Forever*, they did none of the above. Like Jeffré, the artists seemed to want their involvement under wraps too. But I'm getting ahead of myself. At this point in the story, early February 2011, there were no artists attached to the project, just Jeffré's assurances to Chris that there soon would be. And maybe Jeffré would have pulled it off, personally smooth talked the artists into the Tribute show, but Jeffré by his own choice was invisible, in the background, under wraps. So Jeffré handed his contacts book over to his "team" and let them get on with it.

CHAPTER 3.
MICHAEL (HENRY)

"Everything beautiful and noble is the product of reason and calculation"   Charles Baudelaire

Firing up a major bit of investment from the City of London requires numerous people with varied talents to nursemaid the cash from one bank account to another. Brokers, investment houses, market makers, and bankers all line up to deliver the specific and unique services required to launch a publicly quoted company. Binding all this together are the lawyers, and Michael Henry was and is a master at this type of work. It's how he and Chris met, during the formation of Online Classics, and it's how they have continued to work together, on film funds, on refinancing packages, and most recently, on *Michael Forever*.

Michael is not only a skilled lawyer, but the author of about seven metres of legal tomes all about media contract law. His efforts in this area form the template of most English business contracts, and he would often get a frisson of lawyer excitement when he saw his own words re-penned by another and presented back to him for execution. For a non-lawyer, with a non-legal brain, it's probably most useful to measure his output by the length of shelf space that his works occupy in any decent law firm. One can, from prop houses and interior design emporiums, buy books by the metre. The previous owner of my hotel did just that. How else can you explain the twelve volume biography of Campbell-Bannerman that adorned the lounge? Book yardage makes your house look good, and you learn-ed (unless it's unreadable dreariness about a Scottish liberal politician). Law firms are no different. It makes clients feel comfortable to discuss matters with someone seated in front of rows and rows of books. It's as if all that knowledge is flowing off the shelf, through the lawyer at the desk and on into the client at the astoundingly speedy rate of £500 an hour. It's impenetrable knowledge too. The tomes are dark coloured, the titles etched in gold. Each series is unique. You have to know what you are looking for when you reach for one, and know what to find as you flick through the thin pages of dense type. None of them have graphic representations of smoking blondes on the front, or ranged endorsements on the back. You won't see:

"*Vicarious Liability in English Law* sets a new standard for this kind of writing. It's a real page turner from start to finish!"

"He was a loner; ex-CIA, ex-husband, ex-solicitor with no way out – until one day a hedge dispute in a quiet suburb changed everything, forever."

"Also by the same author: *Vicarious Liability in English Law Volume XII*: it's never the fault of the one to blame!"

It's also quicker to visualise Michael's prodigious output by yardage than attempting to measure by weight (about 2 tons) or by colour (mostly burgundy) or by thickness (very).

But it quickens the blood, this writing lark, and Michael Henry was no different in this regard. Having slapped down a million words on the minutiae of contract law, he turned his talent to translating Baudelaire, presumably into English, which he did with enough success to get his efforts published. Hence the chapter header departure from MJ lyrics. Intellectual and clever, Michael Henry even looks like the French poet he is an expert on, but with more hair. He is ever polite (except when stressed, at which point he tends to bark rather foolishly). Michael Henry may not be the antithesis of the popular view of lawyers, but certainly is the very opposite of Jeffré's LA based legal team. The two cultures were to clash violently, and nothing, not even hindsight, could have prevented it.

When Chris returned from Los Angeles that September, fired up with Jeffré's big idea, the first person he spoke to was Michael Henry. For Chris, the Michael Jackson tribute was a perfect fit with Limelight – the investment vehicle he and Michael had set up earlier in the year as a source of film finance. There have always been lots of wealthy investors who, when it comes to showbiz, seem to lose the critical faculties that made them wealthy in the first place. They get a bit of glam-blindness and pile in to projects that, were they in the toilet bowl industry, they would avoid by miles. No crapper however, looks crap if Keira Knightly is sitting on it – does it? But there was hard core cash behind Limelight, because it rode the wave of tax breaks the British government has made available to boost manufacturing. If you make something (a film, a pram, a toilet bowl) you get tax credits which you can borrow against, so funding your production and providing the investor with some return.

Michael, used to advising on these matters, readily signed up to be a partner in the venture. He would no longer suffer the twin frustrations of clients either heeding his advice and making lots of money, or ignoring it and making none. Michael would now advise himself, and reap the benefits of so doing, himself.

Like Chris, Michael Henry strove for the big league. A thin, sharp man with a brittle and humourless nature, Michael used the law as a scalpel like weapon, carving, teasing and moulding commercial law, maximising the use of tax incentives and creating edifices needing only some creative talent to become money making machines

With his usual skill, he set up an investment vehicle, Park Place, to control the money coming in from investors and from tax reliefs. Then he made an operating entity, Global Live Events, to would produce the event. And on the third day he rested.

By the start of 2011, the skeleton of a structure was in place. Michael would provide the legal expertise and a ready access to City investors. Jeffré would, at arm's length, provide the vision, the artists and the show. Chris would provide the stage, the venue and look after the television and media aspects of the event. The Limited Liability Partnerships set up to support the skeleton were Chris and Michael as Park Place for the money, and in turn Park Place, Chris, Michael and Jeffré as Global Live Events. Why a Limited Liability Partnership (LLP) and not a limited company (LTD)? – Because the tax regime for an LLP means it's a much more efficient structure for the kind of transatlantic enterprise that everyone envisioned. Jeffré had the lion's share of GLE, but none of Park Place. In this way, Chris supposed to control the flow of funds to the US, and keep the money at arm's length from his principal partner, La Toya's Svengali and malted beverage supremo.

In February the triumvirate got on the road. Figuratively speaking of course. They didn't actually mount horses or jump into cars to head off on an over the horizon mission, although Jeffré did take Chris for an LA spin in his convertible Bentley, and Chris' head did dutifully spin when Jeffré said,

"Chris, we get this show done and I'll buy you a Bentley just like this one. But first we have to get the Jacksons on board with this, and that's going to be very tricky. They'll manoeuvre around each other, each trying to get the upper hand, they'll form alliances and make camps, and the trickiest of all will be Jermaine and Janet, but given time they'll all come in, because they won't want to be left out in the cold. But remember, Chris, that none of them can know of my involvement, because then they'll figure La Toya stands to make more out of this then they, and they in turn won't stand for that. Once the Jacksons are in, once the world sees this as the family tribute, the stars will fall over themselves to be on that stage Chris."

CHAPTER 4. PAUL "KINGY" KING

Everybody's somebody's fool
The world is the biggest school

From: Andy Picheta
Date: Thu, 28 Apr 2011 16:33:51 +0100
To: Paul King
Subject: concert design team

Hi Paul,
Who do you have in mind for the design team, which presumably will be SET, LD, and sound
My thoughts are, for set, Mark Fisher, Peter Bingermann, Kim Gavin, Willie Williams
For LD: Al Gurdon, Patrick Woodruff, Ethan Weber, Simon Tutchener, Pete Barnes
I'm sure you agree we need major, Grade A talent
Best
Andy

Hi Andy
We had already approached some key people by the time Chris put everything on hold pending the outcome of his trip to LA. However I am concerned not to take any discussions too far until we have something more concrete in terms of an Artist or two.

Because of the nature of what is being proposed people will be sceptical, so we will need a couple of ducks vaguely standing in line at least.

Regards
Paul

It's early April and I'm called down to London for a meeting. Chris has been holding the line at Cardiff Millennium Stadium, but the time has come, he tells me, to put some flesh on the bones for them. They are beginning to doubt the booking, and Chris is concerned that they'll give the bank holiday date to one of the myriad international stadium events that are looking with interest at the August bank holiday Saturday slot on hold for *Michael Forever*. He's been badgering Jeffré, and Jeffré has hired a heavyweight promoter and put him and an entourage on the plane to London. He has added a couple other Ja-Tail execs to the trip, to make up the numbers and show willing. Chris, in turn, has hired a UK promoter, who in turn has hired a health and safety chap who used to be a concert sound man. We are to have meetings in London then head off to Cardiff the following day to talk turkey with the stadium. I can only presume that Chris thought two promoters and a health and safety guy would instantly convince the denizens of Cardiff Stadium that this show was real, and that they should not hand the August date over to the massed bands of mining folk or some other global event that could not wait to get into Wales. But first to London, and to Chris' shiny office on Shaftsbury Avenue. The small and only conference room is full to bursting, and my first meeting concerning *Michael Forever* begins.

I'm introduced to Paul King and Health and Safety man. Paul is in jeans and a leather jacket, looking very rock 'n' roll, which he is, and very 1985, which he was. We immediately find common ground, as Paul used to co-promote with Andrew Miller, who gave me my first job producing music videos in the 1980s. Andrew, you see, as well as promoting concerts, managed Captain Sensible, and had found an up-coming BBC edit assistant called Simon West to make the videos. Simon in turn, found me. It was a fun filled two years during which time we progressed from the Captain and made a load of promos for the likes of Mel and Kim, Rick Astley and some really dodgy bands. One of them, I recall, was managed by a kebab shop chain owner from North London who paid the £15,000 cost in cash in used fivers. It took an age to count the money and each note smelled of chip fat. We spent the lot on a night shoot in Portsmouth docks. The relationship with Andrew ended when Simon decided he had enough of a showreel to move on to a bigger company. I went with him, but lasted only six months, when I in turn decided to move on and work with directors of greater talent. The high point of this brief time at Limelight was production managing the shoot of a T'Pau concert at the Hammersmith Odeon as it then was. Steve Barron directed, it was my first live show in a production role, and I was hooked. Simon went to LA and got his dream, which was to direct movies. The first *Tomb Raider* is probably his biggest credit.

Health and Safety Head, HaSH for short, tells me he's taking a course in advanced Health and Safety, which really excites me and gives me confidence that someone will at least know where the first aid kit is. Paul tells us he likes to take ownership of a project, even if he's just a hired hand, which is equally good to know (although just how much ownership Chris will let him take is another matter). I also meet Pete, who does lighting, production and a bit of set design too. I'm polite, and choose to ignore the jangling alarm bells that have just gone off in my head. If this is supposed to be the biggest event since Live Aid, I'm certain we are going to need some more experienced, more mainstream, more A-list talent than somebody on a course and somebody who does a "bit of everything". I decide however, that meeting one on day one is not the time to air these views. I'll see how we get on, see how the land lies, and have a quiet chat with Chris later. After all, he's hired me for my concert expertise, so he's bound to listen. For the moment, there's no time, even if I wanted to press for a fabulous Lighting Director and superb, TV minded designer to be brought on board, because we move on to our first meeting with some technical guys that do amazing things with mobiles. They have been sent by a couple of investors in the show, who have an interest in their techie companies also. It goes way over my head, but it involves turning your smart phone into money by using special electronic posters that know your mother's maiden name.

"This technology can be applied to *Michael Forever* and make a lot of money," one of them says.

"Good. You've said exactly the right thing. We like money, and lots of it," replies Chris, and I swear I see a little drool forming at the side of his mouth as he does so. Oh Dear.

As the suits from TeknoKomplex or some such file out, the Americans are buzzing the buzzer downstairs and, having successfully avoided any of the numerous oriental massage joints that surround the office, are on their way up.

American promoter Leonard Rowe, just off the plane, is blacker than black. He is a gnarled, grizzled ebony-hewn old survivor who has music in his veins and wisdom in his bones. He has promoted tours with every black act of note – including Michael – he has booked soul stars into 1950s segregated southern states, he has marched with Martin Luther King, and he is so old he probably marched with Martin Luther too, and was probably on hand to co-promote the separation of the sea by Moses. If you spoke to him on the phone you would believe all that and more just from the beautifully resonant timbre of his voice. In person, Leonard delivers what his voice promises. He appears calm, polite, and on the ball. No stranger to controversy, the list of acts he's been sued by would fill a whole season of music festivals. Last year he wrote a book titled *What Really Happened to Michael Jackson*, in which he claimed Michael was killed for his music catalogue. The book was ridiculed, but

Leonard made some valid points about the ruthless nature of today's music business and the frailty of the talent that supports it. With him is Britney or some such, a fat black guy who, despite his corpulence, soon shows himself as a lightweight. I'm not being racist or weightist here. Britney is black, and is fat. Even he must admit that, looking in the mirror, he may see skinny and feel thin on the inside, but that skinny-inside-guy has a lot of lard to punch through if he's ever going to get out.

Chris chairs the meeting, and begins with an outline of the event so far. First the title, apparently much pontificated over by lawyers on both sides of the Atlantic. The words Michael and Jackson cannot be used together in this Michael Jackson tribute, because numerous states in the US have laws preventing exploitation of "name and likeness". These state laws are presented as a uniquely American hurdle, deftly leaped over by calling the show *Michael Forever*. In other countries of course, such protections are in place under laws against what is known as "passing off". In California, the Michael Jackson estate owns the rights of name and likeness, because Michael owned them when he was alive. So *Michael Forever* it is and I am too new in my seat to question whether the nifty word-work is a good thing or bad thing. We move on to the question of who is going to appear in the show. Chris opens his notebook and reads out the following list. I wrote it down as he read, and part of me got very excited indeed.

"Beyoncé, Bruno Marrs, Britney Spears, Madonna, Enrico Iglesias, Lady Gaga, Rod Stewart, Rihanna, Elton John, Lenny Kravitz, Sting, Mick Jagger, Mary J Blige, Jennifer Hudson, Taylor Swift, Celine Dion, Tina Turner, Ne-Yo, Chris Brown, Pink, R Kelly, Usher, Christina Aguilera, Justin Timberlake, Stevie Wonder, Shakira and Prince."

Quite a list. I note the absence of Barack Obama and Nelson Mandela, which shows a level of realism unavailable to Jermaine Jackson. A few actually made it to the show, and Jennifer Hudson nearly so. Britney (the one in the room not the one on the list) then chimed in as talent director, telling us that each and every one of the listed acts had expressed a specific interest in doing the show. They had all been approached, talked to and would soon be signed. Contracts were being drawn up as he spoke. Managers were in daily contact. Everybody wanted to pay tribute to Michael. All these artists were a certainty, and more would surely follow.

Chris then talked about the date, August 27. Michael's birthday. Actually the nearest Saturday to Michael's birthday, which fell on the 29th. But a bank holiday Saturday is certainly prime time for a multi-artist concert event as big as Live Aid, and a great time for a one day Michael Jackson festival. Leonard then took the floor and delivered, in his stentorian tones, what I still remember as the "Five Guys Speech". A lot of it was grandmothers and egg sucking, but what a grannie! And what eggs! To place the voice, mix Morgan Freeman with Darth Vader, replace the menace with a weary hope, and you're there. The delivery is slow. Real sloooow, like an ancient twelve bar blues player settling himself on his Louisiana porch.

"We need five guys," he began, "five guys who are our guys, not stadium guys, not artist guys, but our guys. We don't need no Live Nation guys, because those guys will hate this show, they'll try to kill this show just like they tried to kill Michael's show. So we need these guys, and these are the guys we need. We need a guy on top of the merch-and-ise. He needs to know every shirt, every stand, every hat and every poster. He needs to answer to us, not the venue. We need that guy. We need a guy to handle the pro-duc-tion, not a talent guy but a pro-duction guy, a guy who knows every light, every trussing, every cable; a guy who will answer to us for the shed-ule, not a venue guy, our guy. We need a guy to run the hospitality, to take care of the corporate people, the money people, to make sure the venue don't get clever, because they will try to get clever, and if we don't have our guy they will get clever and rip us off. We need a guy to look after the talent on the ground, not a venue guy, not an artist guy but our guy. A guy who knows every limo company and every hotel and who can work with the city and the po-lice. We need that guy.

"That's what we need," and with that he sat back in his chair, all tenored out.

"That's only four," I said, "Who's the fifth guy?"

Leonard looked at me as if I had just spat on the freshly hewn commandment tablets he had helped Moses bring down from the mountain. Wearily, he leaned forward. Quietly he said, "You'll know who the fifth guy is. We need that guy," and collapsed back. His assistant quickly gave him a can of Coke with a straw in it, holding it up so he could suck a slurp without moving. Then he looked at Chris.

"Chris, you've gotta get the City to contribute. This deal with the pitch is huge. The City should pay for this. We're bringing millions into the City. Talk to the mayor. Talk to the Boris guy."

He didn't mean Boris of course, he meant Cardiff Councillor Delme Bowen, but who knew – I had to look it up just now. But first, the deal with the football pitch, sacred ground to Welsh players of rugby, but an impediment to a music event: In addition to paying the stadium £350,000 to stage the concert there, we have to pay for the pitch to be removed and replaced.

This costs a further £250,000. Everywhere else, the promoter pays to cover the pitch with specially designed plastic decking, which allows light and moisture through so the grass keeps growing, but spreads the weight of the audience so the grass is not damaged. This costs a fraction of £250,000, but, as I was soon to learn, nothing costs a fraction of anything on this show. In Cardiff, however, the pitch is made up of pallets which have layers of soil and nutrients with the grass on top. These squares bond together to create a playing surface. The pallets aren't designed to carry much weight (thirty rugby players as opposed to twenty thousand music fans) so have to be removed, one by one, leaving a concrete surface. The good news, Health and Safety Head (HaSH) cheerfully tells us, is that trucks can drive on the concrete, so the load in will be quick and efficient.

Second, the location: Chris had convinced himself, and everyone else, that Cardiff was a great alternative to Wembley. The stadium had obviously reinforced this view, pointing out that their catchment area extended as far as Birmingham and London. Indeed, when the old Wembley was being torn down, and the twin towers replaced by a giant arch, Cardiff Millennium was the temporary home of English football. But, as Chris now and not for the last time pointed out, Cardiff is not in London, it's not even in England, but in a different country (Principality actually), called Wales. The Americans looked at him blankly. They thought Cardiff was in London. Then the questions: How far is it from London? Is there a time difference? Does it have an International airport? Can I fly there from Dallas, or Nashville? Are you saying it's principally a country?

On discovering Cardiff was two hours by train from London, and in the same time zone, they became even more confused. Another country is just two hours away? How is that possible? Countries are eight hours away by plane in the US. It's definitely not London, right? Right. Chris continued to further point out that the stadium grandees got their noses very out of joint when they heard suggestions that Cardiff was an English city, and their stadium an English stadium. Cardiff stadium, however, is owned and run by ex-rugby players – so noses out of joint is quite usual for them. I waded in to help.

"Cardiff Football Club is in the English Premiership, and the English FA cup is sometimes played there."

"Soccer, right?"

I Google some more Welsh stuff to help them understand.

"Yes, that's it. Also, Christian Bale, who plays Batman, Queen of Hollywood Katherine Zeta Jones (Mrs Michael Douglas), and *Doctor Who* are all Welsh."

By now the Americans are completely befuddled, and glance at each other nervously as if some dark plot has just been revealed to them.

"So Gotham City is in Wales?"

"This doctor guy, he looks after the chick from *Zorro*?"

"Yes, yes and yes. Look, here's the border"

And with that I get Google Earth on my iPhone and show them. Wikipedia then informs me that the first king of Wales was Cunobelinus, but I hold back from sharing this information, because I know that the Americans would undoubtedly confuse him with the pleasuring of ladies.

* * *

The following morning we meet at Paddington to catch the 9:30 to Cardiff. It's fast, smooth, efficient and comfortable – at least in First Class. It would become a common journey. The Americans have all brought their passports, and take them out to show the train guard. We all have a good laugh about it, except for Leonard, who is asleep. Two seamless hours later, and the short walk from the station brings us to the security entrance, where we are met by Alex, nearly seven feet of Welsh rugby muscle. Handshakes all round. Alex crushes my hand in the strongest grip I have ever encountered, delivered by the biggest paw I have ever seen on a human, and I try not to wince. But for an hour afterwards I'm unable to make a fist or hold a pen.

The first time entering an empty stadium in which I am to work is always a splendid moment. I can sense the energy that bounds around the place on a show day, I can feel the anticipation, the excitement of crowds past and future. I connect with the stories the walls could tell. And, because I am with the client, I get to go on the pitch. This is usually a very big deal, because nobody is allowed on the pitch. If you've been on a stadium tour, you know you don't get to go onto the pitch. Stepping on to the pitch at Wembley, or Old Trafford, is like stepping onto hallowed ground, but if you are with client, you don't get cursed. Here at Cardiff it felt good, but not that great, maybe because it was a rugby ground not soccer, and not Wembley. I came back off before everyone else piled onto it, as I could see the groundsman haring round from the other side – not across the grass of course, but around the sidelines. I smiled at Alex, and he smiled back. I could tell we would get on. So I re-joined the group, all staring and looking and pointing, but I could get no feel for the place, so I left them to their pointing and started to climb up the stands. Cardiff has three layers, called Lower, Middle and Upper Tier. The highest seats in Middle Tier are about the same height as the lowest seats of Upper Tier. From up here the view was pretty good. The seating was well designed, so even the other side of the pitch seemed close. I wandered off to try and get higher, but my phone beeped an incoming text from Chris: "Meeting starting. Where r u?" So, now to find the meeting room. A quirk of the construction of the Millennium Stadium is its regular oval symmetry that, at one end, is rudely and roughly interrupted by Cardiff Arms Park. This old stadium, with its block stands, forms one end of the new stadium. Two tiers of straight-on terracing stuck onto the back of the old existing building. It means the oval is incomplete, and you can't get from one end to the other at the north end. Annoying, especially when you are several levels higher and a whole stadium away from the hospitality suite that has been earmarked for our meeting. I figure out my geography, climb down over the seats and run across the pitch, again. I fully expect to get yelled at, but nobody says a thing and I sneak into the meeting.

Chris is reading out his list of artists, Britney is assuring everyone that they are all as good as on the plane, and Leonard is dozing. We make some progress on the contract between the stadium and GLE, which, although agreed, has not been signed. The public reason proffered by Chris is that a host of detail needs to be sorted out. The private reason seems to be that as soon as the contract is signed GLE has to pay the venue £150,000 – which GLE doesn't have.

Because here's the deal with the investors, over two dozen in all. Between them they have pledged two million pounds, the vast bulk of which is to be released only when certain minimum event conditions have been met. These are that four Jacksons plus Janet Jackson plus three other A-list stars have signed to do the show. Until these conditions are reached, Chris only has about £200,000, released to him as seed money. Jeffré is spending this fast, having hired Leonard, Britney and other members of his three ringed circus. Chris seems to be spending very little, apart from travel costs. The signing of the Jacksons is on Jeffré's To-Do list. The A-listers seem to be the province of Britney. So the contract issues with the stadium remain deliberately unresolved, kicked into touch as it were, where Chris and Michael Henry really want them to stay.

We talk about the layout of the stage in the stadium. There are usually two options: Theatre style, where the stage is at one end; and in-the-round, where the stage is in the middle of the pitch. Each has advantages and disadvantages. Putting the stage at one end, as Take That did, blocks out anything behind the stage, up to a quarter of the seating. There is also an area of floor that is taken up by stage, barriers, safety areas, cameras and thrusts. The capacity is then around 65,000. Putting the stage in the middle of the pitch area creates a more intimate show, as the audience is never too far away from the stage. The artists just have to remember to turn around now and again, and play to all parts of the venue. In-the-round is always more expensive to stage, because screens have to be seen by everyone, the stage has to be clear of sightline obstructions, and everything has to come up from underneath, as there's nowhere to put the wings. Filming an in-the-round presentation requires more cameras, more cranes, more everything to capture the action where-ever it is pointed. Servicing the show from under the stage means the stage has to be higher too, which in turn affects the view of those watching from what little floor space remains available for audience. The capacity for an in the round presentation is also around 65,000, because areas of the stands are blocked off ("killed" in industry parlance) by the ground support structures that hold up the lighting grid. For a bit of football of course, rugby or otherwise, the design capacity of 74,500 is available for sale. Veteran stadium rockers U2 designed their 360° tour to maximise attendance. In a brilliant piece of lateral thinking they combined all the advantages of both options by being at one end yet still in the round. With this set up, they were able to sell all the stadium seating and half the floor space as well. The support legs for lighting and PA were made as thin as possible, obstructing only narrow wedges of seating, and the end result was a record breaking crowd of 73,354. The 360° screen was made up of hexagonal sections that rose and lowered, as well as separating to form a lattice. All very cool, very expensive, and designed and lit by two of the industry's most senior practitioners. Chris has chosen to follow the U2 concept, and hopes to beat U2's record for the number of people watching the show. I make a mental note to get more cameras, more cranes, more everything to cover a three-sixty presentation. I also wonder about the increase in the technicality of the staging. U2 rehearsed for months. We shall have a week. U2 is one act of four people who have worked together for 35 years. We shall have over a dozen separate superstars, yet no wings for easy on and off stage movement. At least we learn at this meeting that we have a house band and that all the acts will perform with the same set of musicians – so we only need to worry about individuals. This cheers me. The death of a live-to-air multi-act show is always in the turnarounds – getting drummers on and off takes an age unless you set everything on a rolling riser, a mobile platform that can be wheeled on and wheeled off in seconds, sometimes even whilst the drummer is playing. In the round of course, there is no backstage and no wings to wheel them into. But we have no bands performing, so it's not an issue.

We also talk about Take That, who sold out every one of their UK concerts in about three minutes. When Take That tickets went on sale, the Ticketmaster site crashed from the demand.

Chris tells us that *Michael Forever* is the biggest concert since Live Aid, a once in a lifetime experience, a unique chance for the fans of Michael Jackson to pay tribute to the star in the presence of his family. He wants to beat the sell-out record set by Take That. He wants Ticketmaster crashing faster, for longer. He wants to beat the attendance record set by U2. He wants 80,000 people in a stadium built and licenced for 74,500. Chris is riding high on a wave of wow; he knows we have a winning show, a high concept product, an amazing event. We talk about Don Mischer, the show director that Jeffré has hired to put the event together. Don is going to come up with the stage design. His experience as producer and director is legendary – any big TV event in the States is either directed or produced by Don Mischer. Unfortunately Don is a bit busy producing and directing all those shows so there is no stage design as yet. Without one there is no footprint of the stage in the stadium, so there is no way of working out the capacity. The stadium's stern directress of operations is clear in this regard. First comes the stage plan then comes the safety stuff, the barriers and minimum distances and standing audience densities, and escape lanes. This is followed by resolving sightline issues created by the stage design and the seat kills (the way of describing unusable seating in a venue, rather than any kind of wholesale slaughter of the audience whilst seated) resulting from ground support structures, screens, public address (PA) stacks and, of course, TV cameras. Once all this is known, the capacity can be determined and the tickets printed. We are a very long way from that moment. I do a quick calculation, starting with the 27 August show day. Tickets should be on sale three months before, so at the end of May. That gives us six weeks to figure all this out, six weeks to design a set, six weeks to build a show, six weeks to sign the megastars, six weeks to put something together to market to the world. Phew.

Here's what I know at this point. Here's the beginning of the yawning chasm that will eventually engulf us all, although at the time I didn't recognise it as such. There is a world of difference between selling a concept to a client and selling a product to a consumer. The client buys a concept based on track record, on the pitch, the presentation, the treatment, the plan. The client buys the person with the concept. The consumer, on the other hand, buys a product, a known entity, a tin with the ingredients clearly labelled. Chris had been very successful in pitching to broadcasters and selling concepts. His consumer facing experience however, was nil.

"Here's the programme idea, and here's one similar that I've made before," he says.

The commissioning editor at the BBC, or Channel 4 or ITV or wherever then says, either:

"No thanks, I've got three like this already," or:

"This fits with what we're looking for, we want a music programme, and Abba/Shakespeare/a musical is right up our street – thank you here's two hundred grand/a million quid".

My favourite pitch story concerns Wayne Isham, pitching to Def Leppard's manager Peter Mensch. It's a lunchtime meeting in a Chelsea restaurant. Peter asks for a treatment for the music video for *I Wanna Touch You*. Wayne hands him a paper napkin. On it, he's written "trust us". Peter approves the deal, tells Wayne he has $150,000 to spend and we're in Bray studios one week later.

What no commissioning editor ever says is "this is crap, I'm not buying it". That part of the process happens much earlier, in preliminary meetings designed to sort the wheat from the chaff.

So getting TV programmes made is about selling ideas by selling yourself and your idea, but no consumer, no end user, has ever bought an idea. Consumers need to see the product, and then they make emotive, emotional decisions based on needs, hopes, aspirations, on greed, desire, peer pressure, word of mouth, on brand loyalty, on a whole host of complex thoughts and feelings that businesses and their marketing analysts spend fortunes and entire careers trying to understand. Consumers rarely say "this is crap, I'm not buying it'," except quietly to themselves, just before either buying something else or walking away.

But we don't need consumer marketeers, because Chris has hired rock 'n' roller Paul 'Kingy' King, who's sold concert tickets forever, and who should now be wading in with words of wisdom and guidance. Except he is quiet in the meetings. I think he's realised how far we are from a marketable, promotable product. He knows we need the acts announced, so the consumer knows what they are being asked to buy. He knows we need the stage designed, so he knows how many tickets he has to sell. He promises to have a poster in every chip shop in South Wales, but first he needs to know what to put on it. Paul King knows we will need what is known in marketing terms as a "call to action". The action is buying the ticket. The call is why you should.

After all the talk about staging, about a house band, about keeping it simple, Britney says he's definitely going to sign Take That. In fact, he's going to talk to Robin Williams that very day.

On the train back to London, at least during the Cardiff – Bristol leg, Chris asks me how much we'll get from ticket revenues. I look at the U2 plan, suggest that our stage will not be as large, and then I look at the U2 ticket manifest for Cardiff. Chris goes through each section of seating attaching pounds. He starts at £75 and gets to £195 for the prime, middle tier seats. We create a Golden Circle right up at the front of the stage and price that at £250. I urge him to have something a bit cheaper, and suggest the north stand, the area of seats that will effectively be behind the stage. I suggest a price under £50, and he reluctantly agrees. We add up the projected ticket revenue, which comes to a shade under ten million quid – seven million once the VAT is taken off.

"That's quite a ticket price."

"This is a once in a lifetime experience, the ticket price of which is going to be a small part of the audience's spend. They're gonna come from Europe, Japan and the US, they're gonna spend thousands on plane tickets and hotels. It's a price structure that compares to festivals, although admittedly not one day festivals, and it's cheaper than Wimbledon, the Cup Final and any opera you care to mention. I don't think it's that expensive."

One thing I've learned since I've had the hotel, is that the product, be it a hotel room, a pair of trainers or a concert ticket, is worth what the customer will pay for it. I have the nicest place in this part of Scotland, but if the price is too high, I sell few rooms, and the few customers I do attract moan like crazy, because they feel they are paying too much. Still, seven million quid is a lot of moolah, and it should be enough to pay for everything, leaving all the media revenue as profit.

My instincts on the ticket price aren't mollified by Chris' views however, so I try again.

"Seventeen year old fans of Justin Bieber just don't have two hundred quid to spend on a ticket" I try, pointing out what I think is obvious

"But they know where they can get it" comes the response, offering a glimpse into a lifetime of daughters smiling at daddy for the cat, the dog, the pony, the private education and the overpriced concert tickets.

"Not all daughters are as fortunate as yours" I tell him, but my words fail to impress. Chris sees the customers as he sees himself; affluent and ready to spend big bucks on their entertainment and on keeping their children happy. I'm left with a consolation prize of some £45 seats in the North stand and a sense that the price is just too high.

We go through all the media revenue. The show is live-to-air, to TV, cinema and big screens in stadia around the world. Leonard and Paul have links to WWF, the wrestling franchise, and Chris tells me they have agreed to take the show. The show will be recorded, in 2D and 3D HD video, for TV and feature film presentation later on. It will go out on DVD, on download and every other medium you can think of, and some you can't. I groan inwardly about the 3D. It is, even at this time in the spring of 2011, a waning star. It's cumbersome to produce, expensive and bulky. We have been talking about an open stage, yet here we are also talking about putting five or six camera rigs the size of Volkswagens in front of it. Chris tells me not to worry. He's been on all the 3D courses and he knows we can do it with just three cameras and lots of conversion of 2D into 3D later.

"How much of Avatar was 3D?" He asks, rhetorically. "Less than twenty minutes!" is the self-delivered answer. Then he jumps off the train at Bristol Parkway, and leaves me returning to London and then Scotland with much on my mind.

* * *

It's early May and I'm driving down the A9 to Edinburgh, where I am to catch a late afternoon flight to Cardiff for a meeting at the stadium the following day. Normally I would travel from Inverness, but this morning option is not available because I have a hotel full of Slovakians that I must disperse first. It's a family and a business, and they have come to Speyside to learn about whisky. They own a distillery producing vodka called *Goral* (mountain man). The father is about five feet high and as many wide, some of which is fat but the rest muscle, presumably from hauling barrels of vodka around for sixty years. In fact he looks like a vodka barrel, and seems to run on a daily barrel load of vodka. The mother is five feet wide and as many high, and she runs the petrol station they also own. She runs on vodka too, or perhaps their own brand diesel. The rest of the party is formed of strapping sons and beautiful girlfriends, managers and sundry workers. During communist times the factory produced industrial ethanol, but the collapse of the central fixed market and the onset of capitalism meant they had to adapt or die. Hence *Goral* vodka. Presumably the factory's output is no longer pumped into cars in the gas station, just into the drivers. But they are fantastic characters and their culture is very familiar to my Polish roots (my mother was born and raised just over the border, on the other side of the same mountain range). They are also a handful for my hotel staff, who don't really know how to respond when offered a breakfast shot of *Goral* (take it, down it, smile). So I stay to supervise their farewell lunch before renting a car and heading south.

Emma, Chris' attractive assistant calls. She tells me not to get on the plane. She tells me the meeting is cancelled, and that Chris is leaving for Los Angeles in the morning for a crisis meeting with Jeffré. Don Mischer has dropped out because he's doing the 9-11 memorial show. The Jacksons are proving difficult. There's nothing to discuss, in Cardiff or anywhere else. I turn the rental around wondering who is going to pay the cost of it. I question Emma further but she doesn't really know what's going on, which is how she likes it. I get back to the hotel to find the Slovakians departed and four bottles of *Goral* left as a present in the bar. I drink one.

> *From:* Chris Hunt
> *Date:* Thu, 12 May 2011 15:03:16 +0100
> *To:* Paul King, Andy Picheta
> *Subject:* Concert update
>
> *I'm just back from the US. The Jackson brothers agreed the wording of their contract yesterday, and will sign shortly. But then we need to get Janet, and then the initial guest artists, before we can announce. I'm guessing that points to early June to go public.*
> *I'm about to recommend to the US guys that we now move to October 8th. Do you agree? We'll decide for definite by Monday.*
> *Paul, we should meet next week with Julian (and Andy by phone unless you'll be in town) to regroup. Wed or Thurs works best for me. While I think the date change might bring Don Mischer back in we will still need to get the floorplan ready asap.*
> *Andy please talk to Angela about OB units etc. so we can get availability and quotes.*
> *Chris*

My first conference call on this job. I dial into something called Pow Wow Now, and a soothing, Joanna Lumley-sounding female voice asks me to enter my pin. I'm asked to announce myself, then she introduces me into the conference. She tells me there are four people on the call, and then leaves me to my own devices, while presumably gathering up some more callers. Others join and soon there are loads of Americans, and Paul, and HaSH, and Michael Henry, and Chris. But no Jeffré. As ever with these things, it takes an age for everyone to sign in, and then there's a peculiar protocol to follow when speaking. The time lag between saying something and the others hearing it means you have to wait for a gap, and then talk. You cannot easily interject, or cut across someone, as you can in a face to face meeting, because the delay causes the speaker to either stop talking or ignore you and carry on. If they do stop, there's always a doorway moment: "You first, no you first, no you, no I insist". Nobody goes through the door until somebody leaps in. It's a bit like being on a walkie talkie, but you don't have to say "over". It seems that Jeffré's entire three ringed circus is on the call. There's Paul and Jim, Leonard, and a Ron, Britney – of course – a lawyer called Michael, but not our lawyer called Michael. There's Juliette, who is introduced as the show PR. Juliette starts to say hi but is cut off because she is in a car, driving somewhere.

Chris makes small talk with the Americans who he has seen but a few days ago, while we all wait for Jeffré. I begin to imagine all these people, hooked together by just a telephone wire and some computing. I layer my memories and perceptions of Los Angeles into my thoughts and try to picture the other callers. Leonard and Courtney are the only ones I have met, so they are easy to visualise: Leonard is in an airy office with his assistant at his side, who has a can of Coke with straw at the ready. He's sitting back, nearly dozing but not quite, and his feet are in bright yellow chicken slippers. Britney is lying on a massage table, breathing a little heavily, as four Filipino boys rub vegetable oil into his rolls of fat. He is naked and glistening, like a seal just out of the water. One of the boys is making a scale model of the Golden Gate Bridge using drinking straws, and anchoring the structure by sticking the straws into the folds of blubber on Britney's back. Visualising the others is harder, less fun, and not as homo-erotic. Jim I imagine behind a very big desk, chewing on an unlit cigar. He is after all, a Hollywood producer and production company owner. Paul I cannot place, not even if he is black or white, but his voice is thin so I imagine him to be thin too. And in drag. My mental picture of Michael the LA lawyer is coloured by the TV show LA Law. He doesn't sound particularly handsome though, but I do see him in his law office, on the eighteenth floor of something glassy and big, with rows of Michael Henry's books behind him. Then there's Kingy, calling from his bedsit in Reading, and our dear chipmunk featured Health and Safety Head, HaSH for short, because he is. There's no doubt in my mind that he is in some dingy pit, probably a portacabin, wearing a Hi-Vis jacket and safety helmet while a fax machine spews out safety manuals. His assistant is similarly attired, but in stockings. Office work can be very dangerous, and the Hi-Vis jacket informs everyone where you are – in the office.

Have I described Chris to you? Chris Hunt is tall and ginger. He has ginger freckled skin and a ginger face and ginger hair. He's so ginger that he reacts to sunlight only marginally less spectacularly than a vampire. He has a big frame, so he carries his over-weight quite well, but recently he's been travelling and eating (you need serious willpower to lose weight while travelling first class and living out of five star hotels), so he's beginning to look very heavy. He has strange teeth. When I first met him he had positively rodent like front teeth, like a gerbil or something. In fact they were more like double ivory doors behind which lay his wisdom teeth and his masticated lunch, the latter sometimes poking through and trying to get back out. At some point in the noughties Chris got all American and had his teeth fixed. The dentistry is very fine but even Beverly Hills orthodontistry was challenged to get those two squirrel incisors looking completely human. But they did what they could.

Two questions pop up while we wait, delivered by one or other of the American contingent. I forget who posed them, but I suspect it wasn't Britney.

"Why does this have to be in England?" is the first, and "Why can't we do this next year?" is the second. Somewhat alarming one might think, putting the fundamentals under the spotlight in this way just months before the show. But if Chris was concerned at the way the Cousins were shifting (thank you John le Carre, who first coined the phrase in reference to the Americans, at least in literature. It so perfectly describes the relationship), then he did not miss a beat.

"It has to be in the UK because twenty per cent of the funding comes from UK tax breaks, which we will lose if the show is staged anywhere else. It has to be this year, because that is the deal with the investors and they will sue us if we don't go in 2011."

I postulated that another Blue Riband, A-Class event in an Olympic year might suffer from too much competition. Looking back on this view I may have been wrong. Hordes of Chinese volleyball enthusiasts, Japanese Tai Kwando fans and steroid driven American sprinter supporters might have made a difference to the eventually appalling ticket sales. I mean, once you've supported your country in your chosen sport, waved your national flag and shouted yourself hoarse having become an instant expert in the scoring systems for synchronised diving, women's team ten metre air rifle shooting and mens' team pursuit cycling, you may be at a loss for the evening, and a bit of MJ magic might just be the thing. Were the show in London. But I was partly influenced by a report from the London Theatre Association, which expects a substantial downturn in business during Olympic fortnight. Who knows. Time will tell and we can all be super-clever with hindsight.

Finally Jeffré joins the conference call, apologising

profusely. He has been in the Department of Motor Vehicles renewing his driving licence. Mobile phones are not allowed in the building, and he was told to either switch it off or step outside. As he had queued for four hours, he chose the former option. Just as at the DMV, Jeffré has attended the conference call to renew something: everyone's faith in the concert. The Jacksons are taking an age to get on board. Janet and Jermaine remain outside the fold. There are family tensions over this show. Jeffré tells us we need more time to bring everybody in. Britney tells us all the stars on the incredible list read out in Cardiff a month before were ready to sign, but the Jacksons have to sign first. Then it's a family tribute and then they'll come flocking. We'll have to fight them off.

"I'm sorry Sting, you are just not of-the-moment enough for Michael's tribute!" – that kind of thing.

Having renewed everyone's faith in the concert, there is a roar of agreement for the new date, to give Jeffré time to get Janet on board. The show is rescheduled for October 8. Chris says that although we lose the link with Michael's birthday, the new date is within a day of the anniversary of the start of Michael's solo career, with the release of Michael's first solo single, *Got to Be There* on October 7 1971. So that's Okay then. Having got everyone gung ho again, Jeffré disappears back into the foliage, back to the background. Juliette rings in, says "Hi," and is cut off again.

I amuse myself by redoing the reverse schedule for the new date. Nobody pays any attention to it, and I don't expect them to. Any plan is just there so you know when you are deviating from it. In a creative enterprise things take as long as they take. But working backwards from October 8 and assuming three months of ticket sales, I write "tickets on sale July 8". Then

I allow a month to build expectations and create a buzz, so I write down "announcement June 8". I do this immediately after the conference call, on Monday May 16, and I realise that we have exactly three weeks to design a show, sign the artists and tell the world what we are doing. I add a whole load of other stuff, like when to hire TV directors, lighting designers, stage designers, artist liaison managers, line managers, stage managers, dressing room managers, transportation captains, travel managers, hotel co-ordinators. I highlight the key decisions and when they need to be taken. Decisions about tickets and merchandise and loads of TV stuff like show durations, hiring music clearance agents and the deliverables, which are all the things you have to give to a broadcaster in addition to the master tape.

I list the suppliers and when they should come on board: TV facilities, sound recording trucks, lighting, satellite upload trucks and the satellite time needed (loads, because we need two channels for 2D to send it everywhere, and 4 channels for 3D). We need to pin down the duration of the show, and to do all of that, and the design, we need Don Mischer's replacement to tell us what the show is, and for Jeffré to tell us who is in it. I send off my schedule. Chris thanks me and tells me it's useful. Jeffré thanks me with an exclamation mark! Sent from his iPhone!

I have a long conversation with Chris about the venue. Is Wembley available for the new date? Will Wembley work that late into the year for a music show? Will it be too cold for the artists and audience, will it rain and really dampen the spirits as well as the clothing? Chris thinks Wembley will cost a lot more, and that we should stick with Cardiff. To be honest, I don't know what I think. I've been told everyone will go directly to Cardiff and rehearse there for a week before the show. Chris argues that hotels will be a fraction of the London cost, and that rehearsal facilities, offered by the Welsh National Opera and arranged by a friend of his, will be cheaper too. While my gut tells me that such a major international event should be in London, the budgetary advantages of Cardiff seem to loom large as a positive reason to stick with Wales. The roof too, is an important consideration. The Millennium Stadium roof closes completely, unlike at Wembley, and keeps the rain out. It also, I am told, completely changes the ambience of the building, turning it from a stadium to an arena. So Cardiff it remains.

* * *

From:HaSH
Sent:*19May201113:52*
To:*Pete;Pete;Andy Picheta;Paul King;Chris Hunt*
Subject: *Drawings and Briefing Notes for Monday's meeting.*

Hi All,
I have sent everyone a link to a file system called DropBox: when you log in you will find a drawings file marked MJ Concert and all the drawings I have so far are in there. Let me know if anyone has any problems accessing.
Our first design meeting is confirmed for 11am Monday 23rd, at Limelight Media's offices, Third Floor, 62 Shaftesbury Avenue, London W1D 6LT
Attendees at the meeting will be:

Chris Hunt, LimeLight Media: Overall Project Director.
Andy Picheta: Heading up Film & TV Management
Paul King, Stadium Events: Promotion, Marketing & Distribution
Pete: Lighting & Video Design
Pete: Sound Design
Pete: Staging & Rigging Design
HaSH: Health and Safety Head: Design team, production & procurement head.
AssHaSH : PA to HaSH

Having talked to everyone I am confident that we have the beginnings of a concept for the show. In the drawings file you will see the footprint of the stage setup used by the U2 360 tour. Our intention is to emulate what this footprint achieved in maximising audience capacity and a VIP enclosure capacity of 2,000.

So far we are considering the gloved hand as the stage platform with the forearm acting as a link into the north stand giving our artist access point. We need to consider how we are to use the fingers as stage thrusts. We are currently working on the principal that we will have a fairly sizeable house band, plus we will also need to have room for dancers etc. Having the VIP area in such close proximity we need to keep the stage height low but also have the capacity to house all of the services below.

Current thoughts on the overhead rig is to use the tilted fedora hat as the feature, probably housing the video screens that can drop out of the hat and possibly using the band of the hat for further LED panels to give both image and solid colour. I think we will need to consider a grid through most of the roof area to accommodate the stage lighting, plus audience lighting for TV, overhead camera tracking plus flown follow spot positions.

The priority outcome from the meeting is to agree the stage footprint including VIP areas and barriers etc. plus camera positions so that we can calculate any seat kills prior to the imminent press release and tickets going on sale and ideally to produce drawings or at least 'roughs' for a meeting in Cardiff on Thursday so we have some very tight initial timescales to meet.

If you have any more questions prior to Monday then please email me. Looking forward to seeing everyone.
regards
HaSH

...All of which is complete news to me. Chris had obviously been busy, beavering away with a determination not to allow the absence of a show director to delay the all-important ticket manifest from being finalised. I have not been asked about the stage design, nor involved in the discussions, and I realise on reading the email reproduced above, that my plan (to sit back and find how the land lies before pushing for some proper world-class people do some proper world-class design, and - crucially - some proper, world-class lighting), may not have been the ideal thing to do. Because here we were, on the cusp of the greatest show on earth, looking at a design created by a Health and Safety chap, who seems to have promoted himself to Head of Production, Procurement, Environment and Design (HoPPED). But HaSH has HoPPED onto not just the design, which would need to be a disastrous mishmash before it affected the TV presentation, but the lighting as well, which was crucial to a great TV show. These vital elements, so incredibly important in our kind of multi act, fast turnaround, live-to-air show, have been put together by a man in a high visibility yellow jacket working out of a portacabin in Norwich. This was bad. I was supposed to be looking after the media, and I had singularly failed to do that, because I had stayed my hand and not pushed, from minute one, for a decent lighting guy.

Historically, shows are either filmed live on first presentation (like Eurovision) or once they have bedded down, once all the wrinkles are ironed out and the artists have settled into a performance that works (unless there are good reasons, as with *Lord of the Dance,* to shoot them early). The stage lighting is designed to work as a crucial part of the audience experience. Whether in the theatre or on a rock 'n' roll stage, the lighting is an editor, showing the audience what to look at and what not to look at. Tone, colour and the amount of light create mood. Whilst these tenets hold good for TV, the limited range and adaptability of the TV camera when compared to that of the human eye means the balances have to be completely different than in a concert which is not being recorded. Crudely put, 2D video needs a ton more light than the human eye, and 3D video needs a ton more than 2D. We also don't need lighting as editor, because we have close ups and mid shots and tracking shots and crane shots and reverse shots and all kinds of shots to keep the viewer looking at what's important at any moment. Filming an existing show means the show has to be re-lit. This used to mean bringing in a film lighting person, who in turn would bring in audience lighting and more lamps for the stage. In days gone by some show LDs (Lighting Directors) resented the intrusion and the changes to "their" lighting, and although most of them now understand the different media and work with the TV director to translate the show lighting, I needed an expert in both live and TV.

What I had was HaSH, and a team with very little information, very few credits, coming up when I Googled them. I had planned and hoped to light this show once, by an adaptable lighting director who understood both media and would make the thing work for both. The calibre of proposed artists on the stage also called for one of the world's best, someone who would enhance their performances by working with them, but also someone who would get the key lights right so the artists looked good on camera. However good HaSH and his team were, if you've only ever done small water colours you're going to bring the wrong brushes to the Sistine Chapel ceiling.

Still, off I went on the damned early FlyBe from Inverness to Gatwick, and turned up at Shaftsbury Avenue at the appointed time. I was actually several hours early, having got into Gatwick at eight and into Soho half an hour later. I settled down in the Costa under the office and waited for somebody to turn up and unlock the door. Media folk in Soho tend to start around 10 am. As I waited I tried to figure out a new game plan. Given that it's pretty hard to fuck up a stage, yet very easy to screw up the lighting, I chose to concentrate on the latter. But I could do little until I had more information. And I should have paid attention to the stage.

We are crammed into the conference room. Stadium plans are spread over the table. They show the playing surface and the lower tier of seating. Chris tells us the design concept, as developed by him and Jeffré, is the stage as giant glove, and the lighting rig a fedora hat with a video screen as the hat band. The design is terrifying in complexity. We debate for a while whether the hand is a hand or a glove, and I insist it should be a sequined, sparkly glove. One of the Petes assures me that's not a problem. I insist it should sparkle like Michael's glove sparkled. He tells us he can put in LED panels so the glove can become another projection surface, working with the big circular screen in the rig. This one will drop down for projections and fly up when not in use. Another Pete tells us about the special, cutting edge scrims that can be placed over the flown speaker stacks. Normally, no soundman on this earth would encourage putting ANYTHING in front of his speakers, but this material is so new, and so amazing, that it is transparent to sound so won't affect the noise. This gives us another two projection surfaces.

Next we talk about the position of the hand. The initial idea to have the forearm over the access tunnel, and so the thumb at the back of the stage, is reversed by Chris who wants the fingers as thrusts into the audience. So the thumb and forefinger become two thrusts at front stage left and stage right, and the little finger is at the rear. Instead of Michael's gloved hand presenting the show to the audience in a natural way, Thumb at the back and little finger edge forward, it's twisted so the hand is tipping away, thumb forward. It looks and feels weird, but nobody seems to notice.

I am asked about camera positions, and say I don't know until I've seen a plan and stood in the stadium. I've decided I'm not going to let the absence of a TV director get in the way of camera positions, just as Chris has decided to design the show himself in the absence of a designer. Unlike Chris I'm not going to commit to anything until I've got an expert in the room so for now I'm going to take every camera position I can think of, then double them to be sure, then add another ten for comfort. At least that will leave a shed load of tickets set aside for cameras, and any director coming on board will be spoiled for choice, and have the flexibility to position the cameras wherever he needs to. I didn't point out that it was the province of the TV director to choose the camera positions, and we were even further away from that position being filled than we were with the show director. I wasn't going to have the TV blamed for holding up the ticket manifest.

I had discussed the TV director with Chris, and a number of names came up. Chris wanted Hamish to direct the TV, but of course Hamish worked for, and co-owned, Done and Dusted, the live event production company Chris had brought into DCD Media a few years previously. Chris' cunning plan was to hire Hamish as a freelancer, something he knew was allowed for in Hamish's DCD/Done and Dusted contract. What he didn't want was to hire the whole caboodle of director, producer and production company, because he figured that he already had two out of those three (me and Iambic, his own company)

"Why should I give Done and Dusted the production fee when I can keep it for Iambic?" he asked. (Production companies work on a cost plus basis, each line item of expenditure marked up by a fee for doing the work. This is known as the production fee and is in addition to producer and director fees, which sometimes are not marked up) The answer to Chris' question was plain – he shouldn't. But success with this approach required a bit of flirting with Hamish, which so far Chris had yet to do. I'd only met the guy twice, so I was not the right person to get him on board. Chris had made him a millionaire, so he probably was the right person.

Adding a further layer of desirability for Hamish to direct the TV was the presence, on the GLE website, of about half a dozen Hamish directed, Done and Dusted produced TV events, like *Victoria's Secrets*, *Robbie Williams in Concert* and many more. Chris may have already sold Hamish as the director to Jeffré, who in turn would have sold him on to La Toya, Katherine and God knows who else.

In the meantime, the Shaftsbury Avenue design meeting was drawing to a close. We had a hand as the stage, which I kept reminding everyone was a glove, not hand, and an empty glove at that, because Michael is not there. We had a fedora hat as a lighting grid, with the hat band a screen. And we had two thin, narrow projection surfaces on the flown speaker stacks. We add another screen for good measure, one that will rise and fall in front of the band to present specific video material. All of this needed to be drawn up for a meeting in Cardiff in four days' time.

* * *

I have, as is my wont, jumped into the vacuum of the VIPs. Servicing this part of the market has been an important part of rock show income for quite a while, and the enhanced VIP packages create a lot of revenue while giving the hard-core fan something to treasure. I've had a little experience at the hotel in designing packages that offer a load of added value for quite a small outlay, packages that enhance the guest experience and help us sell more rooms.

It's not much, my experience, when weighed against the need to craft "once in a lifetime" experiences, but it's all we have, especially as Paul Kingy King is not particularly forthcoming. In fact he is so backward in coming forward, with anything, that I begin to wonder why he is here.

My nicest hotel offering is the Whisky Wisdom package, a two night break that steeps the customer in a complete malt whisky experience, without of course steeping them in whisky. They get a broad ranging whisky tasting at the hotel delivered by our resident Whisky Ambassador (me) that shows the difference between Speyside, Islay and Highland. They learn about the distillation process, and the way that process, followed by ten or more years in an oak barrel, gives Scottish malt whisky its flavour and colour. They go off to a distillery, and have earnest distillers talk to them of the minutiae of production for hours on end. They go off to a cooperage, to see the barrels being refurbished. They come back to the hotel, and get a whisky themed dinner with whisky in everything accompanied by the whisky that's in everything served in a glass as they eat. And if that isn't enough, they get a genuine, full blown Scottish Highland piper (they are really cheap up here, except at New Year) piping away by squeezing dead sheep innards into his armpit and creating a noise that reminds me of cats being skinned alive from the inside with only a wine bottle and a tin opener as tools. Now, *that's* a package – and I've sold three since I've been here.

This experience, terribly limited as it is, is streets ahead of any VIP package creating experience available anywhere within the team. Chris, as explained earlier, has only ever sold programme ideas to commissioners, and company ideas to investors. Paul King has only ever sold concert tickets and something very dodgy that landed him in prison (more later). HaSH has only ever sold Hi-Vis jackets, and his production team is very adept at putting up the stage and lights for product launches at the local supermarket. And the Americans? Well, Jeffré is invisible, and even if he wasn't his experience seems to lie in the realm of malted beverages – as does mine, but at least you can get pissed on Scotch whisky – and his troupe of jugglers haven't sold a bean of anything as far as I can figure. So here I am, filling the vacuum, and designing VIP packages for the concert.

One of the things that Leonard had raised at our first visit to Cardiff was a concern about servicing the artists equally and fairly. It was a wise comment, because nothing stirs the blood amongst the glitterati more than one of them being perceived as more glittery than another. So we've decided, in the interests of equality, to treat them all equally. I came up with a plan for a serried rank of identical Winnebagoes (big American camper vans), parked up with picket fences and garden furniture and a central marquee with bar and a green room and a press area. Then I came up with a VIP marquee next door, a massive tented village of bars, buffets and comfy chairs, with giant screens onto which the show would be piped, of waiters and sommeliers and decorations and a huge, feelgood, happy place where every VIP would feel very 'I' indeed.

To make all this work I proposed to rent Cardiff Arms Park, a rugby ground right next door to the Millennium Stadium and indeed sharing some of the fabric of it. The Millennium north stand is formed from the back of the Cardiff Arms Park south stand. At the time of building, the financially challenged rugby cohorts of Cardiff Arms Park refused to agree a deal with the lottery funding flush rugby legions of the Millennium Stadium. So instead of bulldozing Cardiff Arms Park into the ground and completing the Millennium oval, adding some car parking space and some more retail outlets, something a bit special, the architects had to work around a dilapidated, shabby stand and incorporate it into the design of the pride of, and new home of, Welsh rugby. So my plan was to cover the pitch at CAP – no palletised grass here – and have half of it for artists and the other half for VIPS. I then put together not one but three packages, each escalating in exclusivity. I thought I'd call them Bad, Dangerous and Thriller – crass I know but hey, I was swept up in the moment.

So the BAD package, the basic bronze VIP product, consisted of a Golden Circle ticket, access to the VIP enclosure right next to the artist dressing rooms (true – but I didn't mention the ten foot high security fence with screens, security patrols with dogs, mines and razor wire and trigger happy, AK47 toting freelance Somalian killers that would separate the VIPS from the stars), a free buffet and bar and a goodie bag of merchandise which included a branded umbrella to keep them dry on their 300 metre walk from VIP tent to stadium. Next was the DANGEROUS package, which had everything the BAD package contained but had the added extra of an invite to the after show party, and a meet and greet with "some of the artists performing in the show". I figured two dancers and a backing singer, and maybe a stagehand could be persuaded or bribed to spend three minutes in the VIP tent. The final, best and very golden THRILLER package included everything the previous two packages included, but in addition was a special gift designed especially for the occasion by La Toya Jackson (Star Ice anyone?), attendance at Friday's soundcheck, hotel accommodation, travel to and from the stadium by limo, and a meet and greet with the Jackson family. You can clearly see my thinking. In any other major show, this kind of stuff is very tdf (to die for). Fans would, I figured, kill for these packages. At least the rich ones. What I didn't understand at the time, was that fans of Michael were not fans of the family. I had however, done some package research. Bon Jovi offer a stage-side package for fans where you get up on stage, in an enclosure of course, right next to the band. Paul McCartney offered a sound check deal, similar to the one I'd constructed, with great success, but charging just under a thousand for the experience. The price for my packages: £995 for BAD, £1650 for DANGEROUS and £4995 for the ultimate THRILLER experience. Total revenue: a million quid. Cost of provision: about £320K. That's a 62% margin after VAT, which is what most retail operations try to achieve. You see, the infrastructure, the travel and hotels, staffing and food and drink were the expensive items. The rest of it was, like the cooperage and whisky custard, almost free to provide, but inaccessible, dream level, behind the scenes stuff for the fans. Or so I thought.

 I circulate my plans to my leaders and associates. Jeffré thanked me with an exclamation mark! Sent from his iPhone! Chris enjoyed the bottom line, and Paul Kingy King didn't respond, choosing not to take ownership of anything other than silence and inactivity.

 Off we go to Cardiff, for a big meeting to sort out the stage, the ticket manifest, the VIP packages, hiring the CAP (Cardiff Arms Park) for our artist village and VIP world and, in the afternoon, a meeting with Ticketmaster. But first the ticket manifest, the stage plan and the camera positions which, in the absence of anything else concrete have taken on a totemic quality in the minds of the team. Not knowing precisely where the close up camera is going to be seems to be holding up everything.

Tell me where the stage is and I'll tell you where the close up camera will be. Tell me if there are any duets and I'll tell you how many close up cameras there will be. And I'll tell you something else for nothing – wherever the close up camera goes is where there will be three or four other cameras too. Two will be primarily for mid shots and two shots, and one will follow the action, in a loose mid or a full length shot. They will all form a stack between 25 and 40 metres from the stage front. So, again, tell me where the stage front is and I'll tell you where at least four of the cameras are going to be. Until I get a director on board I can't be specific about anything else, because the reason to have a director is so he or she does all this, and the last thing they will want or accept is the producer telling them where their cameras are going. But I've directed enough stuff, even been nominated for an Emmy for some of it, to be able to make some intelligent guesses as to where a top class live concert TV director will want to put their cameras. But I can't do that until somebody, anybody tells me where the fucking stage is going to be, where the centre of the stage is going to be, where the front lip and back of it is going to be. Because all I can see out there is a load of grass and some seats. Anyone?

HaSH promises to have detailed plans available by the end of the week. I thank him and promise a camera plot as soon as I get the information. We move on to the disabled viewing areas. At Cardiff as elsewhere these are prime positions, usually large, level platforms and often eyed greedily by TV directors as great places to put a camera crane. I am told categorically that this is not on. There are minimum requirements enshrined in discrimination law as to the numbers and availability of disabled viewing. Kingy tells us that the price for these is usually the same as for the surrounding seating, but the carer comes free. I feign astonishment and argue that this is discriminatory to able bodied people who are not allowed to bring a carer for free. Kingy then tells us that it's quite common for unscrupulous fans to hire a wheelchair so they can get their mate in for nothing. Sales of disabled access tickets are the province of the stadium directly. Alex cuts off any further discussion before I am given an opportunity to make a total cock of myself and perhaps end up in court for a hate crime against someone with no legs. Chris agrees to the status quo. We talk more about loads of stuff, about security and curfews and trains. We discover that the trains stop at 9:30 in the evening, so our midnight finish is going to leave a lot of people with nowhere to go, unless they drive or come by coach. I ask about coaches and servicing package providers like coach companies and travel agents and Kingy tells me he will look into it.

  The team takes a look at my VIP packages and Alex is concerned that these might affect his corporate sales. I argue that the fan who wants to be in a box up here is different to the fan who wants to be at the front of the stage. Corporate quaffing is Alex's domain, hardcore fans who want to meet La Toya and drink Star Ice are mine. I ask that the stage be as low as possible, so the fans in the front have a good view, and so the close up cameras, which will need to be on the eyeline in height, won't be too high to spoil the view for everyone behind them half way up the middle tier. I'm assured the stage will be as low as possible, no more than five feet high. We break for a sandwich lunch, which is a pale echo of the marvellous spread put on when we came down with Leonard and co. Then we decamp to the CAP next door, and another conference room overlooking another pitch. This room is very small, with a little kitchenette area, and the groundsman makes instant coffee with lukewarm water, so the coffee crystals float on the top and refuse to dissolve. He hands out the floating coffee grounds and pale tea including the teabag in canteen-thick cups and a half a bag of Silver Spoon. The CAP people are pretending to be tough negotiators, but it's plain they don't have two teaspoons to rub together, and that they'll do exactly as the Millennium Stadium tells them to do. We talk about some game of rugby or other that is scheduled for the beginning of November and the groundsman is concerned the pitch won't be repaired and playable. I look out of the window at the sea of clover and dandelion that has overtaken every blade of grass out there, except where deep puddles reflect the pale Welsh afternoon sunshine, and I'm about to say something when Alex tells them not to worry, he'll get the WRU (Welsh Rugby Union) to change the fixture. How provincial is that. You can't see the FA shifting the Cup Final for a concert. Maybe Cardiff is the right place to be after all?

We trudge back to the corporate box for our meeting with Ticketmaster. As we walk down a narrow passageway and out onto the street, a route that my VIPS will have to take (which is why I've budgeted to give them umbrellas), I mull over what I need to know. Cardiff's terms of trade are that 25% of tickets go through the Ticketmaster site. This is the premier ticket seller in the UK. There is no event they do not sell tickets for. Chris does not want to use Ticketmaster, at all, or maybe he wants to use them a lot, I'm not too clear as he keeps airing both views, but "fuck Ticketmaster" seems to predominate when we are reminded they are a part of Live Nation, a massive, US owned conglomerate that in the past ten years has bought up every meaningful venue, promoter and music company in the world. Founded by entertainment mega-impresario Barry Diller, Live Nation had revenues in 2010 of $5.3 billion. Leonard had warned us about Live Nation, and how they would want to destroy our show – only because it was not their show. Live Nation owns the vast majority of every concert you have ever gone to. And if it doesn't, then chances are that AEG does. AEG is a subsidiary of Anschutz Holdings, a privately owned company run by Phillip Anschutz and is about half the size of Live Nation. Mr Anschutz is rated as the 31st richest American, worth about $7 billion. Anschutz Entertainment Group is one of the biggest show promoters in the world. They are the guys who put together the *This Is It* series of concerts in their own venue in London, the O2 Arena. Chris sees Live Nation/AEG as the evil empire. Responsible for Michael's death. Responsible for failing to put on a suitable Michael tribute concert. Hated by the family, by Jeffré Phillips, by Leonard Rowe. Given that Live Nation and AEG are competitors, industry behemoths and rivals, I'm not clear why they have been lumped together into an axis of evil, but there they are, with the Michael Jackson Estate making up the third part of the triumvirate of hate for *Michael Forever*.

Chris spends some time describing the nature of the enemy. This is what he says, which is probably an echo of what Jeffré has told him:

"Michael was killed because he couldn't do the London shows. His contract was for ten shows, but AEG sold tickets for fifty. Michael was in no fit state to do one. AEG could not insure him for *This Is It*, so they stood to lose tens of millions of dollars if he failed to perform. That's why they filmed the Staples Center rehearsal with so many cameras – they knew Michael would never get to London, never perform at the O2. So they set out to secure what assets they could, and then they got rid of him by overdosing him with his own medicine. The surveillance footage from cameras around his house is missing from the night he died. Who came and went in the hours before Michael arrived back from rehearsals?"

Chris then tells us exactly who arrived at Michael's house, about half an hour before Michael returned from rehearsals on that fateful day. He says a name. I'm not going to repeat it in a published work, because I'll get sued to death, because the name is the name of someone very high up the food chain. Very high up indeed. Scarily so. If you really want to know, phone me and I'll tell you. Chris continues the tale, perhaps as woven by Jeffré. He tells us the name enters the house, asks for Michael, and is told by the staff he is not in. The Name says he will wait for him, in Michael's quarters, and tells Dr Murray to wait in his. Michael returns home, and is alone with the Name. Then the Name leaves, and half an hour later Dr Murray finds Michael dying in his room.

The room is silent, and agog. Chris has painted us a picture of a very powerful enemy indeed, one that will go to great lengths to protect their bottom line. But he has not finished, and he moves on to the Michael Jackson Estate and John Branca, its controller.

"Branca was Michael's lawyer for a long time, but was sacked in 2002. After Michael's death he comes out of the woodwork waving a will, signed by Michael, giving him, Branca, control of the estate. At a very generous commission rate, far higher than normal. Michael had told everyone he had no will, that he wanted to die intestate, because under California law his wealth would then pass directly to his children. The signature was not like Michael's usual signature. The family challenged the will, but broke off the challenge and Katherine accepted a stipend and a house for her and the children. In punishment for her action against them, and to keep her compliant to their wishes, the Estate is deliberately keeping Katherine poor. She only gets $9000 a month to look after Michael's kids, which is a lot in a general sense, but very little in Beverly Hills to look after the kids of the King of Pop. The Estate pays for everything, utilities, security, school fees, the works. But they have threatened her many times that they'll shut her down, cut her off, if she doesn't toe the line."

Wow. After a long silence I ask whether the Estate, existing as it does to maximise the revenue from the legacy of Michael, would not be interested in a deal on *Michael Forever*.

"Not a chance," says Chris, "the family won't do anything with the estate. They hate them. They won't do anything with AEG either, because they blame AEG for Michael's death. This is why there has been no tribute concert so far, because the only meaningful tribute is one by the family. That's why getting the Jacksons on board is so crucial and vital."

"So with all these really powerful enemies out there, hating us and our show, why haven't they shut us down?" I ask.

"Because, so far, they don't know we're here," comes the worrying answer.

This information, presented by Chris as the truth behind Michael's demise, is fascinating, scary and sensitive. I am to hear it voiced several times again in various meetings, and the reaction is always the same; a stunned silence, a frisson of surprise, followed by a shrug and a sense of getting on with the work at hand. I think Chris told the story in an attempt to paint a picture of the size of the conflicting forces ranged against the concert, as painted for him by Jeffré. I retell it here as I heard it, but I also had to do a little research, to see what else is out there, to see whether it could possibly be true.

With regards to the estate and how John Branca came to be its administrator and executor, I found most credence in Jermaine Jackson's account in his book *Michael Jackson Through a Brother's Eyes*, which I found in Tesco for 99p. (Well done for being in Tesco. Not so good on the 85% markdown – forgive the author to author snipe). Jermaine and other commentators describe a marked deterioration in Michael's physical and mental wellbeing in the final months of his life, brought about by the strain of preparing for the *This Is It* show. John Branca, it appears was brought back into the fold by the concert organisers AEG in an attempt to surround Michael by people familiar to him. Yes Michael sacked him in 2002, but maybe he wanted him back in 2009.

Chris told us how the signature on Michael's will was unlike any other, but Branca was Michael's lawyer and close confidant for many years, so if anyone knew what Michael's signature was like it would be he. Michael reportedly told La Toya and everyone else he wanted to die intestate, so all his wealth would automatically go to his children. Now I don't know about California Law, but I know that dying intestate in England is a very bad idea, because there is nobody to look after matters, and the vultures will gather very quickly, arguments will ensue, and the result will be that nobody wins, except the lawyers.

So I picture Michael, tired, worried, sick, driving himself too hard, struggling to find the physical strength to work. His financial troubles are mounting, *This Is It* is a way out, a way to secure the future for his kids, but the massive focus and energy and effort required to build a show of this size is a huge drain on a frail man weakened by illness and time away from the touring stage. Many doubted whether he could do it, but Michael knew he had to. It must have been so hard, to force an aching body, and a genius creative mind cluttered by finance and management, to concentrate on the show. So when Branca says "Michael, I can take care of this," it can only be seen as a huge load lifted. And so what if the terms are more generous than Chris and Jeffré's idea of "normal" – the cost is still much less than the years of legal wrangling and combat that would follow an intestate death. The family, led by Katherine Jackson, mounted a challenge against the will, but eventually they backed down. In return, and as legal guardian for the children, she is looked after by the estate, although at this time, in mid-May, that "looking after" is, according to Chris, provided at the bare minimum. Do I believe John Branca stole Michael's estate? – Nah. Do I believe, as I am soon to discover that many fans believe, that the Estate is the embodiment of Michael's soul, spirit and talent? – Nah. The fans are naïve, as I was later to tell them: The Michael Jackson Estate is not Michael, it's just a lawyer with the keys to his house.

Did the concert promoters want Michael dead? Again, this part of the conspiracy theory is difficult to square with the known facts. Leonard Rowe had written something similar in his book, suggesting Michael was killed for his music catalogue. This catalogue, of thousands of popular songs, was co-owned by Michael and Sony, and held within an entity called SonyATV. Jermaine writes that Michael had to put up his portion of the catalogue as collateral to AEG.. No insurance company would touch Michael because of *Dangerous* and on-going health issues, so he and the show were uninsurable for his non-appearance. Jermaine tells us that Michael effectively insured himself, with

Sony ATV as the equity. No wonder he was worried and nervous about his ability to do the show. According to Jermaine, if Michael failed to deliver he would lose everything. With the catalogue in hock, AEG were covered financially whether Michael did the show or not. A successful comeback would open a huge treasure chest for all concerned. A failure would still net AEG millions, but not bode well for Michael. It was in nobody's interest for Michael to die. Everybody made more money if he was alive.

To see Michael as a victim is not wholly accurate – he needed *This Is It* and entered into a business arrangement with AEG, who put up the cash, and took the risk, albeit underwritten by the catalogue. AEG believed in Michael Jackson, at a time when few others in the industry did.

Yet according to Chris, Michael was killed by this axis of evil, at the hand of men so powerful that they were able to set up Conrad Murray as their patsy, the fall guy to take the rap for Michael's demise.

"Michael's death will never come to trial", Chris confidently predicted. "Murray will cop a plea, do a year or two inside, and get a handsome payoff when he comes out. Neither AEG nor Branca want the whole truth to come out in a courtroom."

With the help of Jeffré, Chris has convinced himself he is on the side of the angels, rooting for the battered widow and the orphaned children. He is Zorro, Robin Hood, Luke Skywalker and all of the Magnificent Seven, ready to fight the powerful yet evil empire on behalf of the downtrodden, the sick and the hungry. Or maybe he has fallen in love with the idea of four hundred million dollars. Either way, I begin to worry for my friend.

But back to Cardiff. In the afternoon we sit down in one of the stadium's corporate boxes for a meeting with Ticketmaster. Chris wants to do a deal to see if they would take all the ticketing, despite having lumped them as enemies of *Michael Forever*. We are joined by some more stadium management. Alex has been with us all day. I had been training for days with one of those grip exercisers, a spring loaded double handle that you squeeze and release, to be ready for the handshake with Alex. The hardest thing was not to grunt, wince, or show any effort as I used every molecule in my body to counter the incredible force exerted once again on my hand. I smiled, and I made it through the ordeal. The training meant my hand was usable again within minutes. It took longer for my face to relax out of the fixed smile that had been frozen in place by the effort and the pain.

The meeting with Ticketmaster does not go well. They tell us they will keep all the ticket revenue until after the show, to protect consumers from cancellation of the event, and themselves from demands for refunds if it goes ahead. They express polite surprise that GLE needs the ticket revenues to stage the show. Behind the manners lies a lack of trust. Michael Henry is outraged, as is Chris. The discussion moves around the issue of the refunds, which Ticketmaster and the stadium keep control over. Chris believes it should be the call of the promoter whether to refund someone because the toilet is too far from their seat, or the popcorn queue too long. The opposition disagrees. Chris accuses them of playing fast and loose with his money. An acrimonious discussion develops about the way the show is financed and insured. Not only do Ticketmaster express surprise and concern that the ticket revenues are required to stage the show, but they go on to suggest that the insurance cover, as negotiated by Michael Henry, is inadequate.

Chris and Michael consider their financial standing and characters are being impugned. Here they are, with an amazing project and a cast of thousands, and some ticket seller is openly doubting their word and their abilities. Michael reminds the meeting that he and Chris are FSA approved financiers. The pair are especially angry that the stadium is colluding in what they see as an unwarranted and unprecedented offence. Chris threatens to walk out and stage the show elsewhere. Ticketmaster says "suit yourself," and Alex looks glum.

We coldly part ways and Alex's handshake is for once bearable without a dedicated training programme of hand development. I decide to ride with Chris in his car as far as Bristol so we have a chance to talk. Bullishly and very naively I suggest we don't need Ticketmaster. If this event is as huge as we believe, we can sell the tickets anywhere, through any medium. The fans will seek them out, flock to whatever online stall we set up. Paul King calls to say the same kind of thing, and we convince ourselves we have turned a defeat into a victory. We are going to sell the tickets ourselves. Who needs the experts, when Zorro is in town?

One side effect of the Ticketmaster meeting coming to an acrimonious conclusion was that we never got to discuss the pricing levels for the tickets with the those who made a living selling concert tickets. It would have been invaluable advice, although I'm pretty certain it would not have been heeded.

> *On 6 Jun 2011, at 16:32, Chris Hunt wrote:*
> *Just a note to say that nothing much has happened since we met. The stadium is looking into taking the 'risk' of the ticket money returns and we are in the process of establishing our own bespoke ticketing operation. It is not clear how this side of things will pan out yet, but we have a fallback position courtesy of our investors*

if all goes wrong with it so please do not fee concerned that the event is at risk because of that ambush. Alex at least had the grace to apologise.

This should not hold up any other activity, except that we should keep the stadium thinking we may move out and therefore we should not send them revised floorplans etc. – we should however get them done and ready as we had discussed previously. I shall look forward to seeing them!

All best
  Chris

Hi Chris,
Thanks for the update, Pete is in the office this week and working on the revised floor plan. I should have it back in a couple of days. I will post it into the DropBox and let everyone know when it's there, and post it up in PDF format so that everyone can view it. Once we have agreement we are going to lay a grid plan over the top so that we can reference camera positions easily.
Fingers crossed for the contracts, once that is done everything this end will follow on very quickly.
Regards
HaSH
Health and Safety Head

More delay, as we pretend to the stadium we are about to up sticks to... where exactly? They know and I know it's bluster, and pretty unconvincing bluster at that, but Chris is adamant we teach Cardiff a lesson for their perceived perfidy. It took HaSH three weeks to come up with a plan that made any sense when studied. I don't know why. Maybe he was holding out to get paid some money up front. Maybe he was so spooked by the Ticketmaster thing that he didn't want to invest any more time in the project. Later I was told that Cardiff's plans, the base ones that we were to use for detailed design, were wrong and showed loading points in the roof in the incorrect positions. Who knows, but eventually we all had something to look at. I put pen to paper, found my old scale ruler and came up with forty three possible locations where a director would, could, might want to put something. I had areas for cranes and dollies and static cameras, on the floor and on the stage and in the lower, middle and upper tiers. I had remote trackers in the rig, a hot head bang in the centre above the stage, and cameras everywhere else I could think of.

I went down to Cardiff and walked every position with their lovely box office lady. I warned her that these were estimated positions. I explained that until the stage is up and there is somebody on it, we cannot be sure that Camera 26 is going to be in rows 1 and 2 of Block 34 in seats 12, 13, 14 and 15. It may have to move up a row or two, or down, or along, or into another block completely. We know we want it around here somewhere, but if we concretely say "here" at this early point in the proceedings we will invariably discover that the sound department have put up a forest of antennas for their radio pick-ups, or the lighting department have put a lamp at the opposite side of the arena that shines right down the lens of this camera, completely wiping it out. Camera 26 then needs to move, last minute and unplanned, and it's going right where the Feeney family from Stockport have settled in for an evening of Michael, thermos flasks of tea and those corned beef sandwiches that Dad likes so much (on thick sliced white bread mind), at the ready, and they don't see why they should move, even with the offer of better seats elsewhere.

I know the concern from the team about a lack of precise information about the camera positions is a bit of a red herring, a bit of smoke to cover the myriad other very basic things that have not been done, but I'm not going to let my department be the wanting one. I prepare the lovely box office lady for a world of re-seats, so when the Feeneys arrive and find a camera in their seats, they are immediately and politely redirected to Row 1 of Block 32, really good seats at the front of the tier so they have a ledge for those corned beef sarnies and a much better view of the stage. Everyone is happy, even the stadium stewards, because they are the ones that have to deal with the public, and forewarned, forearmed, with great seats ready to hand out, they can do so effectively.

CHAPTER 5.
THE PAROJIM

Everything begins to set us free
Can't you see, I don't wanna walk away

The hiatus continued during most of June. Mid-month, Chris suddenly flew to Los Angeles, apparently to persuade Jeffré not to pull out of the project. The Jacksons had still not signed, Katherine had not formally given her backing and show director Don Mischer had either suddenly become unavailable because he was bought off by AEG or, more likely, had only ever said maybe to the job and – when pressed – decided it was not for him. It depends whether you climb onto the conspiracy bandwagon or stay on the side of sanity and what passes for normality in this business.

As we waited, for some Jacksons, for some acts, for some direction, for the word, I remained in my Scottish Highland fortress, trying with increasing desperation and failing with increasing frequency, to find someone that could manage the place while I was gone. Not knowing whether I actually would be gone or not made this process somewhat tricky. I hired one girl who was really strong at interview. She showed style, class, and a knowledge and feeling for hospitality. I hired her, and she never turned up for her first day. I hired another who proved to be the laziest, scuzziest most disgusting female I have ever had the misfortune to lay eyes on. Okay, I shouldn't have hired her, but on first meeting she had scrubbed up a bit and made all the right noises. Once hired, she would disappear for hours on end, hiding in the rooms and texting her boyfriend – what a lucky man he must be! She was never where she was supposed to be, always late, always mucky and grubby but not in a good way, and she set fire to the cottage accommodation that we make available to staff. She lasted a week. Another one turned up after being hired, worked one shift and then disappeared, taking three bottles of whisky with her.

I had been spoiled you see, because for over two years the place was looked after by Dom, a mid-twenties chap from some place in Lancashire called Baking Tray or something. He wasn't particularly experienced, but he really, really cared about the place and the guests. His work ethic outshone nearly everyone else's in the hotel, including mine, which meant some of the staff didn't like him. On his own in the cottage, he professed to being a writer, but I never saw anything he wrote. The first spring he was here I decided he needed some female company, so I put out an ad and hired Helen. My plan worked, because they were shagging within weeks, Dom was happier and more content, and the pair of them lasted until April 2011. Helen didn't really like people that much, which meant my dogs were brilliantly looked after, but the guests less so. She went off to babysit thirty-five Schnauzers for some mad American woman in northern Spain. Dom took a TEFL course and joined her. He's now teaching Spaniards English, and doing very well.

* * *

I get a call from Chris to come down to London, and as he's paying I immediately oblige. Not for anything to do with the concert, but a follow up meeting with BBC gatekeeper Sam Anthony, whom we met up in Glasgow. The Bristol office had been beavering away coming up with ideas for what used to be called documentaries, then Fact-Ent, and now "Knowledge". Sam Anthony is Head of Knowledge at the BBC, which I suppose means you can ask him anything, but only if you are at the BBC when doing so. Anything outside of the corporation is a mystery to him, not part of the knowledge he is in charge of. Part of his remit is Head of Knowledge for BBC Scotland, but this is a very part time role, as there is very little knowledge in Scotland generally, and even less at the corporation. It means he is only in BBC Glasgow about one day a month, so Chris and I have travelled to London to present programme ideas to BBC Scotland in London, so they can be shown on the network and the BBC can claim to be engaging in the regions.

Security badged and through the turnstiles, we march down corridors to the lift area. Much has changed at Television Centre, or TVC to the knowing, since I was last here. Franchises have sprung up everywhere; there's a Costa Coffee, a KFC, two branches of WHSmith, an M&S Food and for all I know an H&M, Wallmart and a Poundland, where packs of used staples and rejected programme proposals are on sale at knockdown prices.

Chris' mood is thundery and bleak. He confides he hates this process, of kowtowing to people he considers inferior, of jumping through a myriad hoops for a commission worth very little. He wonders why he bothers: I tell him that with Michael Forever a success, he will never have to again. I can smell his desire to turn his back on this mediocre documentary rubbish for BBC4, his desperation to join the ranks of the A team, his longing for recognition as a major player.

Shakespeare and my Brain was originally pitched to Channel 4, and was to be presented by Alan Carr – the histrionic camp one with glasses. The comedian was to be wired up to a brain monitor and then fed some Bard. This would light up those areas of the brain which react to chocolate, and Alan Carr would get all excited. An expert would witter on and add some science. Commissioners at C4 thought it had merit, but not enough, presumably because Alan Carr is always excited, so there was no emotional arc. One of Chris' elves then reworked it for the BBC by replacing Alan with Simon Russell Beale. Our leading Shakespearean actor would be wired up to a brain monitor and recite some Bard. This would light up those areas of the brain which react to Shakespeare and Simon would get all thespian and recite some more. Surprisingly, Sam turned this one down, presumably because Simon Russell Beale is always going to get excited about Shakespeare, and so there's no arc of discovery.

The Song Detectives featured some professor of music and a sidekick touring the country to track down songs in the local community zeitgeist. A sort of X *Factor* meets *Hairy Bikers* outreach programme but without Simon Cowell, or the X, any factor or chefs on motorbikes. I kept calling it *Songcatchers* for which I was reprimanded many times. Chris had shot a teaser, which he had brought with him, but neither Sam nor Chris nor Sam's assistant could get the DVD in the meeting room to work, so Chris had to describe the teaser. I don't know what Sam got, but I got two blokes standing in a flock wallpapered living room listening to some old woman warble some working class "proud to be a steelworker" bollocks while trying not to choke on her false teeth. I never saw the teaser, so I never knew if I was right. Surprisingly, Sam turned this one down, presumably because of the lack of interaction between the two presenters, and lack of anything on the teaser DVD.

Deciding that the future of Iambic's Scottish ambitions were hanging by a thread, I waded in to the increasingly desultory meeting with an off-the-cuff idea.

"What about steam trains?" I asked nonchalantly. "There's at least three lines operating in Scotland, and one of them goes to Hogwarts."

"Brilliant idea. Steam trains always play well, and there's

nothing else like it in the pipeline," said Sam. "One worthy of pursuit. Find the narrative arc, write the treatment and have it on my desk ASAP."

Oh God. The last thing I wanted to do was make some crappy documentary about steam trains. Chris didn't know whether to thank me for salvaging something from the meeting, or berate me for pulling the rug from under his elves.

Despite stealing Chris' thunder in the meeting, I find myself invited by him to the Derby. Chris is a member of the RAC Club, and they have a swanky country house right next to the race course at Epsom. For Derby Day they put up giant marquees, barbeque skewers of whole cows and entire pigs, set out tables of ten and sell them to their members at twelve hundred quid a pop. Chris had bought one, but didn't seem to have eleven friends that wanted to come, so he was handing out last minute invitations to whoever was within reach.

The package came with a pass to the Queen's Enclosure, where one could, along with ten thousand of her closest friends, watch the race with the Queen. To enter this most inner of Establishment sanctums, one had to wear morning dress. Now for me this usually means the boxer shorts from the day before, but a sense of disquiet, a niggle that the Queen had something different in mind, drove me down to Moss Bros where I was fitted out to look exactly like the doorman at the Dorchester Hotel.

I drove down and met my fellow guests. There was a round lawyer called Bard, his schoolmarm wife who was actually a doctor, Michael Henry and wife, an accountant called Michael Barton and his pretty blonde spouse, and me. My date for the day was a charming young chap called Joe MaCarthy, who ran a film fund called Octopus. Of Chris there was no sign, so we stood around and wondered whether it was the done thing to open the champagne without the host present. Eventually thirst overcame protocol and we got stuck in. Chris arrived very late and very dishevelled, looking as if the doorman at the Dorchester had demanded his suit back, and had fought Chris for it. Chris' brittle wife Jacquie came too.

Having consumed several sides of grilled and properly fatted calf, it was time to get to the races. A minicoach took us the thousand yards from Woodcote House to a back gate on the borders of the golf course. From there we walked about a hundred yards along the B290 and entered the racecourse and crossed the race track to get to the Queen's Stand. What a fine leveller is The Sport of Kings! Here we were, dressed like toffs to a man, parading through a throng of England's finest. Sunburnt girls in Kiss Me Quick hats, dads and boyfriends in singlet string vests, mums with their knitting in bags as big as their hips and gor blimey uncles with wads of cash. Uniformly they took the piss, as a string of overweight ponces dressed as for a cheap wedding, sweated and struggled their way to their moment with royalty.

The royal party, together with a bunch of Saudi sheiks were out inspecting the horses. I joined the crowd creating a tunnel of admiration for Her Majesty leading to the steps and the entrance to her stand. Once she (she? Can one ever refer to our Queen as she?) and Prince Phillip had passed, I felt it was time to move in and find my fellow Derby-ists, from whom I had become separated in the milling multitudes. Up the steps I went, and through the glass doors into a lobby thronged with people, all smiling and pointing cameras at me. In front, by contrast, was a clear run, just a few morning suits between me and Elizabeth II. Instantly I realised what had happened: I had inadvertently joined the Royal Party! The hotel concierge outfit had served as a uniform that made me uniform. There was no difference between me and the rest of the Queen's entourage. I smiled and kept moving, giving a little wave here and there. Some ten metres on the queen turned left and entered a lift. There was space for more people, it was not full, Otis would allow up to twelve persons. I could have kept going, got in too, but discretion forced me forward, away from royalty and back into mere Moss Bros rental.

"I didn't see Kate Middleton" I said to the group, on rejoining.

"That's because she was behind you in the procession" came the answer.

Later, on a search for the toilets, Mrs Barton and I found ourselves entering a large room on the fourth floor, tables groaning under the weight of food and champagne. The occupants were at the far end, on the balcony watching the race. We quaffed a glass of Krug and departed, too full of cow to be tempted by the delights on offer. Back in the corridor I saw the name on the door for the first time, as it softly swung shut.

Duke of Westminster. The toilets were further along

* * *

The drawings of how the stage will look finally arrive. It's a performer's and TV director's nightmare. The thumb and forefinger form two thrusts protruding diagonally into the auditorium. The band is in the centre of the palm. This is difficult for the stage director and performers, because there are only about four feet from the front of the band – who, inexplicably, are in a pit – and the front of the stage. Most of the floor space is on the two thrusting digits, which are about sixty feet from the centre, and double that from each other. The 'V' they form is within the barrier, so the nearest a performer can get to the audience, in the centre, is about eighty feet. This is madness. The bond between performer and audience is the crucial, most vital thing that gives any show its energy. We might as well not bother with Cardiff, hire Pinewood studios and do the thing at a fraction of the cost. Like I said, the stage design would have to be a real disaster to affect the filming, and so it has come to pass. I forcefully make my points, but Chris vetoes any changes to the stage. The audience issue is addressed by hiring extras to fill the stage side 'V'. As our employees, they are exempt from the health and safety rules governing audience. The fact there's not much room for the artist to perform, and nowhere to stick a camera to film them, is not addressed.

> **From:** Andy Picheta
> **Sent:** 08 June 2011 15:16
> **To:** Chris Hunt; Paul King; HaSH
> **Subject:** version 3
> The gaps between fore/index/wedding are 1.5m at the widest point. The gap between wedding and pinkie is 2.5m
>
> The distance from tip of thumb and tip of forefinger to the barrier, and therefore the audience, is about 6.5 to 7 m, which is a heck of a way. There is no front and centre on the stage, because such a point is 11 metres from the audience and therefore too far for the artiste. There's at present no area for much lateral movement (and they do like to run up and down the front of stage). As it stands the centre camera track would be a single track between tip of thumb and forefinger rather than broken in 2 as shown at present. Unfortunately, this gets just side shots from distance as most artists will spend most time either on the thumb or forefinger. There is nowhere for the God Dolly. I'd get rid of the press pit (give 'em VIP tickets) and reduce the barrier to tip distance by half, so it indents at the centre and keeps the audience as close as possible across the entire front
>
> Or turn it around so the thumb is at the back, giving a much straighter edge to the audience

Best

A

You may well be right about the press pit and barrier to pit distance but I like the orientation and size of the glove now and we should work with it, and work out the barriers, press, camera tracks etc. around it. Front and centre will be between thumb and forefinger, which seems fine to me.

Re VIP numbers we should go with 2500 standing plus 700 per side seated (i.e. one tier of seats each). This is masses!

Thanks all

Chris

So the boss has spoken, the stage is what it is, and the media presentation of the show (the filming that is going to live on in perpetuity, the four hundred million dollar value, the placement of cameras and everything else that needs to go into capturing this event), is all going to be governed by a twisted, convoluted shape that has, for very good reasons, never been used before in a stadium. And paramount of those reasons is that it doesn't work. I hope the replacement for Don Mischer sees the folly of this design, and we have time to change it.

From: "Chris Hunt"
Date: Fri, 24 Jun 2011 21:36:41 +0100
To: Paul King; HaSH; Andy Picheta
Subject: Jackson concert
Hi guys

Jeffré has joined the fray in Los Angeles and is claiming a lot of success, with deals agreed, contracts sent out, and the firm intention to announce the little gig on July 8th, exactly 3 months ahead of the concert.

While some Jacksons will clearly hold out as long as they can, he told me last night that we have others plus apparently Lady Gaga, Usher,

> Ne-Yo, Prince, Shakira, Stevie Wonder, Celine Dion and Jennifer Hudson on the hook, and most of the others we wanted not far behind.
>
> We've had a false dawn or two and this may be another but it feels more real this time.
>
> Keep keeping the faith please gents...
>
> Meantime Ron Weisner is I'm told looking at the floorplan and will come back with a few thoughts soon. I suggested to Jeffré that the thoughts should be of the 'wow, fantastic, off you go' kind.
>
> To infinity, and beyond!
> Chris

More transatlantic conference calls. I'm getting quite used to them. We talk about merchandising, and the website, and the amazing marketing opportunities. We talk to a whole load of people who are not Jeffré. The man Jeffré chose to front the US end of Global Live Events was Paul Ring, a music industry exec, band manager, ex-promotions guy at Universal, and all round pop biz insider. One of the foot soldiers rather than a high flyer, Paul Ring took his place alongside various other Rons and Britneys and Jims as the face of Global Live Events in the USA. A kind of Parojim (PAul, ROn, JIM – geddit?) of execs, but made up of not just these three, but others too, faces of a corporation but without the power to make any decisions. I think there were about a dozen of them in all.

The lack of a show director is finally addressed. Jeffré hires Ron Weisner, a music industry veteran, ex-manager of Michael, ex-everything and now a successful TV show director, staging, amongst other things, the annual BET (Black Entertainment Television) Awards. He knows everybody and is widely respected. On hearing his name I Google him and start to relax. Ron has a bit of the A-list about him. Although hiring him, Jeffré at the same time voices concerns that, because of his close links to the Jacksons and Estate lawyer John Branca, Ron may ultimately sabotage the show. Ron is not to be trusted. Ron might be a covert operative for the axis of evil, or he might not. Meanwhile Ron has no idea he has been hired by Jeffré, because the actual hiring was done by the Parojim, who are getting increasingly flaky. On one conference call the subject of the artists comes up, as it often does. Who is on board, I ask. The answer comes back as vague yet as promising as ever. My heart sinks. I met these bozos in mid-April, when they assured us that the entire world of entertainment was ready to walk on and perform. Here we are, a whole two months later, and they still haven't actually even asked anyone! Fucking Hell! What have they been doing? Perhaps Ron can add some much needed structure to this thing. I meet him on a conference call. Another deep, luxurious voice. He immediately tells us that he will sort out the artists, that many on the list are actually not available for October 8 (Fucking Hell, again!), but that he is certain a high profile, A-list event like this will attract the talent. He is also of the Michael firmament, having managed both him and the Jacksons. So he is very much in the loop, and I'm cheered by the gravitas he brings to the show.

At the very end of June, just a week before we launch, the Jacksons finally sign their contracts. This has been a long and drawn out process, because at Jeffré's insistence they had to sign in the presence of Jeffré's lawyer, so I'm told. They have been known, you see, these tricky Jackson fellows, to sign something and then say they hadn't actually signed anything and that any signature was a forgery. Not an un-signing, you understand but a non-signing. Even though they had signed, they would argue that actually, they hadn't. As a result, it had taken three weeks from the agreement of their deal to the application of ink on the contracts, in the imposing office of Jeffré's lawyer Michael Morris. The event was probably videotaped, audio recorded, and actually carried out on a memory foam mattress that was immediately sent off for DNA profiling and setting in plaster.

The signatures mean that we actually now have an official Jackson tribute to Michael, and the tentative plans for a July 8 announcement start to firm up. But there is much to do, because much has not been done.

Of vital and early import is a PR company. Somebody to handle the expected flood of press enquiries, to develop stories, to keep us in the news. I had discussed this with Chris, and neither of us wanted a repeat of posh upper class twit PRotty swanning about and charging fifty grand to say "Yah, Oh Yah," kissing the air either side of both cheeks "Muah, Muah!" and ending up delivering a half page at the back of Tatler. I suggested Mark Borkowski, having first met him when he launched *Lord of the Dance*, and also looked after Flatley, but Chris went with a company he had used before on some classical documentary thing or other. The media plan, which had come about during one of the meetings at the stadium, probably at their suggestion, was for the LA press conference to be beamed live onto the big screens in Cardiff. Very quickly however, the disadvantages of such a provincial venue came to light, with no journalists showing the slightest interest in travelling to Cardiff to watch a video screen. A London conference was soon added to the mix, relegating Cardiff to a local event. With Chris off to LA to lead the announcement with the Jacksons, and Michael Henry deemed unsuitable to be the public face of anything, it fell to me to be in charge of the London press conference.

From: Leigh

Sent: Thu 6/30/2011 6:30 PM
To: Angela
Cc: Andy Picheta
Subject: RE: Press conference - Michael Forever The Tribute Concert
Hi Angela
Thanks for this.
We have had a little more feedback from journalists (bearing in mind they have no idea what the announcement will be). Both BBC News and the Guardian have come back to say that they would be unlikely to send someone in person (as they have limited resource) but they would be likely to pick up the story and run with it later on. They did comment that if the announcement was going to be 'monumental' then they would consider sending someone but that it is a long way to go for most London based journalists.
Apologies for not having more positive news. I think it's incredibly exciting and would love to be a part of it but I don't want to promise you a campaign that we may not be able to deliver on.
Let me know your thoughts.
Many thanks,
Leigh

From: Chris Hunt
Sent: Thu 6/30/2011 11:35 PM
To: Angela Hall
Cc: Andy Picheta
Subject: Re: Press conference - Michael Forever The Tribute Concert
Todays conf call - they are now daily, screwing up my holiday nicely - indicated that at least 3 Jackson brothers will be at the concert and press conf, plus Katherine and Joe. Guest artists with agreed contracts but not signed yet their end are Stevie Wonder, Ne-Yo, Chris Brown (slight visa issue there), Prince, Lady Gaga, Beyoncé, Madonna, Mary J Blige and Shakira. Maybe only 5 or 6 can be announced Friday week..Maybe Leigh should leak these names carefully - I'm told it should make the 9pm News - to gauge reaction. Do we need a London venue to hold the press conf as well/instead? If so can they fix it?.
C

From: Andy Picheta

Sent: 01 July 2011 10:21
To: Chris Hunt; Angela Hall
Subject: RE: Press conference - Michael Forever The Tribute Concert

There's a conference call with Franklin Rae later this morning (Friday) to figure out a strategy. I think we should be REALLY careful with Madonna's name until there's a deal memo. To do a press conference in London will of course make the Cardiff one just a regional thing. We're basically inviting journos to watch TV so the stadium venue is more spectacular - the story will break huge anyway and an announcement from Cardiff at least emphasises where it's gonna happen
Andy Picheta
Producer
Iambic Scotland

Well, at least I stopped Chris from announcing Madonna performing at an event she probably (then and still now) knows nothing about. Do what you like, but don't piss off Madge – ever. The distance to Cardiff from London already seems to be a factor too. Why don't people want to spend over two hours on a train to go to South Wales? Beats me. And yes, Iambic Scotland makes a brief appearance at the email signoff there, the sum total of its contribution to the TV universe.

Anyway, now that I've taken on press duties, as well as media and VIP ticketing, I dip a toe into web design. It seems nobody has thought about the website for the event, despite this being the province of the Parojim. There is the Global Live Events site, built originally to impress La Toya enough to believe what her manager Jeffré was telling her, but it was full of projects belonging to Done and Dusted, the live TV and event company Chris had negotiated into Digital Classical Media PLC. Yes, some Placido Domingo programme Chris had made back in the nineties was there too, but much more prominent were shows for *Victoria's Secrets*, Robbie Williams concerts, and surprise surprise,

Cats and *Joseph* too. Global Live Events was presented as quite a player, yet hadn't actually been involved in any of the credits they listed, except perhaps indirectly. I point this out. I also politely suggest it might be a good idea to, sort of, um, have a website, with a domain name like michaelforever.com and should someone like to look into that? The Parojim jump to it with that typical American gung-ho, boo-yah! approach that they have to most things, and a day later, which is fast for these guys, we have the dot com. I then suggest that maybe we should get the dot co dot uk also, as the concert is in the UK, and off they go again, no doubt high fiving all the way to the domain shop, and come back with that one too. Well done chaps! We have the correct domain name that matches the event name with seven days to go to the launch date. When they ask, I tell them not to worry about securing the Brazilian, Polish or Malinese addresses. What we don't have is a website, so the Parojim jumps about some more and hires a very laid back gent called Meerkat, who, you know, does the web design and speaks something called Aitchtee-Emel, which is a language, apparently. Meerkat has a phone number with a 310 area code, so I imagine him in some shack on Venice Beach, surf boards stacked against one wall and sack loads of high grade Mexican Number One against another. There, in the dim afternoon half-light of a Pacific sunshine that fingers its way in through the closed shutters, the beams barely making it to the surf boards through the thick haze of marijuana smoke, sits Meerkat, his young yet prematurely aged stubbly face eerily lit by the glow from his screen. A couple of bikini clad nubiles laze around, drinking iced peppermint tea and gazing blankly at the fan slowly rotating above them. He assures us all, on yet another conference call, that it's gonna be really cool, and yeah, sure it'll be ready, but in a cool way.

Later on in this first week of July, there is a brief pause in the daily conference calls. Jeffré is away and wants everyone to gather on the phone on Friday, seven am LA time, three pm in London, and sometime in the afternoon in Scotland. We dutifully dial in and get Pow Wow Now-ed into our virtual meeting room. As we wait for Jeffré the Parojim twitters again about putting the whole thing off to next year, and Chris again, less patiently this time, explains why that is not an option. Then Jeffré joins, and tells us we have to postpone the launch. He needs more time with the artists. His team have reached out to everyone, and are planning to send out some beautiful invitations to them all, personal invitations from Katherine Jackson herself and no doubt full of red and gold swirls. I cannot believe what I'm hearing. Months of work, all of it unpaid, and we are no further forward than we were in early April. Jeffré is insistent, but also calm and charming. Give him just two more weeks and we'll have the greatest announcement there ever was, of the greatest show there ever will be. Everybody agrees to this second major postponement of the project. A new date for the launch is set, Monday July 25. Twelve noon, live in LA, with feeds to London and Cardiff. A great announcement, with Katherine and the Jacksons and La Toya and a host of stars all present, all announcing together. I set about rescheduling the London arrangements, while Chris' most senior elf tells the stadium in Cardiff.

The list of outstanding things that need to become in-standing grows longer. Primary of these is a way to actually sell the tickets. Michael Henry has been dealing with this, and he's found an independent ticket agent called Tix-Me who have assured him they can handle the expected flood of applications. What Tix-Me don't have, or aren't prepared to offer, or Chris and

Michael aren't prepared to use, is their own arrangement, their own merchant ID, with a credit card clearing house. So Michael is dealing with this too, getting a merchant ID for Global Live Events from WorldPay. Without this in place, we cannot sell the tickets to anyone wanting to pay by card.

Every time you or I use a card to pay for something, either in a store or online, the payment is processed by a clearing house. They act as the collectors between the merchant, the customer, the credit card company, and the issuing bank. It took me about two weeks to set one up when I bought the hotel. Mine is called Streamline, and it is a part of WorldPay. In the case of GLE, WorldPay are being either difficult, or protective of their own interests (depends on whether you accept Chris' combative stance or just see the complexities the other guy is working with) because they want weeks to make the necessary checks, and they want to hang on to all ticket receipts until after the concert. So we are back to exactly the point at which Chris walked out of any deal with Ticketmaster, because they wanted to keep the receipts too, but we are several weeks closer to the concert, and just days from the announcement. Michael Henry is also negotiating the insurance for the event. The policy is crucial for all concerned – investors, WorldPay, Cardiff Stadium and our brand new ticket agent. Nobody wants to be caught out should the event cancel, not least the insurers, who are holding out for a strict definition of what is, and what is not, going to trigger any cancellation claim. War won't. Terrorism won't. Non-appearance by an artist won't. Ash clouds will. Burning down of the stadium will, and so will non-appearance by more than half the artists – even if they don't appear because of ash clouds, which I think is a bit of a result, given how travel insurers have been running a mile from ash cloud disruption since initially getting caught out by it early last year. If the ash cloud comes from an inferno at the stadium we are doubly covered.

We are back at the stadium to finalise the ticket price. Tix-Me are there, as of course is bone-crusher Alex. I've warmed to him now, and have incorporated his handshake into my regular training routine. The stadium box office managers have been working on the manifest, and everyone is nervous of the ticket price. I try some direct questioning of the "what do you think?" kind, but everyone backs away from any criticism of the pricing, which is still the same as Chris put down on that train ride back in April. I've persuaded him to have some "cheap" seats, but even these are, at £55, twice the price of what I believe a cheap seat should be. At £249, the Golden circle tickets are really expensive, even though they offer both a lower tier seat and access to the front of the stage. I take Chris through the sliding glass doors of the hospitality box and out into the stadium.

"Chris, every expert in that room thinks the ticket prices are way too high, and they sell concert tickets for a living. Are you sure you want to price at these levels?"

His answer is to go back in and tell the experts they are cowards.

"This is the biggest live event in the UK since Live Aid. People are going to come from all over the world, and the ticket price is going to be a small part of their expenditure. We have the greatest artist line up a stage has ever seen. Take That sold out in minutes, which shows their pricing was too low. I am not going to make the same mistake. These are the prices."

"What happens if we go on sale at these levels and then have to move the price?" I ask.

Paul King quickly replies: "Then we're dead, and we lose all credibility with the punter."

"We're not going to have to lower the price," says Chris, adamant he is right, resolute, unbending.

So the die is cast, but the ticket price itself is not the only issue needing resolution at this Cardiff meeting.

WorldPay, like Ticketmaster before them, are insisting on holding on to the ticket revenues until after the event. This is a problem for Chris, as he does not have enough investor money to get to the show. The cashflow is dependent on a sponsor, which Jeffré is working on, and until such time as the sponsorship deal is finalised, there ain't enough money. So Chris needs to get the ticket receipts in early. And someone has come up with a plan to do just that.

The secondary market in concert tickets is both bugbear and major revenue source for artist and promoter alike. Managers and promoters set the ticket price, and promoters sell the tickets at that price. If the price is too low or the concert too popular, the tickets sell out in minutes and, minutes later, appear on eBay and other ticketing sites at vastly inflated prices. A £75 Take That ticket can be worth five times its face value, and sometimes all that extra profit goes not to the band but to operators in the secondary market. Of course the promoters also allocate directly to the secondary market, and share in the income over the face value, but they don't have control over the price. It is to gain that control in the secondary market that someone, and I'm not sure who, has hatched a plot to sell the tickets by a sealed bid system. That way the secondary market is directly controlled by GLE, and all that enhanced revenue goes straight into their pot. Unfortunately the insurers have spiked this approach, saying they will only insure the face value of the ticket, while WorldPay have said they have to be prepared to refund any full price paid, so creating a chasm of risk. As the money would be spent on staging the concert, there would be no cash available to make these refunds, which is why WorldPay won't agree to release the funds.

So someone has a second bright idea about the secondary market. Instead of a sealed bid for the ticket, the purchaser pays the face value of the ticket and makes a sealed bid charitable donation, thus separating the ticket price, insured and held by WorldPay, from the enhanced value, which is a non-refundable charitable donation. These donations are used to pay for the concert, and replaced by the ticket revenues when WorldPay releases them. The expectation is that the donations will be greater than the ticket values, so the charities will get some money up front, and a big pay day once the ticket money is released. So instead of the tickets going on sale on a certain day, a registration and bidding process commences on that day instead. At the end of the registration period, the highest bidders get their tickets. I think it's complicated, and I think the part about not refunding the donation stinks, and I tell Chris so, adding my concern that Michael Henry is justifying the structure because 'it's what touts do'.

> *From: A PICHETA*
> *Sent: 13 July 2011 11:40*
> *To: Chris Hunt*
> *Subject: ticketing options*
>
> *Chris,*
>
> *I've been mulling over the proposed sealed bids system for the tickets and I see a major flaw in trying to limit liability to the face value of the ticket. This fundamentally goes against consumer legislation existing since Augustus legislated the sale of garam. To argue that "it's what touts do" is to put us right up there on Watchdog's most Wanted list and would irreparably damage this event and our reputation going forward. It's also the kind of email comment that loses court cases when trotted out in front of a judge a year down the line. I imagine the*

reason behind trying to limit the liability is that the insurers won't cover any enhanced value. If that's so then we shouldn't do it. We certainly should not present ourselves as shyster tout rip off merchants, nor should we move forward with the sealed bids system unless we can offer a money back guarantee if the concert fails to happen in the substantively advertised form.

I've not copied Michael in on this. I'm going to duck the call with Tix Me. I'm in the London office

Best

A

From: Chris Hunt
Sent: 13 July 2011 11:50
To: Andy Picheta

Don't duck the call.

We already know we can't limit the liability to the face value and won't try. BUT

Today's cunning plan is to make the bid an uplift on the face price by way of donation to the 37 Jackson charities, so they buy the ticket for face value and give the rest to charity. This is cleverer than it looks as we are allowed to use the cash ahead of donating it by creating the condition that the money will be payable to the MJ charities out of first position receipts audited on the concert as a whole.

By the way I have incorporated your budget into a cashflow including all the budgeted US costs. See the attached (still in draft form).

C

I claim a partial victory at the time, but we remain saddled with a clunky, difficult and complicated system for selling very expensive tickets, and although it has some plus points, it is one born not from purity of motive, but engineered through the needs of cashflow. Everybody signs up however, and any doubters keep very quiet indeed. I've stuck my head out and said my piece, as I believe a good subordinate should. Now we move on.

Tix-Me is run by two very nice chaps called Paul. One of them is even called Paul King, just like our so far invisible promoter Paul King. All three Pauls wisely point out that Tix-Me is going to need to control the website, because they will add the purchasing interface to Venice Beach Meerkat's design. But first Chris asks me to negotiate Tix-Me's deal, away from the 12% commission on every ticket sold that they are asking for. Alex at the stadium tells us that Tix-Me is in administration, but the second Paul King is reassuring as he talks of separating the bulk of his organisation from the fallout of HMV going under. So that's okay then.

Chris also asks me to get the Princes Trust on board as one of the two or three charities that will benefit from the concert. Somewhere between LA and London, during the night, someone decided there should be only two charities, not the thirty seven Michael was involved with. I've also started asking the Parojim about merchandising, and the souvenir brochure, and the press packs for the London launch. Paul King points out, from the comfort of not doing very much at all, that I'm spreading myself too thin. I'm becoming all five of Leonard's guys, and I need some managers to take up some of this shit, because things will soon start dropping through the cracks. But I can't hire anybody because there is no money, nor will there be any until the minimum event conditions have been met and the investors release more funds. It has become plain however, that the original conditions, of four Jacksons plus Janet plus three major A-List stars is not going to happen, at least not for a while, so Chris trots off to the investors to persuade them to amend the conditions. He argues that three Jacksons, plus Katherine, plus Jeffré's own artist La Toya is almost as good as the original

Jackson requirement, and three A-listers are soon and surely to follow, although maybe not in time for the announcement which is now one week away. I never hear how this discussion with the investors goes, but days later there is still no money. I haven't yet, in mid-July, been paid a cent, and I've been working on the show for over three months.

Time to finalise my deal and get paid something. With anyone else I would never have committed so much time and effort without a fee structure in place. But Chris is a friend, and I didn't want to burden him – laugh if you will.

I sent Chris a proposition back in June, but he didn't respond. I dig out the relevant paperwork and set about structuring something that will work for him, and for me. I ask for a base fee, to be paid in stages along with the cashflow for the event – so a little up front when the minimum show conditions are met, then stepped payments on the 8th of August and September, with the final 1/3 due just after the show. I also put in some participation, or profit share, which is paid to those who contribute creatively to the event. It covers the licence of the creative rights I am creating. I look at my involvement and put in a small percentage from ticket sales, a flat rate for the VIP ticket revenue, and a very small percentage of TV sales. All this, in the business, is known as back end, and all my suggestions are based on standard industry practice. I also put in some accommodation expenses, which will pay for a short term rent flat in London, and finally £500 per week, £71.50 a day, for living, travelling, and incidentals. This last one I insist is paid in cash, as I have never successfully recovered the cost of any cabs, phone calls, pens, mousetraps or light bulbs from Chris' company Iambic without providing receipts, surveillance camera evidence, and countersignatures from persons of good standing, all in triplicate, on any production I have been involved in. I am determined not to be caught out on this one, so I make it my priority. Chris comes back, trimming here and there but basically agreeing everything except the £500 per week incidentals. He is outraged and offers £100. We settle on £150, which is just £21 per day. I know there are families with that as a weekly budget, but I'll be working twelve hour days in the heart of the city, where a bottle of water is two quid. Ah well, time to lose weight anyway.

* * *

We have another conference call with Ron. He tells us he's approached the Black Eyed Peas and Prince. The latter is very difficult to get hold of, because he sacks managers every week so nobody ever knows who to talk to. The Peas are the opposite. The have managers everywhere, and all of them are talking, all of them are in the loop and all of them want a say in the negotiations. The fees for the Peas goes from a half to two million dollars, although the half million was probably never the fee except in the minds of Chris and the Parojim. Jeffré immediately suggests that Ron is sabotaging the Peas involvement, or sabotaging the concert by offering them too much money, or taking a kickback because Ron's fee is actually not that big. We are told not to trust Ron, because Ron and Branca are "tight". I don't believe any of it. I see somebody who talks a great deal of sense, who has a realistic view of artist fees for shows like this, and he's being side-lined already, only a week into the job. To be fair, Chris resists the paranoia of Jeffré and the Parojim, and I believe we are making some progress with the artists at last. Unfortunately, Ron has not made any meaningful comments about the stage design, focusing on the artists and what they are to perform. On the subject of lighting he sidesteps the issue, suggesting that the TV director should choose the lighting guy.

It's a wise approach, and will mean one of my objectives, to light the show only once, will be met. But as yet, we have no TV director, as Chris has not yet spoken to Hamish. So we have no lighting director. Meanwhile the lighting grid is being designed by HaSH, because the stadium need it to finalise the manifest, and he's doing so no doubt whilst wearing a safety harness because working on a high stool raises several health and safety issues..

The week before the press conference is manic. I'm still in Scotland, at the hotel, but I'm not able to focus on anything because I'm on the phone or answering emails all day every day. My son has come up for the school holidays, the hotel is very busy, and my bitch is about to give birth. None of that matters. The Better is very understanding, although her teeth do grit a little when I take a call just as our black lab Tilly begins to squeeze out the first pup. The call is from Chris, informing me that we still don't have any artists. I offer the puppy, and tell him another is on the way. I also crack on with the website and the other stuff, but find the liaising with the Parojim an uphill task. I was moved to complain to Michael Henry, as I was getting nowhere fast. He in turn received acres of emails from the Parojim assuring us they were 110% on the case working seven days a week, without sleep or even toilet breaks, to get the job done. I pointed out that Americans often confuse activity with progress. But Jeffré really helped!!

> *Michael,*
> *I had the understanding that the programme and website is being put together by Steve Wills. I have offered assistance in arranging local printers but have not had any communication as yet.*
> *It's not supremely urgent yet, but I think a couple of months*

lead time would be useful to at least reserve the print capacity - we don't need to lock content down for a while yet. The website however is a different matter - that needs to be on the UK ticketing servers in 8 day's time. The announcement surely must feature the website where people are going to get tickets. The address should be all over the logo board. Which we'll need in the UK as well. Is anyone on this?
Thanks
Andy

Thank you everyone for moving all of this needs along rapidly! We will DEFINITELY have the website address somewhere were the world can see it. Paul please have Steve incorporate this somewhere were the world can see.

More later!
Jeffré!

Sent from my iPod

Done! Paul will be emailing you to set this up!

Thank you!

Jeffré!

So there we are – Jeffré has made it all work, without ever becoming visible. In the process we discover Bungalow Artists Group is actually the creative force behind all the stuff we need. Who the fuck are they? Where did they come from? And why? This shape-shifting of the Parojim is very confusing. Leonard seems to be no more, Britney too has disappeared from the conference calls and email chains. Somebody called Steve has turned up, with design credentials from the heart of MJ, according to Jeffré! Yet none of them seem to be achieving very much at all. Vital information about the satellite uplink, to get the LA conference into London and onto the Cardiff screens, is not being provided. The website design is not coming forward, but it's um, gonna be really cool. The old GLE site is still up, and still parades Hamish Hamilton's work as its own. I get fed up with the logjam and try some sarcasm.

> *On Jul 19, 2011, at 11:50 AM, A PICHETA wrote:*
> *will someone please, before you all disappear for lunch, address these two issues:*
> *1. book a satellite and camera and truck and crew to beam the press conference to London*
> *2. get all the done and dusted stuff off the www.globalliveeventsuk.com site (and the American equivalent)*
> *Pretty please*

From: Jeffré
To: A PICHETA
Cc: "parojim1@parojim.com"
Sent: Tuesday, 19 July, 2011 19:58:45
Subject: Re: TWO URGENT MATTERS

Hello Andy!
Don't worry about us running off to lunch, we don't do lunch under crunch time like this, lunch becomes a luxury that we can have at the moment. :-) Jim has already secure a satellite truck for this press conference. Jim could you please have Eric remove all items from Buber 2 below.

On Jul 19, 2011, at 12:00 PM, A PICHETA wrote:
I'm so glad that lunch is still for wimps!

FUNNY!
Sent from my iPod
 Jeffré' Phillips

On first contact, the Prince's Trust had directed me to their Cardiff office, but once the scale of *Michael Forever* dawned on them, I was quickly summonsed to a meeting at their

Regent's Park headquarters, located in one of those imposing cream buildings on the east side of the park. It's quite functional inside however, full of messy notice boards and cluttered desks. I sat down with two ladies from the trust and explained what we wanted to do. Michael supported 37 charities, and we felt that to spread the charitable donations from the show that wide would also spread them quite thinly. So for clarity and simplicity, we had selected the Aids Project Los Angeles, which Michael set up with Quincy Jones, as the American beneficiary, and we wanted the Prince's Trust to be the UK charity for the concert. Our reasoning was that Michael was a supporter, indeed he had once performed at a Prince's Trust event, and that the profile of the PT fitted in with the concert. Chris also felt that a fifty-fifty split between the US and UK was right and proper, given that the show would be staged here.

Given my past experience with charities, I fully expected a "why should we?", but the Prince's Trust, in the form of the two ladies before me, were smart enough to realise the potential, experienced enough with music events to understand how it all worked, and keen to take part. The Trust, they explained, has a mechanism for getting involved in events like these, which is to licence their famous Fleur-de-lis logo, based on the Prince of Wales' own crest, to the event organisers. This licence forms the minimum guarantee income for them, and ranges from £5000 upwards. I knew better than to ask for their royal, given as he's future king and all, so talked about the chances of one of their celebrity ambassadors getting involved, maybe as a co-presenter for the show. The ladies got quite excited about this, and suggested their ambassadors could collect a big cheque from the promoters on the stage. They were less excited about the structure for raising donations, the complicated bidding system, and needed this explained twice, although even then I don't think they clearly got it, probably because I wasn't explaining it properly. When, quite reasonably, they asked why we were doing it this way, I could only say we were hoping to control the secondary market to the benefit of the charities rather than ticket touts. Although true, it wasn't the whole truth, because the whole truth would have to include the parlous state of the cashflow as the driver for the charity donation scheme. I told them about the scheduled press conference and how it would be nice to have them on board in time for it. They said they would think about how to proceed. I thought the meeting went quite well, and reported back to Chris, as he climbed aboard his flight to LA and the press conference, that the Princes Trust were up for it.

Unfortunately, few others were. Just hours before the announcement, late into the night of the 24th, Chris sends out an email with a new plan, one to take account of the complete lack of any artists actually signed to perform on the show. Here's the email, and my somewhat hysterical response:

On Sun, Jul 24, 2011 at 9:09 AM, Chris Hunt wrote:
Nearly 7 hour delay on flight so arrived late and had meetings from 2300-0100 LA time, just finished.

All OK BAR we don't have much to announce by way of guests but seem to be getting them in next week. There will be Peas, Prince, and something from Gaga and Beyoncé but if we sign the deal memos now we'll be wasting millions - they're holding us to ransom because of the announcement date.

So we are going to tease the world at the press conf, have the Jacksons speak, the head of one of the charities speak, announce the event but none of the line-up. Then say there is a 10 day countdown to the tickets going on sale, we'll announce the acts gradually leading up to a second press conference, this time in London, the night before the tickets go on sale.

Not ideal but it does guarantee the word about the concert gets around, and keeps it hot. It also gives us longer to get the ticketing sorted, which entre nous is not a bad idea.

Am now going to sleep so don't call! Been up 27 hours.

So looks like a press conf at the Dorchester ballroom late wed Aug3.

Chris
From Chris Hunt

Why would they be any cheaper later?
Here we are, months down the road, and not one single act has signed.
WTF?
A

It's not all rosy in the cyber garden either. Meerkat and his skunk addled beach bum cohorts have come up with the design for the website. It's red and gold. And not in any way that could ever be termed subtle, classy or clever. There's loads of both colours; deep red velour curtains with an empty throne and squirly golden MF crests everywhere. Two Hollywood interpretations of what a suit of armour might look like stand either side of the throne, saucepans or some such in front of their genitalia. It's beyond horrible and so very very tacky. Michael's designer designed it, they cry – but I wonder whether Michael's designer, without Michael to guide and direct him, is such an asset to us after all. I tell them to lose the suits of armour, tone it all down and put a microphone in a spotlight in the centre. But that's just the imagery. All the functionality, the pages of info, artist details, Facebook, Twitter interfaces, and the vital ticket sales page have not yet been done, because the

UK team at Tix-Me, having got as far as they can, have to wait for the Parojim to pull their fingers out.

A small detail develops into a slew of emails and conference calls: the Americans have naturally written the date in American, as Saturday 10/8/2011. I point out that to the rest of the world this means the concert is in two weeks' time, on August 10, and we don't have a venue booked for that day, which is not a Saturday anyway, but the Americans, who like five year olds don't get irony, fail to understand the problem. In the end we settle on presenting the date as Saturday Oct 8th 2011, but it takes two days and a lot of hair pulling to sort it out. The other bit of west coast wonderment is that the site has been built only in Flash, so it's not visible to a quarter of the internet, or to anyone with an I-Phone. Well done guys, pass the duchy on the left hand side!

We obviously need more time, which I imagine was the theory behind the bright idea of a countdown clock and turning the Jackson conference into a "teaser". I recall the countdown was dreamed up by one of the Parojim, from experience gained marketing videogames. What didn't occur to me or anyone else at the time, was that a countdown to the on-sale date of Call of Duty 17 is a very different thing to the countdown to the on-sale date for tickets to a concert without any artists attached.

The first builds anticipation of a known product and part of a brand, the second to just an idea, nothing of note to anticipate, a concept too slowly forming into something saleable. If the artists had us over a barrel because of the imminence of the press conference, they now had us over a whole warehouse of barrels, their negotiating power increasing with every tick of our own self-imposed clock. One compound word springs to mind to describe all this, and ain't "blockbuster", it's "clusterfuck".

Tix-Me need more time too, to sift through the fog of Meerkat' efforts and create something that at least works around the world, but it won't be ready until Wednesday at the earliest, so we don't have a website to announce either. At least Michael Henry has finally signed the deal with the stadium, because they were not going to let us announce a concert in their house without having the contract in place. So we have a venue, but little else.

CHAPTER 6.
RON WEISNER
Every day create your history
Every path you take you're leaving your legacy

Announcement day, and it starts early for me. I'm on the seven o'clock flight from Inverness to Gatwick, and I leave the hotel at five am. The phone is already going, as it's nine in the evening in LA and there is, as ever, much to do. The Parojim have finally booked the correct satellite time, on the correct birds, for us to get the signal in London and Cardiff. I don't know if it needed the cajoling, threatening and bullying to get this done, or just to get them to tell us it was done, but it was the one thing I couldn't take over, because the originator of the signal has to book the satellite, and uplink to it. The users then book the downlink. That's international treaty, and the Parojim are for better or worse, originating the signal. I'm to look after the five pm London announcement, and I've drafted in Paul King, because I think the promoter should be there to promote.

The day is spent fighting Meerkat to get the website released to Tix-Me, fighting the Parojim to get the elements we need to make London look like LA, and fighting Tix-Me over their contract, which has suddenly sprouted about fifty grand's worth of additional costs. I'm also finalising the press release with Juliette, our LAPR (Los Angeles Press Relations). That's when I can get to talk to her – she seems forever to be driving somewhere and losing mobile phone signal. She badgers me for detail on the Princes Trust, to which I answer that we are not yet in a position to announce them as partners, because we haven't agreed terms. Although we cannot use their logo at this time, there's nothing to stop us saying we are going to make a substantial donation to them. It's cheeky I know, to associate us with them in this way prior to doing a deal, but I genuinely believed they would do rather well out of this, and without any artists to announce it would be nice to announce something. Juliette asks me for their boiler plate, but I tell her that they will need it in the winter to run their heating. Juliette finds this hilarious, and explains a boiler plate is the paragraph that they would use to summarize their charity/organization at the end of a press release (I've quoted from her email there, which is why there's a 'z' in summarise).

Amy Winehouse is dead. A tragic loss of a great performer. Jeffré and The Parojim don't really know who she is. The PR people aren't too sure either, coming as they do from telly. Paul K thinks it works well for us, one star dies and another is honoured with a tribute – that kind of thing. We debate saying something at the launch, but I cannot remember the outcome.

Sometime around lunch time I get a call from the Bristol office – the T-shirts the Parojim despatched by special courier have arrived at Stanstead airport. Do I want them for the press conference? They had wanted to send someone over with the shirts, but I vetoed the waste of money. It was a nice idea, to have them there for the press conference, and maybe to have everyone on our side wear them, but it wasn't worth spending thousands of pounds on. Unfortunately, so excited were the Parojim about the shirts being designed by Michael's designer that they put down a value in the shipping documentation of $50 a shirt. They had shipped 500, two boxes, and not unnaturally UK customs and Excise wanted their cut. The duty on cotton clothing is 12%, and the VAT is 20%, so the cost of getting the shirts out of the airport would be $8000! (Because first you calculate the duty, add it on, then you calculate the VAT and add that too – they don't miss a trick, these customs chaps!) I said "Fuck it, send 'em back". What they should have done of course, was tag them as samples with no commercial value, because that's what they were. Instead they pinned a Beverly Hills designer boutique retail value on them, over-valuing the tees as they over-valued themselves!

    I trot up the road to the Soho Hotel, where we have hired their cow-hide covered screening room for the announcement. The big screen carries a picture from the back of the room in LA; a long table on a raised dais runs the length of the wall. All of the tech seems to be working and the logo graphic projects nicely. On the screen a large bearded photographer, who I know to be Harrison Funk (get the funk outta here – is that a real name?), is busily photographing the name plates on the empty table. Harrison was Michael's official photographer for many years.

    In the room in London a table of drinks has been set up, and I taste the white wine – which is truly revolting, despite being charged at thirty quid a bottle. I'm sure the journos will like it, as they'll drink anything. Paul King sidles up to me, and suggests that it's best not to make it public he's here, or promoting the show. I say sure, and think that he's not done anything so far so it's not a change he's announcing, just reasserting his invisibility. Four pretty girls from the UK PR company, the one Chris hired because he had worked with them on TV programme releases, stand by the door with clipboards and mobile phones. A pile of glossy folders containing one A4 press release and some bios are ready for distribution. How very exciting! I test the microphone at the podium, stooge around a bit and settle down in one of the very comfortable and expensive cowhide armchairs. I'm not surprised they don't allow red wine into this room.

Wow. So it's actually going to happen. This huge, unique and amazing event, fraught as it has been with uncertainty, money worries and credibility issues, is actually going ahead. And I'm right at the heart of it. I savour the moment, but in a blissful ignorance that this is the last moment of innocence for the event and me in it. After today, everything will change – indeed it will change in about two hours. As soon as we go public, as soon as the concert is announced, everything will become harder, meaner and more difficult. I have no idea, sitting in that very comfy black and white armchair in the basement of the Soho Hotel, that in two hours we will enter the perfect shit-storm of shit, and we will never emerge.

For Immediate Release:

<u>**MEMBERS OF THE JACKSON FAMILY ANNOUNCE SUPPORT OF INTERNATIONAL HISTORICAL TRIBUTE PRESENTED BY GLOBAL LIVE EVENTS**</u>

October 8th Top Artists Pay Tribute to The King of Pop in Cardiff's Millennium Stadium

Los Angeles, CA (7/25/2011) - October 8th mark your calendars because you have Got to Be There to witness the musical event of our life time, a Thriller of a concert tribute to the King of Pop with the world's leading artists will be announced today by event producers Global Live Events with support of several of the Jacksons including Mrs.

Katherine Jackson, La Toya, Tito, Marlon and Jackie. "I have been approached by many people with a variety of ventures such as this, Global Live Events LLP is the first company to present me with a vision that will produce an authentic and memorable tribute that my son would love!" said Mrs. Jackson.

October marks the 40th anniversary of the start of Michael's professional career and will be celebrated with a tribute fit for a King. The concert will be held at the Millennium Stadium in Cardiff, Wales which is Europe's largest indoor arena holding 75,000 fans and will be broadcast around the world to 30 countries in both 2D and 3D.

The event is being produced by Global Live Events LLP a world-renowned event based TV and DVD specialist with offices in London, New York and Los Angeles. Specialising in the fields of the arts, music, drama and entertainment, Global Live is known for creating original and compelling live entertainment and recorded programming featuring music superstars from around the world. We have worked with a wide range of artists including Michael Jackson, Abba, The Beatles, Eric Clapton, Madonna, Placido Domingo and more. The Global Live team has created award winning, ground breaking content and entertaining formats that span a multitude of music genres. We have successfully produced several documentaries and performances, both in the UK and internationally, winning 4 Emmy Awards and over fifty nominations and awards in the major festivals around the world. "We wanted to do something decadent and worthy of Michael's musical genius yet something fun and authentic that you would envision Michael attending with excitement and joy surrounded by talent that he respected and loved," announced Global Live Events President Chris Hunt.

This incredible event will assist in raising awareness and funds for three amazing charities that Michael supported one of which includes Aids Project Los Angeles with the other two to be announced at the press conference. In order to build the suspense and excitement a ten day countdown to ticket sales will begin after the press conference with talent to be announced daily so listen for announcements or visit www.michaelforevertribute.com for additional information. Contact Juliette on 310-555 8189 or press@globalliveeventsuk.com.

But for now, the moment of announcement approaches. On the screen a statuesque woman with a clipboard marshals journos by the half dozen. I presume this to be Juliette, so I phone her to check, and sure enough the Amazonian stops pointing to answer her phone. At least she had signal. Three Jackson brothers file in from the right, as does La Toya and a frail looking old lady. This must be Katherine. They all look quite serious. Chris comes on from the left, big, ginger and bold. A thin man comes with him, and it's not until the close up that I read the name plate and see this is Paul Ring, coordinator of a website that doesn't work, a merchandise expert without any merchandise (other than poorly executed, stupidly shipped T-shirts) and an artist booker who has yet to book an artist.

Okay, we're off. We know there are no artists being announced, just the date of the show, and that it's the Jackson family tribute. What none of us knew, here in the UK, was that the Parojim had prepared a video teaser trailer, called a sizzle. This was played out at the start of the conference. Then the Jacksons and Katherine sombrely read out some prepared statements, ringing of legalese, in stilted, quiet voices. Then

Chris gets up, says something about not wanting to give everything away at the start, about teasing the world with star participant announcements over the next few days, about the website and about the registration process. Then he gives Katherine a cheque for a hundred thousand dollars while mumbling something about a trust fund for her and Michael's children. Katherine seems moved; a tear works its way down a cheek. The journos in London start scribbling furiously, and I decide not to say anything at the lectern, because I am as surprised as everyone else, and annoyed more than anyone. What happened to the coordination? There's a fucking trailer for the show and a fucking cheque for the granny, both kept secret in LA and about which I knew nothing. A TV journo asks for a tape of the sizzle, and of course I don't have one, because I didn't know until ten minutes previously that there was such a thing. I promise to get it to him later that day, and subsequently fail because the Americans email me a low resolution version good only for the internet. The conference ends and I have a swift beer with a Bristol elf or two, before heading back to the office.

Within two hours, Facebook and the internet are humming. Our FB page has started to attract some negative comments, and some topics are beginning to crystallise. Jermaine Jackson and his brother Randy are quick to issue a statement too, focusing on the clash of date between *Michael Forever* and the trial of Conrad Murray.

> *While we wholeheartedly support the spirit of a tribute that honours our brother, we find it impossible to support an event that is due to take place during the criminal trial surrounding **Michael**'s death. As everyone knows, those proceedings commence September 20th, and this **Michael***

Forever concert takes place in **Cardiff, Wales**, on 8 October. In light of this, we feel it is inappropriate to be involved with such an ill-timed event and its promoter, **Global Live**.

Both Chris and Jeffré had been in negotiation with Jermaine for months. Jeffré believed that eventually the senior brother would come on board, although he also knew that, together with Janet, it would be the most difficult signing. Shortly after Michael's death, Jermaine had announced a star studded tribute concert, to be held at the O2. He neglected to tell any of the stars who would be studding it however, and very soon many were publicly distancing themselves from the proposed event. A year later he did the same thing, this time, venue Tokyo. Neither concert came to pass, but Jermaine had it in his head that if there was to be a tribute to Michael, he, Jermaine, would be the one to put such a thing together. As senior brother and self-proclaimed family leader, Jermaine would be in charge, or there could be no tribute concert. He also believed he should get the lion's share of any such event, a view the other siblings naturally did not share. So here was the first hurdle to bringing Jermaine into the fold; the others would only agree to Jermaine being in if he was on the same terms as they, and Jermaine would only agree to be in if he was to receive substantially more. Not that he wanted more just by right, Jermaine wanted more because he believed he should have an input into the staging of the event, he should be a co-promoter and co-event director. Only he, Jermaine, could ensure this tribute, any tribute, was one befitting of the memory of Michael. Unfortunately the other Jacksons, and the industry at large, did not share Jermaine's view of Jermaine's abilities in this area, as they and many agents and artists made it quite clear that if Jermaine was in any way involved in the business or creative side of a show they would not be coming. So Jeffré's plan with Jermaine was to offer the same as the other brothers were accepting, and leave Jermaine out in the cold for now. As the event drew nearer, as the big acts signed, Jermaine would feel the chill and come on board, probably with a face saving executive producer credit thrown in to assuage the bruises to ego.

Word to the Badd, Jermaine, Word to the Badd! Given Jermaine's press release, and the speed with which it was issued and disseminated around cyberspace, I thought part one of Jeffré's plans seemed to be going well!

* * *

Social networking, this new battleground for the hearts, minds and wallets of the consumer, was the province of the Parojim. They had set up the FB page Michael Forever Tribute Concert, and it was attracting traffic immediately after the announcement. There is some excitement, lots of questions about who the artists are, about the charity donation scheme, about why Cardiff? "Is this what Michael would have wanted?" is another recurring theme. There's some negativity as well, concern about the cost of the tickets, and complaints which echo Jermaine, criticising the staging of the concert during the trial of Conrad Murray, calling it disrespectful to Michael. Tix-Me's cyber troopers believe it's possible to nip all this in the bud, with some straight answers, and some positive comments. But for now, I sum up my thoughts in an email to the Parojim, throwing in a bit of flim flam which I didn't really believe.

On Mon, Jul 25, 2011 at 2:11 PM, Andy Picheta wrote:

Paul, Chris your performances were spot on. We must remember however that all we did was announce an announcement. There's a website out there with a countdown clock on it and if, in 9 day's time, we don't have a line up for Cardiff (not on tape from Topeka Kansas or wherever) that is worth paying $400 to see we are all fucked, So talent kings Paul and Jeffré if there's anything I can do to assist then don't hesitate to ask.
A

Sent from my iPhone

By Wednesday of this first week, the dynamic on the Facebook page had begun to change, and started to coalesce into the pit of hate that it would harden into and remain. Virtually all positive comments had been driven off, and the opprobrium was being heaped higher and higher. The press had sniffed out the controversy, not just from Jermaine but the fans also, and started building stories with headlines like "Jackson Tribute Tickets a Lottery for the Rich" and "Fans Join Jermaine in Concert Criticism". Where there is conflict, there is a story. And we had certainly stirred a ton of conflict. The very serious consequence of this was that everyone was now on the back foot. Instead of setting the agenda, we were reacting to events, always one step behind, always playing catch up, and never quite getting there.

Nothing ever happens in a vacuum. We had arrived at this point not by chance, not by design, but as the result of a series of decisions, some made in haste, others from greed or hubris, and a few from the best of intentions. We had arrived here, where the walls of hell were quickly forming around us, because we had fucked up. What really took me, and I think everyone else, by surprise was the speed of the counter-attack against *Michael Forever*. The press launch had grabbed us all by the short and curlies and dragged us over the parapet, exposing our naked arses in preparation for the biggest kicking ever. Much of the mire on our Facebook page was similar sounding – the date of the concert clashing with that of the trial, the price of the tickets, the lack of a line-up. These were the three areas of weakness that increasing numbers of people were commenting on. Key words such as "disgrace", "disgusting" and "disrespectful" were repeated again and again, and it is easy to see the hand of the MJ Estate behind what appeared to be an orchestrated campaign against *Michael Forever*. Looking back, I'm not convinced. The early days of our Facebook page had a lot of negative stuff on it, but also a lot of hope. In the absence of a line up the fans are creating their own "fantasy tribute". Although many of the names mentioned end up doing the show, or at least on Parojim lists, this process unfortunately allows the build-up of huge expectations which are bound to lead to disappointment.

The Estate I think had better things to do than stir negative internet chatter because of an announcement of a show with no artists. All three of the issues raised on Facebook were our own doing – we went with a weak launch that raised more questions than it answered, made an announcement that seeded doubt as to what *Michael Forever* was, and discounted the trial date as a potential problem. I'm unclear as to whether this was due to pressure from the investors to get the show on the road, or pressure on the investors, to get more funds released.

The stadium payment, made because there could be no announcement without the deal signed, had used up pretty much all the available cash. We set the ticket prices, and then put in place a complex bidding system to get out of a looming cashflow hole for the event. And we set the date, not deliberately to coincide with the trial, but in the belief the trial would actually never happen, that the axis of evil which had done for Michael would never allow the trial to take place, but ensure their fall guy Murray took his punishment quietly.

Wrong, wrong and unfair. This clash between *Michael Forever* and the trial, given by Jermaine as his reason for not getting involved with us, and picked up by legions of fans and later the estate, was just a load of bollocks. Codswallop, because what we didn't know at the time, but were to learn within a few days, was that the Estate did indeed have better things to do than scheme against *Michael Forever*. They were finalizing an MJ themed Cirque du Soleil show with the famous Canadian circus. A show that was due to premier on October 2, also smack in the middle of the trial, and just one week before *Michael Forever*. What we also didn't know at the time, but found out a little later, was that Jermaine's book *You Are Not Alone - MICHAEL – Through a Brother's Eyes JERMAINE JACKSON* was going to be published on September 26, just days after the start of the trial. The book title was also to be co-promoted with the Cirque show. So, one show, not sanctioned by the estate or supported by Jermaine, was labelled deeply disrespectful to the memory of Michael because it coincided with the trial of Dr Murray. Two other Michael Jackson related entertainment projects, also coinciding with the trial of Michael's medic, were not disrespectful.

In the first of many attempts to reverse the flow of negativity in the media and on Facebook, we issue an FAQ sheet, which it falls to me to write. I seem to now be at the forefront of coordinating the responses to the media and the swelling Facebook anger, a sixth guy that Leonard never mentioned. Here is a draft – and I can see how on the defensive we already are, just days from the announcement.

MICHAEL FOREVER FAQ SHEET
DRAFT
THIS FAQ SHEET WHEN APPROVED, WHICH IS WHEN THE WORD 'DRAFT' IS REMOVED, WILL SERVE AS A CRIB SHEET FOR ANYONE DEALING WITH THE CONSUMER OR MEDIA, ESPECIALLY THE SOCIAL MEDIA TEAMS IN THE UK AND US
DRAFT
PLEASE ADD/COMMENT BELOW AND CIRCULATE

WHY IS THE TICKETING PROCESS SO COMPLICATED?
We wanted to avoid the usual frantic rush and confusion when tickets for big events go on sale. We also wanted to stop ticket touts making huge sums of money off the fans. Our system is simple and calm and ensures that those applying to actually buy tickets have their tickets reserved for them.

HOW DO I GET A TICKET? WHAT IS THE REGISTRATION PERIOD?
When the countdown reaches ZERO you will be able to register your interest on the website. You will enter your contact details, choose your ticket price level and enter a charity pledge. The registration period will last four days to give everyone an opportunity to register.
At the end of the registration period we will analyse the pledge amounts and allocate tickets to those making the highest pledge

HOW DO I GET A TICKET? HOW DO I PURCHASE THEM?
If you are successful you will be sent an email inviting you to complete the purchase of your reserved tickets. Your charity pledge will be taken at the same time

I CAN'T AFFORD TO GIVE TO CHARITY. CAN I STILL GET A TICKET?
There will be TEXT TO WIN, radio, TV and Newspaper competitions right up until the concert, which will be broadcast around the world so the millions of Michael fans out there can get a chance to see this Tribute

WHAT IF I CHANGE MY MIND AFTER REGISTERING?
If you choose not to complete your purchase your tickets will be offered to the next person on the list

WHY ARE THE TICKETS SO EXPENSIVE?

The prices of the tickets are comparable to major music events such as premium acts, multi artist festivals and other forms of live entertainment. When the line-up is announced you will see just how amazing this concert will be

HOW DOES THE CHARITY PLEDGE DISRUPT THE TOUTS?
If more people want tickets than are available the price goes up. With our system the initial demand is moderated by the charity pledges. We don't get the extra money – the charities do. So all the profit that a tout can take has already been given to the charities. There's nothing in it for them. Global Live Events only ever gets the face value of the tickets

WHY IS THIS CONCERT BEING HELD DURING THE TRIAL?
We have been planning this concert for quite a while, and the trial dates kept moving. We believe that a concert honouring Michael's music will remind the world of his genius, and the great loss the world of music has suffered by his untimely death

WHY HAVE NO ARTISTS BEEN ANNOUNCED?
We want to build momentum in these first weeks so will make announcements regularly. The Launch Conference in LA was about the Jackson family and their dreams for this show. It was important to focus the message on them.

WHY ARE GERMAINE AND RANDY JACKSON AGAINST THE CONCERT?
The Jacksons are a large family with differing views and opinions on how to treat the memory of Michael. We believe, and the majority of the family believe, that the Michael Forever Tribute Concert, which will be about Michael's music, is the best way to do this.

In the final draft we change the structure of the registration process, assuring customers that a charity pledge of as little as £1 will be enough to secure a ticket. This alters what was stated before, which was that the higher the pledge the greater the chance of a ticket. No wonder consumers were confused. And a confused consumer keeps their wallet in their pocket. In the final draft, we also manage to spell Jermaine's name correctly.

On a more positive note, Sky TV are very interested in the show, and interested in doing a multi-channel MJ special evening, featuring the concert and loads of other stuff as well. We try to set up a date to meet, but key Sky execs are on holiday so the earliest available time is in two weeks, on Monday August 8. Now that the schools have broken up for summer, getting execs together is going to be a tricky thing, and will delay decisions and sometimes prove to derail them.

Even more positively, Ron Weisner is coming to town! This is great news, as I know we'll get a lot done, and a lot of creative decisions that are desperately needed will hopefully be made.

Less helpfully, issues with the website rumble on. It's proving hard to find Michaelforever.com, because Meerkat and the Parojim have failed to actually do anything to make it visible. It's not registered with Google, it's got no meta-tags associated with it, and the link on the Facebook page points to a site called michaelfrever.com. A Tix-Me cyber-trooper solves most of these things, including registering michaelfrever.com, but why did they need fixing, why were they not done properly in the first place? We are also finding the transatlantic delay is crippling our attempts to counter-attack on Facebook. Tix-Me have no access to the page, as all editorial control is in LA in the hands of the Parojim. Most of the activity however, comes from Europe. Small numbers of European fans make critical comments which we are unable to answer, or counter with positive ones, because the Parojim deal with it in the LA morning, by which time the comments have been unchallenged all day. This gives the negativists undue prominence, and probably scares away the few genuinely interested customers coming for a look-see. A further issue is the Parojim's inability to do anything other than remove posts they don't like, which sets off yet another round of anger and disbelief from the fans.

The countdown clock, our very own self-imposed ticking time bomb, served to completely panic the Parojim, who were now running around LA desperately trying to sign some acts. They were talking to everyone they knew, and often at cross purposes. Agents, managers, artist lawyers, everyone and anyone who had the smallest bit of access to a name act were being approached, sometimes two or three times a day, by a GLE card carrying Parojim. Each one claimed exclusive status, each one reckoned themselves to be chief talent muckwallah for the organisation. Unaware of their activity, Ron Weisner, under the impression he had been hired to put on a show, was talking to his contacts too, who often showed interest, and confidence in Ron's involvement, but confusion because earlier that day they had taken a call from one or more of the Parojim, offering different terms and a different deal. All this of course, was because the true deal maker could not be seen making the deals. Jeffré is so chameleon that when he stands in front of the Hollywood sign he has a big, white "WOOD" on his front.

Heavyweight agents Creative Artists Agency (CAA) and William Morris (WM) who represent between them pretty much everyone, had woken up to the reality of the show and were beginning to show some interest, but it was all not fast enough for the Parojim, who were reeling in friends and acquaintances from wherever they could find them. Their behaviour was quite bizarre, and the only explanation I can make fit is that bounties and bonuses were being offered for signings. But I don't know now and I did not know then whether this was true. I do know that every day Chris was fighting fires caused by an apparently amateurish approach in

LA.

The longest week of my life for a very long time finally ends – each hour felt like a day, each day like a week. And this is only week one! I sum up some of my frustrations in an unhelpful email to the bosses.

Guv'nors
We need to take the web design and social media strategy away from the Americans. The command and control needs to run from us to them and not the other way around.
They continue to do stuff that fundamentally impacts on the ticket selling side without thought for consequences
They continue to fail to do stuff which is page 1 - even for me
Long version available if you need it

Much as I don't want to hear it I suppose I'd better have chapter and verse of the ticketing impact stuff
C

As requested - the long version

Ticketing ramifications
1. Having a log in/register button for the blog and news feeds will cause huge confusion for consumers who will think they are registering to buy tickets. Advice is not to have blog/news log in/register until AFTER the registration (tickets) is closed
2. No thought has been given as to how TixMe are to collate and administer the blog/newsfeed registration and pages on the website, which they have to do as it's on their servers
3. Other language tags. Together with the blog/newsfeed stuff these first appeared on Saturday evening (UK) with no thought that TixMe would have to prepare usable registration pages in all these languages, let alone t&c pages, confirming emails etc etc. Because of the way the site was built it's not a simple case of giving the script to a friendly Chinaman/Russian/etc. Each site would have to be rebuilt to work in those languages. This is an error in the making of a magnitude greater than doing a Flash only site. It cannot be done in the time because it has not been planned, either in workload scheduling or site design

4. The command line running west to east causes a 24 hour delay for sign offs. With the lack of technical competence these sign offs create a further delay as the UK seeks clarification and further info. As the site runs on UK servers reversing the command line gains us a 24 hour operating presence, because the Americans can pick up where we leave off.

I've given TixMe a command structure which puts them reporting to me who reports to you. It's simple and they get the info they need straight away

Social Media
This is crucial for the success of our marketing
message. Fundamental things have not been done, as of today
1. The Sizzle has not been put on YouTube
2. The Twitter account is not linked to FB

What we DO desperately need the Americans to do is to
1. shoot messages of support from Christina, Justin, Jamie and Kanye and get them onto our FB page and You Tube
2. post photos, the original letter from Katherine, any other stuff on to the FB page
3. get the signed artists to like us on FB and to tweet/status their participation

There's loads more but it's historical (as opposed to hysterical) and we've worked around it. The net result however, is that we have a shit website built in a non effective way that hurts our google presence. Chris, they're crap and in about 48 hours they're gonna start hurting us again.

Well he did ask!

* * *

The lack of any track record for Global Live Events means the big agents are cautious. Not ones to turn down a suitcase of wedge however, they all put their artists, those that want to do it, can do it, are available to do it, in the frame. So late on the Friday night terms are agreed with Christina Aguilera, Justin Bieber and Jamie Foxx. The caution of CAA does mean however, that they want cash up front, on signing, the whole fee. All three million dollars of it.

No dosh, no announcement. And no tweeting, Facebook page linking, press statements, file photographs nor any kind of linkage to *Michael Forever* whatsoever. In all his previous dealings with talent, Chris had paid anything from 10% to a third up front, the rest on signature of the full contract, known as the longform agreement. This many-paged document is where the minutiae of any deal are painstakingly argued over, with lawyers drafting and redrafting for ages. It therefore often follows weeks if not months after the original deal memo is signed and agreed, and sometimes isn't signed until after the event. Whether or not Chris was banking on this delay between signing the artists and paying them their full fees, I don't know. He certainly didn't appear too happy about CAA's insistence, but with the countdown clicking through the hours at a perceived very fast rate, he had no choice but to pay up. Or, rather, the investors had no choice, both they and GLE were caught in a circular trap, in which meeting the minimum event conditions so that money would be released required releasing the money to meet the minimum conditions. At this point, and compounding the cashflow difficulties, one of the major investors pulled out, preferring to walk away and take a small loss rather than commit the bigger sums promised.

Still, we now had some acts in the bag, and more were on the verge of signing. The Black Eyed Peas had either hiked their ask to two million dollars, or never seriously considered the lower amounts being offered, depending again on who you talked to. Ne-Yo, Jennifer Hudson, Smokey Robinson and

Gladys Knight were also close, although as the Parojim had been promising these acts since April, who knew. In the UK, successful boy band JLS have been in touch, saying they really wanted to take part. Ortise is a huge fan, Michael was his inspiration, and please please can they come on the show. Fantastic. We ask them whether they would come to Wednesday's press conference in London, at which we're expecting at least one Jackson brother, where the line-up will be announced. This could all come good now, ten days late, but better late than never.

We have gained access to the Facebook page, Tix-Me and I are added as administrators by the Parojim, who for reasons known only to themselves won't do the same for the Twitter account. I've created a Facebook character called Randy Flagon, because I don't want my friends, school and work colleagues and family dragged into the pit of shit with me. Randy because it's close to Andy. Flagon because the French for flagon is pichet. Randy Flagon, close to the heart of *Michael Forever*, sallies forth to interact with the angry fans. There are already a few regulars. Andres Salinas, from Spain, is quick to condemn, and relentless in coming back to the page to do so again and again. His photo shows an intensely mono-browed twenty-something holding a cat. He probably works in IT. There are several MJ zealots, endlessly posting "We love you Michael!!" and many thoughts showing up the big, big difference between Michael and his family in the minds of the fans

> *Viviana Mjfan*
> DISGRACE!!, and that goes for the entire Jackson family, who have been living of Michael for 40 years. FACT! the jacksons tried this purchase a ticket and inc charity donation during the

victory tour, but Michael put a stop it and gave all the cash he earned to charity himself. Lets get one thing out there, the jackson brothers have no talent at all, Michael was the main man as we all know, and he earned them millions, let the man rest in peace, and just enjoy the memories

Then there is Victor O'Brien, who photographs himself in the mirror and posts:

Victor O'Brien
give it up while you are ahead. In case you haven't noticed MJ fans do NOT support Jackson family's money making endeavors, you need Estate's approval and support to be Official and you don't have it. Ticketing and charity pledge is problematic. The date is right in the middle of the trial, no self respecting MJ fan would party when the man that killed their idol is at trial for his murder. You can't even name a single act and expect people to commit to buy the tickets. Not gonna happen. You'll end up with an event that only a few thousand attend, while thousands/millions protest and hate you for it. Cancel it now, go back to the drawing board, try to get Estate on board, wait after the trial and only announce when you can list all the lineup.

It's cogently and concisely argued and written without a single exclamation mark! From the Estate? – Perhaps. Either way, we should have listened to his advice, acted on it and hired him as a co-producer on the show, even though he was fundamentally wrong in one respect. We were not ahead, but very much behind. Instead of taking heed, the Parojim continue deleting negative comments, which leads to a storm of protest. I wade in trying to keep positive, building anticipation to the August 3 press conference, but I find it incredibly soul destroying, to counter criticism of something I believe in without any concrete facts (like artists appearing) to do it with. But I'm certain we'll get to a strong announcement on

Wednesday, we'll get access to the performers' Facebook pages and it will all gel into a stunning social media campaign. So I persevere. I post things like:

> *Getting close to announcing some headliners and support acts tomorrow!*

But tomorrow never comes. JLS can't do the PC because they're off to Los Angeles. CAA has taken over negotiations on their behalf, because their London management weren't keen for them to be involved. That means a whole new deal, new lawyers, new terms. No Jackson is coming to the UK. There are no acts that can be announced. We are holding out for the Peas. Ron is inches from signing Stevie Wonder. And Justin Bieber has just announced a string of tour dates in South America, with AEG, commencing October 7! It's not all doom and gloom however – the Parojim have signed Alien Ant Farm. Top billing!!

The Wednesday announcement is cancelled, and shortly after that any requirement for a charitable donation is removed, probably as a result of insurmountable insurance issues, WorldPay discomfort, and hopefully a dawn of understanding of how crap the whole thing looked to a prospective ticket purchaser. The countdown clock is frozen in time, much like the incredulity on the faces of anyone watching closely. Another FAQ sheet goes up. The spin is that we listened to the fans. It's incredibly weak but it's all we have. The detractors on FB smell blood, and become even more merciless. There is very little good in this, and I start to wonder if there ever will be. The Parojim regroup, and we hear the wonderful news that an announcement will be made live on CNN, in their LA studios. On Tuesday the 9th of August. So we are to build expectation, again, get the fans excited, again, while somebody, somewhere, gets some singers to agree to sing some MJ songs. I can already tell that the fans are excited. But their excitement is borne of disbelief and wonder at just how crap we have been. Lots of LOLs abound on FB.

> *I can't believe these morons still have no acts*
> *This whole thing is a scam*
> *What a bunch of idiots*
> *We love you Michael!!*

… And so on. Each one, except the last, is a thunderbolt of naked truth that rips into my soul. Each one a well-aimed arrow piercing my confidence and belief in this thing. It's like skidding on ice in a car. You have no control, you can only wait until it stops and hope you still have a usable vehicle when it does. So Randy Flagon retires hurt, after only two days at the front. And nobody steps into the breach. This following post is typical, the poster has a right to be angry and it's from a pissed off customer who wanted to buy. For every one that posts like this, there are a thousand walking away without publicly vocalizing their disappointment.

> *It is now 10hrs since we were supposed to be able to 'register' for tickets and their website is still telling us to 'Standby for further announcements'! Angry and disgusted, just doesnt come close to what many of us are feeling today.! How can these promoters be so cold and callous in their treatment of us!*
> *At least for a couple of hours on Wednesday evening we had an Admin who communicated with us periodically on the FB site. Yesterday evening as the minutes ticked by this 'Admin' had disappeared off the scene. Then we also lost the 'Countdown clock' to be replaced by the 'Standby for further announcements' sign. Then nothing...nothing!!*
> *This whole set up has been a farce from beginning to end, but to leave us all just hanging with not a clue as to what is happening is beyond belief. Many of are now convinced that this Tribute will most certainly*

not get off of the ground. How can it when it doesnt have the one thing needed to pay Tribute to our King - the permission of the people who are working so hard to ensure that his legacy is kept safe from just such charlatans!

The clear tragedy, even at this early point, is that our failure had been of preparation and management of the public interface. If Chris had waited until things were more concrete, if the investors had let him wait, if the Parojim had been calmer, then we would not be racing further and further from the purity of the intent. I begin to wonder whether there was any purity to begin with, or whether the hubris has grown, alien ant farm sponge like, to completely obfuscate anything else. But when you set a date, you need to do stuff in advance of it. When you set a high price for your product, you need to give people time not just to save up for it, but you need to give them the finest, unarguable reason to buy it. Plainly, "Michael Jackson Tribute" (with the Jackson bit removed by lawyers) is not reason enough. Chris accepts none of this. He is bullish/bullying, resolute/stubborn, confident/arrogant. He sees the objections of the fans as an irrelevance, an Estate inspired or conspired minority shouting loudly, so getting more notice than they deserve. He misses the aphorism that it is better to have detractors inside the tent pissing out, than outside the tent pissing in.

It is equally clear we cannot regroup. We cannot take FB warrior Victor O'Brien's advice, regardless of how sensible it appears. We are too far down the road; early October is the latest date for a stadium show, because nobody is going to freeze their nuts off for four hours during the winter. Moving means going for mid-April of 2012 at the earliest, June, July and August are problematic for kit and event competition because of Euro 2012 and the Olympics adding to the already crowded summer festival schedule, leaving May or September. But it appears the investors won't stand for that kind of delay. The money already spent would need to be spent again, and the whole thing would take on the smell of yet another failed attempt at an MJ tribute. Jeffré had disengaged his cloaking device long enough to start wooing alternatives to Chris' UK based investors. He would use these new sources of finance to pay off the existing commitments, use the extra time to win over Janet and Jermaine, and pretty much do what Facebooker Victor O'Brien suggested.

* * *

But until that happens we are stuck on this path of our own making. The lack of signed artists follows a simple story arc, one that begins with the agents at CAA unsure as to who this Chris Hunt guy was, to waking up to a gravy train once they'd received two million bucks for Bieber and Aguilera, to wondering just how the thing would pan out in the face of the hostility and controversy building around it.

Chris' response is to seal the hatches, climb into the bunker, and try to plough on through. I think he needs to bend and embrace a bit, but that's not in his nature.

I head back up to Scotland to support The Better as she singlehandedly runs the hotel in my absence. My woes and worries are given no attention at all. I'm told by her that the financing, the artists and the Americans are not my concern, that I've been hired to support Chris and to look after the filming of the event. All this other stuff I've taken on is because I'm there to help and assist wherever required. If Jeffré takes the whole thing off to 2012 and Japan or Pasadena, and I'm therefore out of a job, then so be it; the TV in room seven isn't working so go and sort that out, mister big time TV concert producer! After a weekend of explaining to Spanish guests that porridge is not a sausage and handling Dutch complaints that the sea bass cooked en papillotte was not peppery enough – it means "in parchment" and not "with paprika" – I am rebalanced and ready to deal again with mismanaged customer expectations caused not by a misunderstanding of horse feed and poncy French cooking terms, but by a complete lack of a) artists signed and ready to promote the show and b) any plan other than to react to the latest crisis.

The confusion and panic within the Parojim has reached a white heat glow of criticality. Headless chickens don't even come close to describing the state of apoplectic near seizure that gripped them. In desperation they were grabbing at the thinnest slivers of straw. The CNN studio date was fast approaching, Katherine Jackson had agreed to appear, and the Parojim had hours left to get an announceable line up together. Thumbs were ground to the bone, contact books soaking up the blood and raw flesh as fingers again and again scrabbled through the pages and pages of phone numbers that were increasingly going unanswered. Somehow Lady Gaga had dropped off the list, apparently pissed off by Parojim antics. But all was going to be okay. The solution was at hand. One of the Parojim was great friends with iconic rock manager Doc McGhee. Doc offered up one of his bands, the Parojim gratefully said yes please, and Katherine Jackson went on CNN to announce the participation in the Michael Jackson family tribute concert... of pantomime metal screamers KISS.

I was in Bristol at a meeting with Paul King and Chris. The purpose was to get a rocket up Paul's arse so he would finally start delivering something, but it ended up with Paul getting more money and a very nice lunch. Paul's backseat position was partly understandable as there had not been anything to actually promote, but I think Chris and I were hopeful of more input, more initiative, more up front noises of support from a seasoned campaigner priding himself on "taking ownership". I reminded Paul he was best mates with Tom Jones and The Stereophonics, two international Welsh acts that would certainly add some local colour to proceedings, and he promised to do what he could. Then Juliette phoned, to tell us that the CNN broadcast had gone well, but there was some controversy over the signing of KISS. The fans were up in arms because Gene Simmons had once called Michael a paedophile. Chris and Juliette began to hatch a response. Juliette would reach Gene Simmons and get him to issue a statement saying Michael was lovely really and he, Gene, was a big fan. It would be kissy kissy make up time and everyone would be forgiven all round. I thought she was dreaming that that would work, and I told Chris, in the strongest possible terms, that he should unsign them now, immediately, tell the world we had made a dreadful mistake and move on. He should find out which of the Parojim had done this stupid thing and impale them on the spike at the top of the Capitol Records building in Los Angeles for all to see what happens to idiots who propagate thoughtless mistakes. Only the toughest, decisive action could even begin to mitigate this fuck up. Even as the ship was sustaining heavy damage, so my stock must have been rising, because I was listened to and KISS were kissed off.

It was too late, and the damage had been done. Thirty two Michael Jackson fan clubs from around the world post an open letter to Chris and the Parojim. At exactly the same time, John Branca and the Michael Jackson estate decide to enter the world of *Michael Forever*, in the form of a lawyer's open letter. What a coincidence! Both documents get huge exposure on the internet, posted and reposted, tweeted and Facebooked, until even Siberian goat herders in the Karelian hinterland are talking of nothing else. Now that's how you do a campaign on the web! Here's the letter from the fan clubs:

> *We, as Michael Jackson's staunch supporters and advocates, refuse to support the Michael Forever Tribute, planned by Global Live Events in October, 2011. Even with the withdrawal of your most recent performer, Gene Simmons, fans feel the damage has already been done. Your apology is too little, too late and does not solve the problems we have with this tribute.*
>
> *Since the initial announcement, through fan sites and forums and a Facebook page (Fans Against Michael Forever Tribute) fans have voiced their concerns about this tribute. One of the initial concerns was how fans were treated on the Michael Forever Tribute Facebook page. The administrators were rude and deleted comments. Therefore, when the announcement was made that Global Live Events "listened to fans" regarding the addition of Simmons, many fans are doubtful. Fans believe that Global Live Events, in an attempt to qualm the media and the Estate, rescinded their offer to Simmons. Simply put, it is not the fans that Global Live Events is concerned with, but negative media coverage, which in turn affects ticket sales.*
>
> *From the timing of this tribute, in the middle of Dr. Murray's trial, to the ticketing prices, to the obscurity over what charities will be receiving the donation, to the no-guarantee policy of performers, the addition of Gene Simmons and dishonoring, thus tarnishing Michael Jackson's legacy was simply the last straw. With the damage done, it will be the fans who work hard to overcome this debacle for Michael Jackson's legacy. Please understand that this tribute is doomed to fail now. Attorneys for the Michael Jackson Estate have written to you about their concerns, and now the Michael Jackson fan base has done the same. Do the right thing for Michael Jackson, and cancel this tribute.*

Sincerely

And here the one from the estate:

Sirs

I represent the Executors of the Estate of Michael Jackson. As the legal caretakers of Michael's intellectual property, we believe it is our duty to contact you directly regarding the growing number of questions that have been addressed to the Estate, as well as multiple concerns that have emerged in recent days. The Estate's mandate is to protect, preserve and perpetuate Michael's legacy. As such, the Estate is the only entity that can grant the right to use Michael Jackson's name, likeness, or any of his intellectual property, whether such use is for commercial or other purposes. We assume you do not intend to use any intellectual property that is controlled by the Estate.

We are aware that "Michael Forever" has the support of some members of the Jackson family, including Joseph Jackson, Katherine Jackson, LaToya, Marlon, Jackie and Tito Jackson and we have read that the event is opposed by Jermaine and Randy Jackson.

We were especially disappointed today with the announcement that the band KISS and guitarist Gene Simmons were added as one of the acts to perform at "Michael Forever."

As I'm sure you are aware, Mr. Simmons has made numerous disparaging public comments about Michael Jackson after his passing. It was extraordinarily embarrassing when no sooner than you announced this "news" that he would participate in your concert that TMZ posted an item noting that Mr. Simmons called Michael Jackson - the man you are purportedly honoring - a child molester, notwithstanding the fact that Michael was acquitted by a jury.

Since "Michael Forever" has been heavily marketed in the media and to fans not just as a tribute, but also as a charitable event, we are concerned that the concert is piggybacking on Michael's good name and charity when the charitable element of this concert is solely voluntary and an add-on to the ticket price. It appears from your interviews and from your website that none of the approximately $90 to $390 per person ticket price is committed to charitable causes.

If the ticket revenue is not going, at least in part, to the charities you outlined as ones that Michael supported, who is participating in the ticket revenue besides Global Live Events? The Estate would specifically like to know what other individuals and companies besides your entity are sharing in the revenues which might be realized from ticket sales for those that wish to pay tribute in some fashion to Michael Jackson.

It also has come to our attention in recent days, from outraged fans, that as a part of your ticket policies, you cannot guarantee your announced artists and that, "If 50% or more of the number of contracted artists attend and perform, the Concert will take place and no refunds will be offered." It is a concern to us that loyal Michael Jackson fans will pay for tickets and not receive full benefit for their purchase, nor will they be able to get a refund if certain artists they paid to see cancel their participation.

Michael Jackson always made sure his fans were treated to concert experiences so spectacular that they would remember the evening for the rest of their lives. He also always treated his fans with the utmost respect. In light of the questions raised above and the confusion surrounding this "event," we are extremely concerned about Michel's legacy, his fans, and the public-at-large. We believe Global Live should address our concerns and those of Michael's loyal fans about "Michael Forever" as soon as possible.

Very truly yours, Howard Weitzman

You'll note the slightly different approach taken by the estate, with no mention of the date clash with the trial. After all, why draw attention to your own date clashing presentation with Cirque du Soleil? But good old Howard manages to dig up some more twigs to throw on the fire, from within the acres of small print in the terms and conditions of ticket sales Michael had been slaving over for months. What was I saying about enjoying your own words played back at you? Not in this case! Howard also drew more attention to the continuing confusion surrounding the charity aspect of the event, which was a much better aimed kick. On the face of it, the Estate has taken the side of the fans, noting the KISS error and shouting 'enough'. But the fact they weighed in, and probably 'assisted' the fan clubs to orchestrate their response, indicated they may have changed their attitude to us from 'this will never happen' to one of 'this might happen, so we'd better do something about it'. Small comfort, to know you've made enough noise to wake the bear!

Chris pens a worthy, wordy and indignant response to the estate, full of detail of rights required and not, of legal positions researched, of counterpoint and counter-blame. Nobody sees it. It sinks to the bottom of the cyber pool, unloved, un-posted and re-posted, invisible. Our web warriors are clearly out-classed, out-gunned and useless.

Even after the KISS debacle, and partly because of it, the lunacy continued. My favourite example concerns the hosting of the show. A few names were bandied about from early on, Eddie Murphy, Chris Rock, Chris Tucker and so on – top comedians with fine hosting track records, any one of who would do a great job. Eventually Jamie Foxx was approached, said yes, and was signed at the same time as Christina. Ron had talked to him, brought him in, excited him by suggesting he did a couple of songs as well as host. Jamie had in the past ribbed Michael for comic effect, and given the post KISS hyper-sensitivity towards anyone who had ever said a single uncomplimentary word about Michael, Jeffré and the Parojim were having second thoughts. So the Parojim thought it a good idea to re-approach, or maybe approach for the first time, who knows, Chris Tucker. One of them went to a gig Tucker was doing in LA, handed around his GLE Parojim business card, and went backstage after the show. He pigeonholed an exec and started talking up *Michael Forever*, and how wonderful it would be to have Chris present and host the show – worldwide TV audience of millions, greatest stars on earth, that kind of thing. The exec is interested, sounds great he says, but was anyone else in the frame to present? Was this a hosting thing for Chris or a co-hosting thing? He was assured that Chris would be the only host, that nobody else was even being considered. It turns out the Parojim was talking to Jamie Foxx's manager. Another fire. Another panic, another artist nearly lost. Ron and Chris (Hunt, not Tucker) between them manage to calm Jamie down, and he stayed on board, with Chris wondering what Jeffré's ship of fools will come up with next.

You might wonder why, mid-August, mid-crisis, mid-misery, I am still on board. I desperately need to believe in this project. I need it for my sanity, for the re-kindling of a career in the doldrums, for the escape from the drudgery of owning a small hotel. This is what I used to do, and I used to do it very well. The hotel had proved to be a costly mistake, I needed an out, and doing well on a concert of this magnitude held the promise of just that. It's why every setback spurs me to greater efforts, why I dive headlong into every gap in the planning (and there are many), toil ceaselessly to repair every hole, to make this into a *good thing*. Chris has hired me to deliver. He has trusted me and I am not going to let him down. We were just a couple of days from announcing Christina Aguilera, Jennifer Hudson, Ne-Yo, JLS, Smokey, Gladys, and Cee-Lo. British acts were falling over themselves to get on board. Chris had said yes to Leona Lewis and Pixie Lott (I know, I know, not exactly a superstar), but Beyoncé was going to record a special piece for us, Michael's band was being hired, more huge acts were just down the pipeline. It could still be a great show. It would sell around the world. Cinemas were interested in taking it live, and I had found an outfit looking to launch a Facebook streaming app with our show, so the whole thing could be seen globally by anyone with an internet connection.

I was also quite angry about the attitude of the fans, posting and stirring and letter-writing about a product that was still in the making. If you don't like it, don't buy it, but don't also deny the right of others to enjoy what you don't. I've never been a fan of fundamentalist zealots, whether Christian, Muslim, left wing, right wing or MJ. An opinion is an opinion, yours just as valid as mine. The unfavourable comparisons between us and Cirque du Soleil also raised hackles: *Michael Forever* clashed with the trial, Cirque du Soleil, premiering in the same week, did not. Measuring the creative merits of each was also unfair, as the comparison was not like with like, as our tribute was a pure presentation of the music of Michael Jackson. A West End theatre show had been running for two years doing just that. I don't know whether the producers of that show had the "permission" of the estate to put the show on the stage, but they certainly wouldn't need the "permission" of the estate to do so in London's West End. And anyway, the West End show was running before Michael's death, before the estate even existed. So I offer my own, limited and no doubt flawed, understanding of the convoluted world of the rights to all things Michael Jackson.

When Michael died all his assets (and debts too) became the property of his estate. John Branca and John McClain are the legal executors of the estate – the lawyers with the keys to Michael's house. Michael's music is owned by his co-creators, by music publishers, and some of it is still owned by the estate.

Rights to images of Michael are owned by photographers, record companies and TV stations. Rights to moving images of Michael are owned by record companies and TV stations. Likeness rights, where these exist, are owned by the estate. American courts and the rest of the legal world long ago recognized that putting moving images with music created new rights separate to those existing in the music and images. These rights are known as sync rights and they are owned by all of the entities listed, and more. Different uses of music require different permissions from the rights holders, and of course different rights holders have different approaches to what they will and will not give permission for. Different regions in the world also throw up additional issues.

So let's take a simple example to show how quickly the complexities pile on top of each other. Issues limited to just the rights as they pertain to Michael – not with performance or the location. I want to put up a poster of Michael and sing a medley of *Thriller* and *Smile*, and I want to do it:

a) In the bath in my house
b) In a pub in Manchester
c) In a street in Los Angeles
d) In a stadium in Cardiff

Oh, and I want to film my performance, with the poster behind me, and put it on YouTube.

a) In the bath in my house. I'm not exploiting anyone's rights, as this is not a public performance. By filming myself singing I am technically creating a sync right, but until I put it on YouTube, and thereby exploit through publication (exhibition) both the new sync right (the song and me on video) and the existing music and lyrics rights (the publisher's rights), I'm not doing anything illegal. Once I do however, there is no difference in legality between a film of me singing in the bath and one of Christina Aguilera singing on stage in Cardiff. One will be better looking and more in tune. If I use a pre-recorded backing track, I need to clear that usage too with the person who wrote the music, the musician who played it, or the collecting agency to which they have assigned these rights. On film, all the performances require a licence from the rights holders (authors, publishers, owners of recordings: mechanical rights holders) of the material before they can be disseminated. (The word there used to be "broadcast", but now that stuff is on the web, on mobile phones and on cable the term no longer applies.) The Michael poster needs clearance too, from the owner of the image and in some parts of the world, from the Michael Jackson estate as the owner of Michael's likeness. This goes for all the films of all the examples where there is a picture of MJ, or indeed a 'likeness', such as a hat and spangly glove presented in a way that is obviously 'of' Michael.

b) In the Manchester pub. I'm making a public performance, whether the pub customers are paying to be there or just trying to enjoy a pint of beer despite my efforts. The pub pays the Performing Rights Society (PRS) a flat annual fee for clearance to play music, whether live or recorded, in the bar. This fee covers me doing the vocals badly, and the original recorded music tracks done very well. They pay me nothing, saying they'd rather have Christina Aguilera do it. The same is true on stage in the West End. PRS payments cover the right to perform all music, whoever wrote it or performed it before. They also cover music and lyrics separately, so that karaoke sessions are perfectly legal too. Sticking a film of it on YouTube, and therefore broadcasting the performance, isn't legal, and it's why a lot of stuff put up on YouTube is constantly being taken down when the rights owners complain.

c) On the corner of Sunset and Melrose. California state law has created a person's right of ownership of their own image and likeness. In Tinseltown, where image is everything and a big part of the economy, you can understand why laws protecting celebrity are important. I have to get the estate's permission to use the poster (image). If I dress up like Michael I need permission for that too (likeness), but only if I am commercially exploiting. My public performance needs licencing too. If I choose the right street, Christina's agent will likely see my efforts, and I'm bound to get a record deal straight away.

d) Millennium Stadium. Not much difference between Cardiff and the pub in Manchester really. For an organized concert, the venue pays the PRS two per cent of ticket revenues, which the PRS, as a collection society, distributes amongst its members (publishers) who pay the authors. Crucially, laws of image and likeness do not apply at the venue, nor on TV and cinema screens anywhere except in California and the other US states where they are on the statute books.

As I've been writing this I've developed the idea into a concept. My performance is going to be called *Bathtime Michael* and in addition to the poster behind me I'm going to have heart shaped bubbles. I've emailed it to a few people and Sam Anthony of BBC Scotland loves this more even than the steam trains and he wants to put it on BBC One, prime time Saturday night, because he thinks it will beat *X Factor*. Great! The BBC, in common with most broadcasters in the UK (I don't know about elsewhere) have a blanket agreement with the Music Copyright Protection Society (MCPS) who look after music in broadcast, including the web, in exactly the same way as the PRS look after public performance, including in pubs and stadia. This blanket agreement gives the broadcasters the right to use music for payment of a substantial annual fee. The BBC won't disclose what they pay, but this is why there is such great music in *Eastenders* and on obscure BBC4 documentaries about Scottish steam trains. The music is free to the programme makers. So my performance, the sync right and the authors' rights to *Smile* and *Thriller* are covered by the BBC's blanket agreement and everything is Okey Dokey? No. Unlike with the PRS, with the MCPS authors may elect to withhold their work from the blanket agreement. Rod Temperton is such an author. I can't use *Thriller* in *Bathtime Michael* unless he specifically lets me. If authors don't withhold their work, they cannot pick and choose which TV show can use their material and which cannot. *Smile* is with publishing giants SonyATV, part owned by Michael and therefore now part of the estate. None of the four credited writers of the track have withheld from MCPS blanket, so I can use that one. Phew! For a moment I thought I'd be left with just the bubbles. I've cleared the poster for UK TV use with Sony, who owned the image and the photographer's rights. As I'm not broadcasting in California, I don't need to clear the poster (image) or my spangly bath glove (arguably 'likeness') with the estate.

It used to be the case that a producer of a programme had to laboriously clear music for every territory he wanted to sell his programme to. The producers wanted an easier path, so they negotiated their own Secondary Uses blanket agreement, modelled on the broadcasters' agreement with MCPS and given the handy initialism PSMPLA. I can't remember what it stands for; any initialism with more than four letters, tops, should be an acronym anyway. CIS Miami Special Investigations never billed itself as CISMSE – it's just too many letters. I offer up PissMaplay – or perhaps not.

Anyway, authors again had the right not to participate, and Rod Temperton again chose not to. But I can now sell the film of *Bathtime Michael* to Estonia and East Timor, and put it on You Tube, so long as I have this secondary use blanket from MCPS. I'll have to block out the poster for the You Tube presentation because it will be seen in California, and I decide against the spangly glove for the same reason.

Now given all that (and there's much more but you're probably as bored reading it as I am writing it), I hope you understand why, when a fan posted:

Cancel this travesty now you morons, you don't have the RIGHT to do this!!!!?!!

I was moved to reply:

You are naive

In the topsy turvy world of hate for MF, calling us morons was perfectly acceptable, but suggesting that the poster with a bagful of exclamation marks (and no fear of using them) had a less than total grasp of the intricacies of music copyright (see above) led to a new wave of bitter anger from the fans. How very dare I call someone naïve! Just for the record, I do think it is naïve to confuse an estate, a depository of property, with the legacy and spirit of Michael Jackson. The former is a contract, law and logic. The latter is music, emotion and feeling. We were honouring the music with Michael's family. I did not then, and do not now, see anything wrong with that.

The fans however, saw any non-estate project as an illegal one. The law, as I no doubt poorly explained, said otherwise. The emotion of the legacy however, was where the fans placed it – with the Estate. They hated Katherine Jackson and the family for ignoring this crucial, emotional contract they had made, for sidestepping the sepulchre they had filled with their love once Michael was gone. They hated Chris Hunt and GLE for trying to exploit it and them, and they would have hated Jeffré too, had they seen him.

By contrast the Cirque du Soleil project was sanctioned by the estate, and embraced by the fans. Cirque is a known and respected brand, with creative integrity and a long track record. When they decided to do an MJ based show, Branca's door was open and a deal was done. Had Chris approached the same door, the question may well have been 'Who the fuck are you?' But we'll never know, because he never did, because he never felt he should. The entirety of Chris' approach to *Michael Forever* was based on what he could do by legal right, what loopholes there were that he could wriggle through. Cirque's view, by contrast, was to embrace the Estate and the fans.

Another major bone of contention with the fans was that we were exploiting Michael. We were called vultures, crooks, scammers and worse, because the estate had not sanctioned *Michael Forever*. Naïvely, (yes, I was naïve, but not in the way 'Exclamation mark man!!!' meant) I thought we would eventually come to a deal with Branca. Once he saw the strength of the product, how we were trying to be true to

Michael, involving so many people that had worked with him closely while he was alive, bringing together the majority of his family, the Estate would come on board and share in the profits. I also thought Ron's close ties with John Branca would be the perfect conduit for such an approach, but Chris thought otherwise and I was forbidden to discuss it. The doors to the estate remained firmly shut, and behind them were the fans, our audience.

But let's look at this accusation of exploitation. The King of Pop, Michael Jackson, was and is one of the most popular recording artists ever. He and everyone else around him earned millions, because millions bought what he was offering. This essential contract, where you pay for your entertainment, is the exploitation, and it's not a negative thing. The exploiters, the end users, are the fans – if there's no interest, if the product is unwanted, there's no exploitation. So presenting a quality Michael Jackson project to a ready market is good business, created and sustained by the market. Somebody has to do the work to make the delivery, and nobody works for free.

So despite all the shit flying around, I believed *Michael Forever* could still deliver what it promised. We had great acts, we had musicians with ties to Michael's work, and we had a strengthening creative team that worked with Michael on some of his finest material. I was still on board because I believed it would come good in the end. We would get through the cash flow issues (and I would be paid), and we would deliver. Crucial to that delivery was Ron Weisner, and he is in town.

He arrives with two beautiful assistants who tend to his every need. Diane is laid back and laconic. Halston has the most beautiful eyes I have ever seen, can only be described as bootylicious, and is a princess. And Ron? He's like Woody

Allen, but not as funny.

We head off to Cardiff, where we stand on the pitch. I had requested a long thin screen across part of the stands behind the stage to give the cameras a background, and the size and position had been calculated to make an impact across the width of the stage. HaSH had decided to move everything forward by ten metres, blaming errors in the stadium's roof loading plans, so this rear screen needed a complete rethink, because with the change in distance it would be an annoying ribbon for the front on cameras rather than the imposing backdrop I envisaged.

Nevertheless we achieved a lot, although Ron tells us that Prince has disappeared off the radar. Apparently he was in Oslo at the time of the shooting and bombing tragedy there, thought the gunman was actually trying to kill him, and has gone to ground. Incommunicado, so no Prince. Ron pushes for gospel singer Yolanda Adams, but Chris is not convinced, arguing that an unknown, non-mainstream performer who is not a global name has no place in this tribute. Instead Chris signs Alexandra Burke, which makes the show a bit ex-X Factor heavy, leading to more criticism from the fans. Ron counters with Jennifer Hudson, and talks of getting a choir. No shortage of those in Wales, and for a moment the rugby players of the stadium get terribly excited. I think they pictured a modern reworking of the famous pre-battle scene from the film Zulu; renditions of *Men of Harlech* from one side of the stadium and strains of *PYT* from the other. But Ron wants a gospel choir, so their dreams of Celtic glory die stillborn.

Ron and I have a heart to heart. Just prior to his arrival Chris was very worried about the need to hide Jeffré from Ron. He wasn't sure how to have meaningful conversations about artists and the nature of the show, or how to present information that appeared inexplicable without the knowledge that Jeffré was in charge. The huge costs of La Toya's rehearsals and needs for instance, the hiring of Heavy D (a Jeffré-managed act) to duet with her, the refusal to accept Ron's choice of musical director, and so on. Ron thought he was in charge of the show, and to an extent he was, but only as far as the walls of Ja-Tail. Thereafter, Jeffré was still the man, visible or not.

But you don't get as far in the business as Ron has without being a smart cookie. He sensed something was off key; he could see the confusion and in fact was daily dealing with it as artists rang him to ask 'wtf?' was going on with *Michael Forever*. He called the band of LA cousins, (Chris' "ship of fools" and my "Parojim"), "the Quenella", a wonderful made up word perfectly indicating a failing concoction. Agents, lawyers and performers all would be asked to participate by two, three or even four different sets of people. Because they all knew Ron, and had no idea who the Parojim/Quenella were, they would all call him to get some sense as to what was going on. No wonder they all wanted their money up front.

* * *

Being all of Leonard's guys is becoming a bit of a strain, so I hire some help. I need some mother figures around, calm efficient ladies who will sort out the tons of stuff that needs dealing with. First up is Telly Mum, someone to line produce the recording and broadcasting of the show. My first choice Flossie, is otherwise engaged, then she isn't, then she is, so I'm a bit late in getting someone, but very lucky to get Dawn, who has done it forever and just gets on with it. She's not really a mum exactly, more of an elder sister who knows what's best, and she is exactly what the show needs. Next up, I need a talent producer. Purple comes highly recommended. She is feisty, Irish and short. Her experience is in looking after talent on major multi-act shows, and she is soon ensconced and doing just that, setting up hotel deals in London and Cardiff, hiring transport managers, looking for rehearsal spaces and a myriad other things. She wears purple clothes, has purple luggage and purple accessories. She gives me purple post it notes with writing in purple ink, rendering the messages invisible. Her hair is red, as far as I can see, but for me her name can only be Purple. Finally and crucially I get Eat Your Hearts Out, one of two of the world's greatest rock and roll catering companies (the other is Eat to the Beat). EYHO is run by indomitable Aussie Kim. She has fed every major pop and rock act since she started in the eighties. When I told her about *Michael Forever* she was in tears – she had done his tours *Bad*, *Dangerous* and *HIStory*, and had been booked to do *This Is It*. She told me a sad story about the aftermath of Michael's death.

A side of Kim's business that has made her unique is the total care she provides to the artists. Her catering is of a very high standard, far superior to most film caterers, but the environments she creates, turning grubby basement boiler rooms into silk draped and soft lit chill out areas, or comfortable, carpeted dressing rooms, are really special. AEG hired her to find and furnish the country house that Michael wanted to live in while in the UK. Kim located a stunning mansion in Essex and filled it with her own furniture, lamps, pictures and tons of other stuff, to create a home. The day after Michael died she was barred from the house by newly appointed security teams, and she could only watch helplessly as her furniture was carted off into storage, presumably by AEG. It took an age for her to get paid, and she never recovered much of what she had lent out. But she was delighted to come on board *Michael Forever*. I got the impression she believed working on the tribute would give her a sense of closure.

I also need someone to look after the money, a production accountant happy to sit in a corner and add up stationery receipts. Chris however, is determined to keep all the money flow in Bristol, close to his chest, and the position remains unfilled. It means there is no central point covering ordering, invoicing and delivery. It's a gap that will eventually cost millions, but at the time was treated as a Chris thing – he was the boss and that's how he wanted it.

With a team in place work starts on the mass of outstanding detail, but I sense trouble ahead because Ron is talking about bringing his talent team with him for the show. These people organize flights, hotels and ground transportation. They run the show, get the artists to stage at the right time, move them from dressing room to media village to lunch to the toilet. I don't see the need for them when we have some strong production people lined up in the UK, people such as Purple who regularly do the Brits, VMAs and other big multi-artist shows. Ron is evasive on the matter, but I insist that local transport, hotels and all aspects of artist liaison in the UK will be Purple's domain. This arrangement leaves the matter of organizing rehearsal schedules in Ron's hands. It also leaves the issue of booking flights up in the air, if you pardon the pun. We create yet another tiny crack that will become a yawning, money swallowing chasm.

On Ron's last night we go out to dinner. There is a strange atmosphere in the air – Tottenham is rioting, the streets of the West End are full of nervous looking police and then there is a power cut over part of Soho. The light is eerie, the shop fronts and neons unusually dark. We walk for ten minutes and find a restaurant with some power. Ron spends the entire evening in the street on the phone to Jennifer Hudson.

* * *

It's all gone a bit surreal. Chris has asked me to come to Cardiff with him to try to get some money out of the local Council, and to confirm the Welsh National Opera (WeaNO?) as our rehearsal space. Surely the former should have been done last September, when there was actually a choice about location and date, and not now just weeks from the show. I cannot fathom what his negotiating strengths are on this one, and neither does the pleasant but surprised council leader, who is delighted to have *Michael Forever* come to Cardiff, in six weeks' time, and she'll certainly allow us to hang signage from her streetlamps on the day, for a fee, but there can be no question of any public contribution to the costs, unless the event was two years down the line. Thank you and good afternoon.

Next stop, WeaNO, where some spotty public arts oik denies all knowledge of anything to do with Michael or Forever, takes us through a warren of discarded wigs and scenic flats to a subterranean troll who scans a timetable board and announces both rehearsal rooms unavailable. I'd known all this already, as I'd got Purple to research everything in Cardiff and found it wanting – in oh, so many ways – and totally unsuitable as a place to rehearse a major show. So I began to suspect that Chris might be beginning to lose it, a little. I try to refocus him on what needs to be done, not on what should have been done last September, and remind him that the TV director needs sorting out. He promises to talk to Hamish first thing.

A few days later and I'm back in Cardiff. The stadium now confirmed, it's time to decide what to do in the President's

Lounge, a four hundred capacity room directly across the hall from the VIP seating. The catering department have set up a tasting, and given that I own a restaurant it falls to me to attend. I take Purple with me from London, as she has a slew of hotel visits planned. Chris' longest-serving elf, a statuesque brunette called Angela also comes across from Bristol. Chris and Michael want the President's Lounge to be the VIP hub of the event, a place for investors, friends and family and Katherine and the children to mingle publicly. It's also the last remaining twig from my tree of VIPness I had constructed back in April, so I was going to make damned sure the food and drink was spot on and as good as I could get it.

Buffet stations have been set up around the room, and in the centre is a circular table laid in white with eight places. Joining us are various hospitality managers, bar managers and the executive head chef. First we are served some meal options for the corporate boxes that ring the stadium around Level Five. There are hot options and cold options, none of them particularly exciting.

"Have you ever been to a Harvester before?"

"If I had, do you really think I'd come back?" is what plays in my mind, but I'm too polite to say it and I imagine the bulk of my co-lunchees are too young to remember the TV ad. There are no cartwheels with sheaves of wheat anywhere in the room to suggest that I am, in any way, in a Harvester. The offered white wine is undrinkable and the red wine good only as a plaque remover. I look at the wine list and hide the duality brought on by equal measures of admiration and astonishment at the prices. Three pound fifty alco-piss is being sold out at thirty quid! I tell the bar manager to bring out something decent to drink and he trots off to set up a tasting on the bar.

The wine list at my hotel is a labour of love. I have about a hundred bins, with an average of three bottles in each available at any one time. It's Euro-centric because that's what I find my customers want, when they choose to spend over twenty five quid they stick with what they know. It means they spend on brand and miss out on some stunning new world wines which offer double the quality of France or Spain at half the price, but they are comfortable with their choice, and that's what counts. For instance I have a 2006 Chateau Moulin de Pey Labrie, a claret from Canon Fronsac, on my list at forty two quid. It's not a bad Bordeaux, but a few pages on is a Parker Coonawarra 2004, at a few pounds more, that is the equivalent of the finest clarets they will ever taste. But they won't because, despite the glowing write up I have given in the notes, they'll go with the Frenchie. The percentage profit varies, from 80% on a glass of house wine down to 40% on the Parker Coonawarra. My house wine costs between five and six pounds a bottle. The wines are carefully sourced to offer the best possible quality. Once a bottle has been opened, it needs to be paid for, so a glass costs between five and six pounds too. The next three glasses are margin. Drinking by the bottle is cheaper – if it costs five pounds to buy it is on the list at fifteen. This rule of thirds cannot be applied to fine wines however, for three reasons. The first is that a bottle costing twenty five pounds will not sell at ninety (seventy five plus VAT) – not in my Highlands restaurant anyway. The second is that anyone spending that kind of money on wine hopefully knows the value of what they are drinking. Thirdly, the effort in buying, storing and serving the wine does not change that much as the price of the wine goes up. So for all those reasons, the margin drops from 69% to fifty and under. Come to my hotel and the more you spend on wine the less I make!

No such scruples appear to be in play at the Millennium stadium however, where the cheapest available crap, wine so bad not even Lidl would dream of selling it, is bought in and sold on at massive margin. Eventually I find a half decent Sancerre which I earmark as the white. The bar manager cannot seem to find a red wine worth drinking so I decide to bring my own in, and negotiate a corkage rate. Even with the fifteen quid per bottle he wants I can deliver better quality for less money than buying off his list.

Now for the food. I don't really care what they serve in the corporate boxes, but I want to make sure the President's Lounge has the best available. The buffet is nicely presented, and the executive chef is pan searing scallops at a hot station. He assures me they are hand dived. I tell him I own a restaurant and I can assure him they are not (the difference, apart from the ecological damage done by dredging for them, is the amount of water that comes out when they are cooked. Dredged scallops are like cheap bacon, giving off loads of water when they hit the hot pan).

We move to the next station, where he serves me roast beef and Yorkshire pudding. I tell him I think this is a bit Sunday lunchtime rather than Saturday evening gala, and I ask him where the beef comes from, and what breed is it. He hasn't the first clue, or the second. I guess it comes from the same place as the part baked, deep frozen bread rolls his kitchens have heated up. Odourless, tasteless balls of cardboard, delivered by the pallet load off a truck with "Total Catering Solutions" written along the sides. This is banquet cooking set to highest achievable financial margin. If you see such a truck outside a restaurant, you should think of going elsewhere.

Sadly, the truck will have delivered there too. Such is the state of British eating out. Factory pre-cooked, fast-chilled and distributed to kitchens where the chef is a product operative most skilled in opening packets and switching on computerised ovens. Whether it's MacDonalds or Gordon Ramsey, the systems are the same.

The catering manager tempts me with a sushi station, which is operated on site by a Japanese restaurant in the city. That sounds more like it, more the kind of thing to have at a twenty first century VIP buffet, something where a human has actually used personal skill to prepare what my VIPs will eat. My confidence in this idea, which being a good one costs extra, is boosted when the restaurant asks whether I want Californian or Japanese style sushi. That's the kind of question that tells you someone is actually thinking about the product. I choose Californian, so the Americans feel at home.

As we finish our tour and I approve this and ask him to think again on that, and he nods and smiles but I can tell he's looking forward to a rugby client who knows nothing about food, who does not have his own "everything from fresh, everything cooked to order, everything sourced locally" restaurant, and will just accept his offerings without comment.

The room fills with office girls from every corner of the stadium. Most of them have come for the cakes, beautifully presented but tasting of nothing much other than sugar and cream, and delivered by that "Catering Solutions" truck. They tell me tasting days are great, because they get the afternoon off to eat fantastic food. I tell them it's not that great, and that I own a restaurant where everything is fresh, everything is cooked to order and everything is locally sourced. I tell them finding Scottish olive oil was a real challenge, but there is a cold pressed rapeseed oil that is very good. They fight hard not to look bored.

The scallop searing station has produced a lot of smoke. I ask if anyone has turned the sprinkler system off and a young under-manager runs from the room. Someone promises they'll fix the smoke problem. Then Alex arrives. I'm quite pleased that I have raised their game for the VIP feeding of *Michael Forever*. I have made my mark, pushed the chef to find something unusual, and had quite a decent lunch. I am as ready as I'll ever be to shake Alex's hand.

* * *

The fear continues. The dichotomy between getting material onto the web and not releasing anything uncleared because an artist hasn't actually signed is beginning to take its toll. When Craig David tweeted his participation he was quickly told to stop it. The new web people threw their hands up – here was an artist willing to say good things about the show, which is exactly what was needed to counter the hate campaign, yet as soon as he did so he was told to shut up, because he was spoiling a major announcement (about KISS, for God's sake!).

The investors appear to be getting increasingly nervous, wheeling out little companies they own from all over the place to "help" us with the marketing and planning and catering and tea. One casualty of the KISS car crash is the PR company that has singularly failed to make any impression in the media. One of the investors owns a media marketing company and he insists they take up the mantle of dealing with the social media aspect of the project. Paul King wheels in a tried and tested rock 'n' roll public relations campaigner and we are fired up again.

They are all immediately at odds with one another, and

Michael Henry spends most of his time as umpire between variously irate backers hurling abuse at the lack of performance from their opposite numbers, and expressing incredulity at the antics of Paul's PR lady, who to me and the sane world appears to have a good handle on what needs doing. By great good fortune this nonsense stays as background clutter and away from the morass of fan-angst and artist tardiness. We have almost completed engineering the perfect storm, and we are setting course to sail our lumbersome, leaking oil tanker right into it.

Looking at our line up, now finally announced, it was clear we needed one more A-lister. Stevie Wonder had been interested because of his ties to Michael, and he would have been popular amongst the fans, but there was some history with the family, and he had wanted Katherine to personally ask him to do it, which she had not been prepared to do. The others in the frame were of course the Black Eyed Peas – BEPS in email shorthand. Founder Will-I-Am was a huge Michael fan, and had produced a number of tracks with him. The BEP fee of two million dollars was not immediately on hand in the bank or anywhere else, so Chris needed to stall. Fortunately for us, Michael Henry tells me, one of the BEP's many lawyers is insisting that the whole fee is paid, in advance, into an account Michael is unhappy about, held, the way he tells it, by someone's cousin's ice cream van business in Puerto Canco, Venezuela for all I know. Not surprisingly, Michael Henry refuses to send a medium consignment of blow's worth of cash into something so unsecured, and the BEP lawyer gets terribly upset, insisting this was standard and normal industry practice. If GLE wanted BEP, they had better follow SOP and pay up PDQ. And how dare they asperse the cousin - the cousin is not only trustworthy, but his Tutti Frutti is famous throughout Latin America. Finding an escrow account acceptable to both sides would take over two weeks.

* * *

As August draws to a close and we pass MJ's birthday and what was to be the show day, Chris and Michael Henry announce they are close to finalizing a refinancing deal involving increased participation of one of the key investors, a hedge fund called QuickDraw run by Sara Giles. QuickDraw had been approached at the start, and were now looking to provide additional funding, including the two million bucks for the Black Eyed Peas. It appears we might now have enough money to get to the show, and once there everything will be very rosy indeed, especially with the outfit I found that would launch a Facebook streaming app for live events. It seems the perfect fit. Jeffré tells us a sponsor is on the verge of signing, the band start rehearsals in LA, and Ron and his team fly into the UK in a couple of weeks' time. I have a production team in place, I still need a director and lighting designer, but for the moment things seem to be moving in the right direction. Ticket registrations are slow, amounting to only about twenty five thousand, but everyone figures this is fairly meaningless. Once they go on sale, they will sell fast. Confusion continues to reign as to what exactly our product is. Issues of copyright and estate sanction have muddied the waters sufficiently for potential customers to believe there won't be any Michael Jackson songs at the Michael Jackson tribute concert. Rumblings continue about the date, the charities, the ticket price, the process of getting a ticket, signing KISS – pretty much every facet of our consumer interface seems to have a serious flaw in it. Juliette thinks somebody should talk to the fans. Chris, having done a series of radio interviews in which he managed to piss off virtually everyone who might want to buy a ticket, refuses. I mentally check Leonard's list of five guys, and realize that somebody is me.

Before I tackle the fans, I set up a text to win competition. Michael Henry had been talking to an outfit promising a global reach, but a study of their terms and conditions showed us, the client, liable for any breach of local regulations in any territory the text to win was active. Since a number of fundamentalist, zealot countries considered text to win as a form of gambling – the US for instance, and as we had no clue what the "local" regulations were: Did we need to have a Pentacostalist sponsor in Alabama? Shroud the answers in a burkha in Afghanistan? Make Putin's birthday one of the answers in Russia? Henry though it prudent not to proceed. So I found another, UK only operator and did the deal. £1.95 per text netted GLE around £1.20. The operator and British Telecom carved up the rest. The prize was an all-expenses paid trip to the show, including hotels, travel, spending money and two empty cans of Star Ice that had been personally imbibed by La Toya Jackson.

To stay the right side of UK gaming and gambling laws there had to be an element of skill, so I quickly researched three answers to a question I formulated: Michael's first solo album was a) *Thriller*, b) *Got To Be There*, c) *Dangerous*. I did this by Googling "Michael Jackson's first solo album" and I took the answer, *Got To Be There* off the Wikipedia page listing all his solo albums in chronological order.

Within hours the fans are emailing the Bristol office.
Hi,
I was hoping to enter the
http://home.michaelforevertribute.com/ttwin.htmlcompetition,

however, I note that the answers to your question "What was MJ's first solo album" are wrong, the answers you state to text are:
A) Thriller
B) Got to be there
C) Dangerous
the answer is in fact OFF THE WALL. With this in mind, I do not know whether it is worth entering the competition if I cannot answer with the correct reply. Are you going to fix this error or should I still enter with an incorrect answer of Thriller?
I hope to hear from you
Kind regards,
Natasha Toft

Emma, Bristol's prettiest elf, wades in less than helpfully

Hi everyone

Who has organised the text-to-win competition? There are lots of emails in Chris's GLE account saying that none of the 3 options are correct, that Off The Wall was in fact MJ's first solo album (I could have told you that – as could anyone with a slightly more than passing interest in MJ)

Maybe this has already been picked up elsewhere, but if not obviously need to rectify.

Thinking I had made a blunder of monumental proportions I went back and checked again, and again. *Off the Wall* was Michael's fifth album. *Got To Be There* was the first, listed so not just on Wikipedia but on at least three other MJ sites as well. I relaxed, told Emma to check her facts and stop sniping, and sent a round robin email calming everyone down. It was definitely a sign of our nervousness though, that we could doubt the truth so quickly, panic so thoroughly, and find mistakes even where there were none.

The conference calls with the fans have been set up so each fan club representative dials in at half hour intervals. Juliette has arranged it so we are using the American conference call account and not our English Pow Wow Now.

The American one is crap. The line is bad and it refuses to recognize the pin code, When prompted I dial it in, 1345, only to hear:

"You have dialled 1 3 8 7. This pin is invalid. Please try again. Goodbye"

More carefully this time. 1-3-4-5

"You have dialled 8 7 8 8 This pin is invalid. Please try again. Goodbye"

And so on. As a result I'm ten minutes late signing in. Not that it matters, as there is no fan person on the line, just Juliette and Paul King. We give it another few minutes, chat amongst ourselves, and hang up, ready to dial in for the next one. I have lived these past five weeks plugged into my iPhone, taking calls and working the emails wherever I found myself. Cafes, park benches, the office in Shaftsbury Avenue, on the train, in a cab – it doesn't matter, I can talk from anywhere. But these important and difficult calls with the fans required a little more thought as to the best place to conduct them. A cosy pub, snuggled down in the snug bar with a pint of ale, held many charms, but the danger of too much ale would be ever present, creating the spectre of a combative drunk abusing the fans, slurring "Yer all a bunch of fuckers!" and so not really presenting the GLE line. Noise, background chatter and worries about signal strength ruled out being on anything moving, and I chose somewhere warm, comfortable and familiar – the dining room of my parents' house. My son was with me, back from his Scottish summer holiday and grown by the experience of looking after five puppies. I had given much thought to what I would say, prepared some notes but was ready to go with the flow. Here are my notes.

DATE and the TRIAL
The path of American justice is a complex one, especially in such a high profile and important case. The trial is due to start one month before our concert. It may not start at all, it may be delayed, it may be over by the time of our concert. What of it gets delayed to next year? Will there be calls for Cirque du Soleil to then cancel their Michael Jackson project? Those responsible for the terrible tragedy of Michaels's death denied us all his continuing genius. Do not let them deny you still. Join with us in celebrating his music. Join Smokey Robinson, Gladys Knight, Christina Aguilera, three of his brothers, his mother, sister and children as we all pay tribute to his music and his life. And should the trial take place without further rescheduling, further legal argument, further distancing from the outcome you want, then what better a way to focus the minds of the jury and the court with a reminder, through music and dance, of just how great a loss was the loss of him

FAMILY OPPOSITION
Show us a large family full of strong characters that all agree on anything and we'll show you the Waltons. Outside of fiction such unity of thought just doesn't happen. Yes some family members oppose this concert. But equally some are actively supporting it. Mrs Jackson, Tito, Jackie, Marlon, La Toya to name but five, 3T and Michael's children are six more. Janet has privately sent us her best wishes but is not yet ready for something like this. Jermaine and Randy are opposed, but Jermaine has tried twice to do something like this without success, and chooses not to support the wishes of the majority of his family.

ESTATE
we at global live have the greatest respect for the estate and the work they do to protect and enhance Michaels legacy. We tread with the utmost care not to infringe any of the rights the estate hold; as entertainment professionals we have a clear understanding of what they are, and what rights (music publishing, sync etc) lie elsewhere. All Michaels repertoire, from age five onwards, that has been published, can be performed at the concert. A substantial portion of the ticket revenue is paid directly to the Performing Rights Society to secure these rights. This money is paid to the rights holders and the authors of the music and lyrics.
The estate does however, retain some rights of great value in the US, and we reach out to them to allow us to present our tribute in the same way

and to the same standard in the country of Michaels birth as we are in the rest of the world. We plead with the estate to give Americans the chance to enjoy this tribute fully, to share not just in the music but in the man. We humbly request the same terms granted to Cirque, on the same basis,with the same result. Share with us and we will share with you.

BOOKING KISS

We really screwed up. Somebody thought it was a good idea, seeing as how they were Michaels favourite rock band. Nobody checked, someone really should have known. We once retorted to a fan on FB that they were being naive for not having a full grasp of music rights and how they operate. Well we were the naive ones, for thinking this was just another show, huge yes, but ultimately just another gig. Nothing to do with Michael is the same as with anyone else. We understand the passion of the fans, we respect it and them hugely. We know we have made mistakes, and we are very clear that working with Michael's legacy is not like any other project. We urge the fans to embrace this concert, join our performers, Michael's musicians and dancers, Ron Weisner's creative vision for the show and make it a pure and complete celebration. And for those that cannot, we respect your wish and ask only that you respect the wishes of those who do want to be there on October 8 in Cardiff

CALLS FOR CANCELLATION

Everyone has a right to choose, and we accept that some won't choose our show. But to demand it's cancellation, to try to deny an audience the chance to hear Christina Aguilera, Smokey Robinson, Gladys Knight, Cee Lo Green, Ne-Yo and a host of British stars sing songs made famous by Michael is just not right in a free society. We're not going to cancel, we will not cave to those who cannot see the love light and joy this concert will bring, we will not surrender to those who would keep Michael's genius in the dark. We will however hold back from general sale, across all price bands, 10% of ticket stock and make it available only to accredited MJ fans.

CHARITY

We have set up a trust fund for Katherine Jackson and Michaels children, one which they benefit from far sooner than any other. We have guaranteed substantial sums to the Princes Trust, and we have an agreed profit share formula in place with them. We have embarked on a vast *commercial project with huge costs, state of the art stage design, and a host of 20 international artists. Our profits are the last to come from this ocean of expense. That's why the tickets are pricier than for other stadium shows, but comparable with big festivals and top line concerts*

Some fans had been attacking Katherine Jackson quite vehemently, and this had led one of 3T, Michael's nephews and part of our line up, to tweet their unhappiness at the vitriol pouring onto their granny. This really upset me, as I firmly believed that Katherine had a right to honour her son's music however she wished, and abusing the mother of your idol is not a proper way to behave. When I put this belief up on our Facebook page the fans screamed back:

We are the true fans of MJ. How DARE you criticize our behavior!!

So I had an additional area of discussion to sashay into should I want, or should the fan clubs want, and in this area, I felt the moral high ground was mine. Paul King announces that he doesn't want to be announced. In fact he's sent us an email on the subject:

On 29 Aug 2011, at 17:11, Paul King wrote:
Hi Juliette
—   Give the fans have been digging the dirt on a number of us, we should not use my full name in any invitation, as I have had a couple of financial accidents in the past, and the last thing we need is to add even more fuel to the fire.
Thanks Paul

We have to stop hiding stuff. We can't introduce you as just Paul A

My reply was ignored and Paul remained hidden under Jeffré's cloaking device. But which of the following qualifies as a "financial accident"?

    a)   Losing twenty quid down the back of a sofa

    b)   Losing a hundred quid on a horse

    c)   Losing a successful management company and a million quid of NatWest's money

    d)   Losing two hundred grand of an old lady's savings and doing two years in prison at Her Majesty's pleasure for it

If you answered 'c' and 'd' you are spot on. One hundred and eighty thousand bonus points if you knew the management company was called Outlaw, and three more if you remember Paul's incarceration came about through his involvement with Global Health Products, and a quack hangover cure developed by a witch doctor in South Africa. Paul was right, it's best not to let on to the fans that the UK promoter of their favourite MJ concert ever is a convicted fraudster, especially as they'd already filled the Internet with descriptive nouns like shyster, vultures, shit-talkers, hypocrites (various spellings, none correct) and more. We love you MJ!!

It's not the falling, it's the getting up that makes the man, and Paul has certainly nothing to prove in that department. It would be nice however, just for once, to be totally honest with the fans.

First up on the phone is Gary Taylor, of the UK's biggest MJ online community and a very unhappy bunny. The allocated half hour proves nowhere near long enough to get into, and properly respond to, his concerns. Juliette doesn't help either, barking at him, threatening him, telling him he is wrong. I lose patience with her towards the end and tell her to shut up. In between Juliet's snapping I try to answer Gary's point about the trial, glibly telling him, because Chris told me, that there would be no trial, that Murray would quietly take the rap, do his time and collect a fat cheque on his way out. Gary tells me I'm dreaming. He tells me of conversations with the defence lawyers, of deals he has done with journalists covering the case, of his preparations to bring his MJ fan subscribers all the news as it happens in that LA courtroom. We agree to talk further, as I sense he may come to understand what we are doing is honourable. I give Gary my mobile number, the iPhone one not the cheap pay as you go I had purchased to avoid being plagued by journos and the Michael lunatic fringe, and we agree to keep having a dialogue. Next, an earnest woman from the Netherlands, who leads with

"Do you think Michael's children are poor?"

This is the fallout from the $100,000 trust fund cheque that Chris presented to Katherine and which surprised us all back at the press launch in July, a day which now seems a universe away. I need to tread carefully here, because I mustn't attack the estate. The facts as presented to me by Chris are these: Michael's children don't receive the money in the estate until they are thirty. Until then, Katherine has her bills paid, her house provided and a stipend of $9000 per month, all at the whim of the estate. The trust fund Chris and Jeffré set up, seeded with the $100K and funded from show profits, was for Katherine alone, a source of income outside of the control of the estate, giving her a degree of independence from people she didn't trust, people she believed responsible for her son's death, people she had challenged over control of the estate. In that light the trust fund appears a good and noble thing to do, especially as it was not requested or demanded by Katherine. But I can't say any of that, other than the "wait until they're thirty" bit, and then I am accused of going against Michael's wishes for his children, against the terms of Michael's will that Michael signed and that California courts found to be true and proper.

I end up speaking to just three representatives of the fan clubs, because Juliette had organized the thing and she had obviously done it whilst driving somewhere because many failed to get through and lots more didn't know about it. I get somebody to reach out to them all again and manage to speak to half a dozen more over the next few days, going over the same ground and the same issues. I get the sense that, although they are not being swayed by my arguments, they are becoming a bit more reasonable in their opposition, moving from "die now you scum!" to "we cannot agree with this". I ponder that while Chris may not be brilliant at making films, or concerts, when it comes to rods for his own back there's nobody better!

So a partial victory, which sadly comes to nothing. Tickets have been on sale for a week and we have sold 327.

In the big scheme of things, this doesn't really matter, but it is symptomatic of the completely arse about face way the whole project has been handled from day one. The weak financial structure, now about to be shored up by Sara Giles and QuickDraw, led to a need for access to ticket revenue because it's the first money in. This in turn meant that the huge marketing power of Ticketmaster became unavailable because their terms and conditions of business held the ticket revenues back, which became the situation anyway with WorldPay, but within a far weaker sales structure. The complex charitable donation scheme was constructed to circumvent this, but had failed to do so because it had to be so diluted, after a press and public outcry, as to be meaningless. And the tickets were far too expensive, three years in to the credit crunch – the market was just not there at the asking price. £6.5 million in ticket revenues is a small part of the $400 million dollar revenue projections that were bandied about at the start of this thing – and even if you take those projections with a huge pinch of salt, the fact remained that the likely outcome as measured in early September looked like this: a $10 million sponsor, $15 million in TV sales and $20 million projected from the Facebook stream – enough to deliver a healthy profit for everyone concerned.

Much better then, with hindsight, to have done a free concert at the O2. Or at least free to anyone with a *This is It* ticket – or something, anything, to show a degree of care towards the customer. We would have lost ticket revenue for sure, but the goodwill purchased would have been huge, a goodwill that would translate to DVD sales and the potential to do it all again, take the show on tour, make a living memorial to Michael's music and give the fans something back. We'd also have saved a million quid by not having to schlep everything out to Cardiff. If only Chris and Jeffré had had that vision! But then, the O2 is owned by AEG, so those conspiracy theories would immediately have popped up. And why didn't the ticket sales matter? Because of the Facebook thing. Yes, twenty million MJ fans were up in arms about the concert, refusing to buy tickets, dissing the whole event, but I bet a fair proportion would have invested the three bucks to have a look at what they hated so much, a peek at the thing that had stirred such strong emotions amongst them, that they had poured so much anger onto. Although it makes difficult reading, the bad press may actually be helping to maintain interest. Or so we kid ourselves. This article is but one of many spotlighting our plight:

The New York Times Online
August 31, 2011, 5:37 PM

Tribute Concert Promoters Fail to Sway Jackson Fan Clubs
By JAMES C. MCKINLEY JR.

The promoters of a Michael Jackson tribute concert tried to dispel the concerns of fan clubs Monday during a series of international conference calls on Wednesday, but leaders of some large groups said afterwards they were still opposed to the event.

For weeks, fan clubs have criticized the promoters for staging the "Michael Forever" concert in Wales on Oct. 8, around the same time as the involuntary manslaughter trial in California of Dr. Conrad Murray, the physician who was caring for Mr. Jackson when he died in June 2009. Several fan clubs have criticized the promoters for not releasing details about how much money from the concert's proceeds will go to two charities that Mr. Jackson had supported during his life. Many have also said the promoters should have reached an agreement with Mr. Jackson's estate before staging the concert.

"In all honesty, they haven't answered any of my questions," said Gary Taylor, the president of the Micheal (sic) Jackson Community in Britain, which has 80,000 registered members. "Where is the money going? Who is benefiting?"

"They just don't want to listen to what we have to say," he added.

Juliette Harris, a spokeswoman for the promoter, Global Live Events, said the goal of the calls was to open a dialogue with the fan clubs and counter some false reports on fan Web sites, among them the charge that none of the ticket proceeds would go to charity and that the tickets could not be refunded. "We are not trying to persuade people or change their minds," she said. "Our goal is to say 'Here are the facts.'"

The opposition of the major fan club groups presents a problem for the promoter, Chris Hunt, a British filmmaker who formed Global Live Events this spring to put on the show. The fan clubs wield influence with many of the people most likely to buy tickets to the events. Mr. Hunt did not take questions from the heads of fan clubs

Wednesday. Instead Global Live was represented during the calls by another executive, Andy Picheta.

The concert has divided the Jackson family. Janet Jackson and Jermaine Jackson — who have had the most successful solo careers — are boycotting the event, along with their brother Randy Jackson, because it conflicts with the trial. La Toya Jackson and three other siblings — Tito, Marlon and Jackie — are planning to attend and may perform.

The executors of Michael Jackson's estate, which is not controlled by any of the siblings, have also raised questions about the charitable intentions of the promoters. They have made it plain the promoters may not use Mr. Jackson's image, name or other intellectual property to sell the concert.

Wesley Noorhoff, the president of the Legendary Michael Jackson Fan Association in the Netherlands, which has 25,000 members, said the conversation with Global Live officials had not swayed him. Holding the concert during the trial and excluding the estate from the project still bothered his members, he said.

"We are still not behind the concert," he said after the telephone call. "The biggest problems we have are the timing and not working with the Michael Jackson estate and not getting all the Jacksons on board."

Noorhoff's position was one shared by too many people. Ticket sales were dire, and serious meetings became a daily occurrence at Shaftsbury Avenue. Tix-Me, investors, lawyers and all manner of suited and not so suited people would traipse in and sit behind closed doors with Chris and Michael Henry. Paul King's PR lady was sacked, as was the social media outfit owned by one of the investors. Both had failed to stem the tide, both had failed to get a positive message out. In came Mark Borkowski and a heavyweight team of crisis managers. We sat in the small meeting room, talking old-time talk about Michael Flately, and Mark told us not to worry. There was time to turn it around. The lack of interface with the signed artists was an issue, as they were all doing the bare minimum in terms of promotion, so we had no links to FB fan pages, tweets or posts or TV chat show appearances. The contracts had been negotiated in LA, by one of the Parojim of course, and no promotional activities had been included in the deal memos. Mark told us to hire a social media team in Manchester that he worked with a lot, and by bullying, cajoling and generally making a nuisance of themselves they began to turn the Facebook page around. They did this by flooding it with statuses (statii?), relegating the negativists to the comment sections of each, where furious debates would erupt between the antis and those who liked the idea of the show. With Borkowski on the scene, Juliette was relegated to dealing with just the Jackson family. This was part of the reversal of who was tail and who was dog, inevitable as we got closer to the show and the action centre shifted to the UK.

    The ticket prices were slashed. The one thing, the one crucial thing that Paul and the stadium warned us not to do had to be done. Not only were they slashed, but then Paul put a BOGOF (buy one get one free) offer on internet discount seller Groupon. The fans that had paid top price (all one thousand of them) were outraged. The fan clubs were outraged (although I didn't see why they should now complain that tickets were too cheap, when they had spent the summer moaning that they were too expensive). Another FAQ sheet on the website, another U turn, another fuck up. Gary Taylor, of Michael Jackson's Greatest Fanclub, is on the phone and email – I ignore him as I have nothing to say that could make anything better, for anyone. The ticket price decision had been taken in consultation with Mark Borkowski.

The mainstream media, Mark told us, was waiting for the event to be cancelled. As he heard this, Chris turned pale and expressed shock and surprise.

"That's not gonna happen," he insisted.

Borkowski continued, advising that the public at large were broadly not just unaware of the ticket prices, but unaware of the concert itself, so the damage by a price reduction would be limited to the activists, most of who weren't coming, and those who had purchased, which was a painfully small number. They were offered partial refunds later anyway.

* * *

This first week in September is the low point for me as I realise the scale of incompetence that I am a part of. The muck from the fans flies in thick and fast, the press and the entertainment world, including the artists supposedly appearing on the show, are waiting for it to be cancelled. Ticket sales are non-existent, and Chris and Michael Henry have descended into a bunker mentality. Because of the negativity, and because we can't get any artist to link to our FB page, the Facebook streamers are getting very nervous and threaten to pull out unless they receive an upfront payment to cover their costs. Having built huge expectations, the Sky TV deal is coming to earth with a bump. All they want now is a two and a half hour version for Sky Arts, a minority channel buried deep in the listings, and a one hour version, which is just forty four minutes of show once room is made for the ad breaks, for Sky One. The first will air a week after the show and the second a week after that. No live-to-air TV anywhere, but cinemas in the UK will take it. I've been against the 3D presentation from day one, yet Chris still persists with it, even though nobody except Sky Arts wants it. The cumbersome nature of the medium, two cameras recording a stereo pair of images onto two tapes, makes post-production incredibly laborious. The offset between the cameras is adjusted during shooting by a stereographer, and each shot requires a different offset. If the shot is moving, the offset needs to change during the move. This can only be approximated at a live event, so the offsets need to be adjusted electronically in post-production. Cutting the show down to 150 minutes, tidying up the line cut, the switching between cameras done live on the night, slapping on some credits and getting the tape down to Sky HQ at Isleworth is achievable in five days for the 2D version, but impossible for the 3D. Sky Arts reluctantly agree to schedule the 3D at some point down the line. They remain the only customers for something that is adding half a million pounds to the cost of the TV, hours to the very tight load in and rehearsal schedule, and huge difficulties in getting the van sized cameras where they need to be to actually deliver a meaningful 3D image. They are also not offering any additional money, so the whole thing is a massive loss leader leading to nowhere. In the bunker, Chris wants to hear none of this. In the bunker, he cannot understand why artists, airlines, hotels and other suppliers won't commit to work for the promise of being paid. The endlessly re-subtitled clip from *Downfall*, forever appearing on YouTube only to be taken down by the film studio, plays over and over in my head. My own version of my own private hell is not about Paul Scoles or English grammar, (two of the most popular ones) but Chris Hunt rabidly ranting about the perfidy of artists, agents, Jeffré, suppliers, crew – pretty much everyone involved really. If you know the film for more than just the Hitler rant in the bunker scene, you'll know that while he was ranting there was some topless dancing going on in the canteen. That's where I'd want to be, but I'm far from a dancing mood.

The stress is beginning to show, and I am so miserable I wonder about contacting John Branca, offering my services, becoming a double agent and his chief saboteur deep in the heart of *Michael Forever*. The thought that I could consider such treachery makes me even more miserable. I look around the office, at the people I have hired in good faith, working hard, believing in the show, not letting the constant trip ups brought on by lack of funds and uninspiring leadership get in their way, and know I cannot desert them, nor can I walk away from a twelve year relationship with Chris. There is nothing for it but to get my head down and bulldoze through it all, get the fucker onto the stage and onto some tape, and get it finished.

* * *

One month away, and it's a good moment to take stock of where we are. Of who's in, and who's out. The artist list is strong, but lacking one more A list act. We have Christina, and Smokey, and Jamie, and Gladys. Chris has signed Pixie Lott, Leona Lewis and JLS. The Parojim have delivered Alien Butt Farm (thanks so much guys!) Ron has brought on Yolanda Adams.

Michael Henry is working hard to get some more money, so we can pay the Black Eyed Peas their two million bucks. They are seen as the key; A list certainly, and performers of such standing that they'll kick-start the ticket sales, encourage sponsors to come on, and because of the rarity of their televised performances, draw a huge TV audience too.

So we are eighty per cent there, a place we should have held back in July, on the announcement day. But life is always what it is, and so rarely what it should have been.

CHAPTER 7.
DAVID

"There ain't no second chance against the thing with forty eyes"

Hamish finally tells Chris that he is not going to direct the TV of the show. Whether he has been unable to get out of existing commitments, or has been playing a waiting game to see how things would pan out (or maybe a mix of both) is not relevant. What is a little pressing is the lack of detailed TV creative one month before the show. I've struggled to get HaSH moving in the right direction and failed, because the one thing I could not do is make creative, director type decisions about the show prior to a director coming on board. I wasn't going to present a done deal to Hamish or anyone else, because they'd change it all anyway. Sure, I could manage the no brainers like a background and the placing of most cameras, all forty possibles I could think of, but I needed to preserve as blank a canvas as possible for the director. Unfortunately HaSH had had his crayons out for months, and the canvas was far from blank. The sooner a director came on board the better, because there was still time to get it right.

I ruled myself out of directing because I was too deep into the show; being Chris' right hand man and Leonard's five guys was enough, and it would cause havoc if I removed myself from the elements I was supposedly looking after. I also had never done live-to-air, and the biggest live-to-air music show in years was not a good place to start. Besides, yet most pertinently, Chris had not actually asked me to direct. So with Chris' urging I rang one of the concert filming industry's stalwart practitioners; Distinguished Director David Mallet. Thankfully he was available. Much of my career is down to two men. Chris Hunt is one, and Distinguished Director David Mallet (DDD^M) is the other. My first experience of DDD^M was driving a minibus full of dancers and sundry crew as he filmed a music video for Joan Jet and the Blackhearts. All I remember is that we bombed around west London, that there was a scene in a supermarket and one involving dog poo, and that filming stopped so Mallet could get a haircut on Portobello Road. I was still at film school at the time, so I guess it was 1984 or thereabouts. Ancient history for some, my youth for me, but I was very impressed by the insouciance of that haircut. A year or so later, and I get a call from a friend who has been hired to work on the filming of Tina Turner's Private Dancer tour at the NEC. He has been told to find three other people to be SkyCam Motormen with him.

I have no idea what that is but I'll happily take the £25 per day being offered, so I say yes and head up to Birmingham for my first ever paid employment on a concert.

SkyCam was invented by Garrett Brown, who also invented the Steadicam. The latter is a harness with a counter-sprung, counterweighted arm that keeps a camera steady when you walk with it (or run, roller blade, ski, ice skate or fly with it). Apocryphally, Garrett thought of the idea whilst walking down stairs at a party holding a glass of wine. The former device, SkyCam, consists of a gyro-stabilised mount suspended between four cables. These cables spool onto computer controlled winches which are positioned as high as you can get them. By letting one cable out, and reeling another in the camera in the centre moves around the sky. God knows what Garrett was doing to think of that! SkyCams are very popular at American football games, and one was brilliantly used at the rowing events during the Beijing Olympics. They are not infallible, and one crashed during an American Football college final last year. There are alternative systems available too, one using three cables instead of four. Back in 1985 however, the kit was brand new, there was only one in the world, and it was being rigged on a music concert for the first time. Previous deployments had brought up issues with the temperature of the winch motors. If the cable didn't collect properly the motors would strain and overheat. Then they would jam and the camera would be stuck in the air. So for the Tina turner concert four people, SkyCam motormen, were needed to monitor the temperature of each of the motors. We were briefed by the young American technicians that had flown over with the kit. The Operating Temperature Monitoring System (OTMS) consisted of one person per winch sitting squished high in the gantry of the NEC and periodically putting their hand on the motor housing. If it became hot, we were to activate our comms (a walkie talkie), and tell the Californians below. We were not, under any circumstances, to talk on the walkies other than to report hotness. We were not to chitter chatter, we were not to radio down with spurious notions of warmness of the housing, we were not to do anything other than holler if the thing became hot.

So up I went, high into the gods, high above the highest seats about three quarters of the building away from the stage. What a view! I was going to see Tina Turner live on stage, from a position unavailable to any member of the public, and I was going to be paid to do so! This was the second epiphany in my film career. This is what I wanted to do. I wanted to work in this exciting, buzzing live environment. I didn't know as what, I didn't particularly care, but I knew I was where I wanted to be.

The concert was being filmed over two nights. I could

hear the director on the talkback, urging the SkyCam to fly faster, lower, to reposition quicker. I could hear the disappointment in his voice as this wizard bit of kit failed to deliver his vision of what it should.

"At the moment it's just a fucking expensive Louma crane," Mallet announced over the comms in his posh public school tones that, then as now, cause shameful embarrassment, yet at the same time create an urge to do better, in whichever crew member they are directed at. (The Louma crane was, at the time, the state of the art remote crane. Because it did not need an operator and assistant sitting on the end of it but utilised a remote head, it was whippier and more agile – ideal for music work. There were two on the concert.)

Stung to action by Mallet's well aimed criticism, on the second night the SkyCam boys let fly. The pod with the blinking light soared and dived around the hall. The 35mm camera mounted below it tore through roll after roll of film, coming in to land and reload every four minutes before shooting off again and delivering swooping audience shots the like of which had never been seen before.

I had been diligently touching the motor housing every minute as instructed. About twenty minutes in I noticed it to be a little warmer. Showing initiative I doubled the frequency of monitoring, and started touching it every thirty seconds. It was definitely getting hotter. I thought about alerting the techs, but I remembered their warnings not to waste their time with tales of how it was a little warm, so I refrained. But the housing got hotter still. I decided to risk their approbation and make contact.

I punched the transmit button on the walkie. "This is motorman three. The motor is getting hot," I said.

"Who the fuck is that?" barked Mallet. Shit.

"Er, my name is Andy and I'm monitoring SkyCam motor three," I said, not understanding that the question was purely rhetorical. I was thrown into further confusion when Mallet responded:

"Get up her legs! Go on! Get up there! That's it! Good!"

I didn't dare speak. The housing was hot and so was I, sweating with embarrassment and the heat from the winch, which had started to make a very peculiar noise. I knew I wasn't to climb up Tina Turner's legs; I'd spent two years in film school and I could recognise a camera direction when I heard one. I'd also painfully and searingly just learnt why silence is so golden on the communications network of a live event film. But I didn't want to die up here in the roof gantry of the National Exhibition Centre, garrotted by snaking SkyCam support wires or pierced by shrapnel from an exploding motor, so I braved everybody's wrath and spoke again.

"This is SkyCam motorman three. The housing is now very hot and the cable is making a noise on winding which it hasn't until now." That did the trick. Mallet told me to wait. Then, in a flurry of instruction and he redeployed his cranes, told two of the seventeen tracking dollies on the floor to shoot something else, and his voice was replaced by the west coast twang of the head SkyCam technician.

"How hot is it?"

"Hot."

"How long can you hold your hand on it?"

"About three seconds."

"OK."

A couple of minutes pass, and he comes back on the radio.

"We need to figure out if it's any hotter. How long can you keep your hand on it now?"

"Ouch!"

"OK."

Several minutes later, one of the Californians is crawling along the gantry towards me. By now the thing is practically glowing, and the winch is making the kind of noise you associate with bearings tearing themselves apart; a million metallic banshees dancing to their deaths, leaving nothing but shards of freshly chewed metal and mortally wounded dreams of a revolution in camera mobility. They shut the system down. I'm instructed to stay in the gantry in case the winch bursts into flame, and I'm given a small CO2 extinguisher for that very eventuality. I sit back and watch the show, wishing I had brought something with me into which I could piss.

Years passed, and my music video career progressed. Following T'Pau with Steve Barron, I found myself filming more and more live shows, until I had become a bit of an expert. Eventually my path crossed again with DDD^M when I line produced the filming of INXS at Wembley Stadium. Fortunately, DDD^M had no recollection of our last collaboration, so the danger of being blamed for the destruction of his SkyCam was avoided. The job was very last minute. I flew to Vienna and got on a coach for five hours to drive to some music festival high in the Austrian Alps, where INXS did not get on stage until one am. I watched their set, had a quick meeting with their production guys and was introduced to the Farris brothers, the brains behind the band. Then I got on the coach and went straight back to the airport and flew to Amsterdam for a further series of production meetings before seeing the show again that night, this time with David. The following afternoon we had meetings scheduled at Wembley.

Forty eight hours without either sleep or drugs took its toll. The phone rang in my dream and I couldn't answer it. Eventually I woke with no knowledge of where I was and picked up. On the other end was one of the production assistants.

I said, bleary and sleep ridden, "Hello. Why are you in Amsterdam?"

"I'm not, I'm in London. You're supposed to be at Wembley in an hour."

Frantically I charge to the airport and get the first available flight. The PA reschedules the Wembley meetings for the following day and they go well. Because I can talk the talk, both the stadium and Brent Council Health and Safety have confidence enough to let us go ahead. Instead of SkyCam we have a helicopter. I learn later that the production company offered to fire me for missing the meeting, but Mallet said no, anyone could make a mistake.

I tried not to make any more. During my time at Propaganda Films running their event TV division I worked with David on Torvill & Dean and Bon Jovi, again from Wembley. When Propaganda self-immolated itself in an ill-conceived attempt to buy its way into the UK commercials market, I went off to PolyGram as a consultant and chosen freelance producer, which led to, amongst others, *Cats*, *Lord of the Dance* and finally *Joseph*. All were directed by DDD[M], who stuck up for me as I battled Lloyd Webber's accountants, and I stuck up for him. After *Joseph*, when the accountants finally won, we parted ways. Eleven years on, and here we were again.

* * *

With Mallet on board, and the delightful Dawn to look

after him, I feel confident the televising is in hand. What appears to be less together is the show we are actually going to televise. Ron has been talking to the artists, developing their ideas, choosing the tracks they were going to do. In the background was the continuing issue with the Black Eyed Peas. They had been in the frame for many weeks, but lack of funds to pay their fee meant the deal was stalled.

I had finally seen their full contract and rider, a fifty page document handed out to venues and promoters around the world detailing everything down to the type of flowers in the hotel suites and the make, model, colour and window type of the ground transport (white lilies, Mercedes, Vaneo, black, tinted – all times two and two separate hotels). That was fine – we had those. We could even put lilies in the Vaneos if they wanted. What we didn't have was the two hours required to get the specified kit on and off the stage during a live show. The BEPs, as headliners, had also reserved half a dozen songs that other artists were also keen to do. So no rehearsals could happen, and the show couldn't get close to a running order, until these matters were resolved. It meant the long and tortuous path of music clearance for TV couldn't begin either.

We knew about *Thriller* and the other Rod Temperton tracks, but we didn't know what else was going to be tricky, because we didn't know what was on the list. I had found an expert in the field of music clearance, but Chris was loath to hire her. He also told me Iambic had a prized secondary blanket licence, a PSMPLA, although an elf later confided that "had" was the correct tense, because it had lapsed the previous year and had not been renewed. Chris was now re-applying for it, as a renewal, but it wouldn't be in place until late September.

I should have been shocked, amazed and concerned, in

equal measure, that the music rights, a cornerstone of any music project, actually more than a cornerstone, the whole building in fact, were being treated so lightly, so 'it'll be alright on the night', but this was Chris all over, and my familiarity with his style muted the alarm bells to a dull headache.

Cee Lo Green tweets that the show is cancelled. This is because he hasn't received either his fee or an airline ticket. My team have negotiated a superb deal with British Airways for the flights, but they won't start releasing tickets without names, and the entourages of all the artistes keep changing, as do the dates they want to fly on. Once the names start coming in, they won't release the tickets without payment, but there is no payment because the Sara Giles deal is still not done, and there is no money again.

The Intercontinental Hotel demands payment up front, seventy thousand pounds, or they will not provide rooms for Ron and his team or the band. Chris gives them his Amex card, to guarantee the rooms until the money turns up. I'm working late one night and ask to stay, so they discount me a room. I give my Amex card to guarantee the room extras, and I am shown to one of their beautiful one bedroom superior master penthouse fuck off suites. Wow. There's a bathroom in the dining room, which on closer inspection turns out to be a fruit bowl large enough for an entire blonde. Sadly I don't have the energy, not even for the fruit, because I'm knackered and the strain of all this is beginning to get to me.

Everyone is demanding money up front. The Cardiff hotels want their contracts signed and funds paid or they'll release the rooms back on sale. Chris doesn't get it and I'm too tired to explain that if you book a room you make a contract so the hotel doesn't sell that room to someone else. We've taken every big hotel in Cardiff, at negotiated rates. I stayed at the St David's in April, on one of the first recces, and found it reasonable, so that's where the artists and top brass are going.

Ron and his entourage have arrived and taken over the small meeting room as their office. Ron's assistant Halston demands an upgrade to a suite at the Intercontinental, because she had to make evening phone calls. I tell her to use the office like everyone else.

Ron has also brought over two travel coordinators, despite my and Chris' protestations that we had people like this in the UK who were cheaper and didn't require airfares, hotels and per diems (a daily cash allowance for food and drink) to do the job. But they were part of Ron's comfort blanket so they came. It meant that the airline ticketing part of artist liaison was out of Purple's hands and deep into Ron World.

I gave these co-ordinators the details of the British Airways deal, the phone number of the department, and left them to get on with it. Picking a huge fight with Ron over this would be pointless, and indeed counter-productive, as would trying to micro manage their work. Purple was in charge of the artists when they got to the UK, the Parojim looked after them in LA, and in between they were in Ron World. Very soon Ron World stopped talking to Purple which meant her hotel and ground transport systems were thrown into confusion, cars going to the wrong hotels to collect artists who were still in LA because they had no airline ticket. The BA deal collapsed because the airline was not given any indication of names until the day of travel – or sometimes later! Nor did they receive funds in time to release tickets, so the coordinators began using their own travel agent contacts in America, buying full price tickets which were up to five times the price of what BA were offering.

There was no control over what the artists were demanding either. Neither Ron nor anyone else had seen the deal memos which had been executed by the legal arm of the Parojim, so nobody knew whether Cee Lo Green's demand for eight first class tickets was a part of his deal or a reach. Eventually I got all the contracts emailed to me and gave them to Ron. Most weren't too bad, with a first class ticket for the artist plus one, and a small number of economy requirements for everyone else. Jamie Foxx didn't want a ticket, he was going to come on his own jet. The Peas wanted a jet. I wondered if Jamie would give them a lift. The one area where the travel demands were disproportionate was in the Jackson camp. Jeffré, La Toya, Katherine and the children and the three brothers between them seemed to need over fifty first class tickets! This was a black hole of potentially epic proportions. Each full price, fully refundable, open return ticket was about $18,000 – so a million bucks to get the Jacksons to London. I firmly requested a spreadsheet showing what tickets were being purchased at what price, but my request was ignored. My request became a demand for this information about two days later, also to no avail. International travel was out of control, with Ron's two coordinators barely hanging on to a bucking bronco, spewing dollars from every orifice, and there was no way to it.

* * *

I have come to understand, on this project and through subsequent research, that Michael was Good. My knowledge helps me to see the molestation trial, the trials by media, the "Wacko" label, all his struggles and difficulties, as the effects of the work of small men, jealous men, men who never saw what many have seen and understood to be the good of Michael. Men like Thomas Sneddon and Martin Bashir, men with hang ups, men afraid of their own limitations, men who believed Michael was abusing his celebrity and wealth because that's what they'd do if they had the same. These were men who saw compassion as weakness, goodness as cynical self-interest, and genius as duplicity. Michael was Good, with a capital, upper case, strong and tall 'G'. His other-wordliness was a part of his talent, and of that there is no doubt.

There is always a balancing force. For everything good, there is something bad. We were working with the memory of Michael. A good memory of a good man. We may have been completely fucking it up, but our motives, or at least mine and I still hoped Chris' also, were pure. We wanted to put on a great show, a show that would do justice to the memory. We finally had some great and not so great acts, and Jeffré, through the Parojim, had put together the house band.

We had guitarist Tommy O, we had Kevin Dorsey as musical director, hired over the head of Ron Weisner, who wanted somebody else. We had a bunch of other musicians with varying strengths of ties to the Michael Legacy. Jeffré had insisted, from the start, that the band should be as 'of Michael' as possible, and pinned the show's music around the talents of Kevin Dorsey. Kevin in turn had his tour manager and sound engineer Doreen Semblance.

Maybe it was the apparent weakness of the Parojim, the lack of visibly stern leadership by Jeffré or the conflict of Ron Weisner wanting someone else for musical director, but this unhappy group of musos quickly inflated their self-importance to that of the show itself. They were paying tribute to MJ despite everyone around them.   Doreen Splendid especially, very quickly showed himself to be the bad to Michael's good, and the most vocalising of this mind-set.

His first contribution, at our first meeting, was to tell us how the band would not travel to Cardiff on the day specified. No discussion, no debate, but an unworkable ultimatum with the expectation everyone would jump around and change everything to suit him. Just so you understand, his approach wasn't:

"I have a scheduling problem and can we work it out?" It was:

"This show ain't gonna happen unless you guys talk to me and fix this"

What a wanker! An evil, twisted orc trapped in a body that once belonged to Jabba the Hutt, nothing passed his blubbery lips that wasn't vile, nasty, or spittle. Doreen had alopecia of the hair and of the soul. He was not a happy camper, and it started with Kevin's travel arrangements. It started there for me. For Doreen it most likely started when he burst from the chest of an unsuspecting astronaut or splatted, squidgy, sweaty turd like, from a shit spewing machine of meanness set to maximum malevolence.

The Parojim had been delighting in the departure of the band for London for many days. Apparently they were a real handful – demanding, bolshie, stroppy and generally hard work for everyone involved. Constantly threatening to walk if this or that demand wasn't met, always moaning about something; the room, the coffee, the ice was too hot, or too cold, or both, the food was late, or early, and so on. The Parojim had had enough, and couldn't wait to be shot of them.

I had decreed, because I thought it was right, that billed talent flew first class, management and supporting talent flew business, and hangers on and junior staff flew premium economy. I thought this fair and protective, in as much as anything was, of GLE's money. Kevin, being billed talent, the musical director and thereby key creative, was booked in first. The band manager was booked in business, together with Doreen Spangle. This arrangement failed to impress Kevin, who badgered Purple to despair, and when that didn't work, he started badgering me. He was polite at first, and his voice, his honeyed voice of molasses slowly dripping into a deep bowl of black cherries, was so bass, so melodious, that it made Leonard Rowe sound like a shrill washerwoman. It rumbled and rolled and vibrated at me down the phone, pitch perfect somewhere way beyond a low B flat, and on its way caused wales to kill themselves from despairing sadness in the darkest depths of oceans.

"Thing is, Andy, I've got a ton of work to do before the show, and there's just sooo little time. I need to work on the plane, and I need Brandy (or whatever her name was) to do that work."

Many would see that as a load of bullshit, others would fall asleep before he reached the end of the sentence, so sloooowwww was the delivery, but I gave him the benefit of the doubt. So I told Purple to get travel to stick her in first on the way here, so they could work, and business on the way back, as befitted her grade on the production. If they needed to work on the way back, it wasn't going to be on my show, so someone else could pay to have them sit together. Kevin hit the roof, but had no argument to offer. He didn't really shout – when your voice is that low and necessarily slow, there's nowhere to go in the pitch and speed of delivery, and you're just gonna sound less cool than when you speak normally. Supposedly, but only on his own website, Kevin is the voice of *Oh Yeah*; the growly double baritone catchphrase heard on *Ferris Bueller's Day Off*. Elsewhere on the internet this sound is credited to Dieter Meier, the vocalist of Swiss band Yello who composed and recorded the song. Whichever is correct, it's not much of a claim to fame, and even less so if it's fictional. A few days later I find out that Brandy is Kevin's girlfriend. His "I have to work" plea was no more than a successful attempt to get his squeeze into first class. Neither of them belong there. Had I known I was being played I would have shipped her over in a box, by DHL.

Nevertheless, I saved the company a little cash, a drop in the ocean of cash that was being squandered every hour. I also pissed of Kevin, Doreen, Brandy and the band so much by doing it I became their public enemy number one. Ho hum once more.

> *From: Jeffré Phillips*
> *Sent: Sunday, September 18, 2011 11:30 AM*
> *To: Chris Hunt; Andy Picheta*
> *Subject: WHAT A DAY?*
> *I'm sure you guys are dying to hear about my day and THE NEW DRAMA! I thought the drama flew to London today with his assistance who didn't get their pay yesterday to add in to his DRAMA.*
>
> *Well today I got a call from Kevin Dorsey, I didn't answer it and then Paul Ring calls me 10 minutes after Kevin did and says Kevin called me and wants us down to rehearsal right now! I called Kevin and he said we can't handle anymore disrespect from the UK and all of us are walking, I need to speak with you and Paul IMMEDIATELY!*
>
> *I'm so sick of people saying they're walking! I'm almost at the point to say WALK PLEASE!!!!*
>
> *Anyway, I get in my car and rush 30 minutes to rehearsal hall, when I*

get there Paul is already there and all the band members are outside of the rehearsal hall, Kevin says we're done! We have never been so disrespected on any production in our lives and we work with everyone. So me playing dumb asked him, "What's wrong, did you all get paid yesterday?" He said yes, we're getting paid every week but the disrespect from the UK is just RIDICULOUS! I asked what happened, Andy sent Dara an email today, which I'm waiting to see, which was so rude to them that it just pissed everyone off, and then SIR Studios threaten Kevin for the final time that if Monday morning came around and the remaining $49,000 isn't paid for the rehearsal hall then you're being locked out. Kevin was mad because his name and reputation is on the line, Jamie Foxx is in rehearsal on Mon, Tues & Wed along with Jennifer Hudson on Thursday and the Jackson's and 3T throughout the week. Kevin told them it would definitely be paid by Friday and he works out of this rehearsal hall all the time and he feels like a idiot every time he walks in and see them.

Then they were angry about plane tickets not being paid and they have families who need to know what's going on, when they are leaving, what time on that day are they leaving, how are they getting to the airport, what airlines will they be on, how to plan properly and appropriately and etc. Now they know it's too late for all of them to get on the same flight and everyone in the band needs to arrive on the same day so they can start rehearsal and not have to wait days for other band members to come in.

Because of everything that has gone on with the band from contracts getting to them extremely late, to not getting any plane tickets, hotel confirmation and any other arrangements as of yet, they want all of their per diem (16 ppl a day @ $100 per person a day equals $30,200) before leaving. They want all of their pay before leaving, which I told them can't happen, so they want next weeks' pay and the follow weeks' pay on Thursday and a half weeks pay before the show and then final payment held here in a verified account so they know they will get it once returning to the states. They also want all their needed petty cash they're going to need while they are there which is another $18,000 before they leave.

So on Monday this is what needs to be paid:

1. S.I.R final Payment $49,000 or they are LOCKED OUT
2. They want their plane tickets paid (roughly $100K now), Hotel & ground transportation with schedules and confirmation numbers in hand

By Thursday this is what needs to be paid:

1. $30,200 in band per diem for there stay in Europe
2. $18,000 for the bands petty cash
3. All of their payroll except half of the last week which they will get once they get off stage but that money needs to be in a verified account here in the US, it's roughly around $275K

Kevin said the he and his assistant will flight First Class as he always has and all band members will flight business class as they always do. They explain that we are professional musician and we work with only the biggest stars in the world from A to Z and this is how we're always treated and we're not going to get treated any less.

Please make sure when they get there they're treated like the celebrities will be treated, they are celebrity musician and they demand to be treated that way... I spent literally hours convincing them to stay on, if they walk over no we have NO SHOW! Let's keep them happy! WEDNESDAY CAN'T GET HERE FAST ENOUGH!!!! I HOPE NOTHING GOES WRONG!!!!!!! This is do or die!

Hope you have a PLEASANT DAY!
Jeffré Phillips

And from a band functionary:

Hello
Yes, Kevin did speak with Andy yesterday regarding Brandy's flight and per Kevin Andy agreed to flying Brandy in the class of service that he requested (first class) RT. Below is Kevin's response to the statement made below about Brandy's return ticket.
"I take this as an insult to my intelligence for someone to authorize a first class ticket and then place my assistant in an economy seat on the return. I refuse for that to occur. I consider this to be a slap in my face after an agreement had been made. This is an outrage as our

needs as the house band and staff have not been considered as we have been met with a lot of resistance and rude comments with regards to our requests. This is unacceptable especially when our team has done everything in our power to save whenever possible as it relates to the hotels, flights and visas. The lack of communication and disrespect is horrible given how hard we have and continue to work to be treated as second class citizens. It has been my understanding that we all are supposed to function as a team as we prosper as a team but as individuals we fail. Some may blame it on the distance and the time difference but NOTHING is worse than someone giving their word and in less than 24 hours stabbing me the back. A man is only as good as his word." NEED I SAY MORE?
Please let me know how Ceire and Andy would like to proceed to quickly find resolution to this problem.
Thanks
Dara

And the one from me that caused all the fuss, sent after several frustrating phone calls and to stop Purple hiding under her desk every time a band person rang the office. This is not to impugn Purple's dedication and ability; she is feisty and confident, but even a character as strong as hers gets worn down by the eighty-sixth whining call.

The policy of GLE is clear and I reiterate it here once more. Assistants travel in economy, talent and management in business. Exceptions are on a case by case basis and agreement in one instance does not set precedence for any other. Kevin made a specific request that he had to work on the flight and required his assistant to do that. His reasoning was accepted that with so little time left to the show he has stuff he must get done whilst in the air. His assistant was duly upgraded. With the show over, I cannot see any reason to upgrade Kevin's assistant for the return as there is no work remaining to be done of such urgency it needs to cost the production $6000. As the producer I have a fiscal responsibility to GLE and I will not allow unnecessary expenditure on this production. This is part of my job and I will not be deflected from it nor told how it should be done.

That I find disrespectful and offensive. We agreed first for Kevin and his hotel suite without question, as well as for anyone who has it in their deal.

Anyway, the whingers arrived, spitting nails from day one. We had booked a brand new facility specifically designed to rehearse big rock and roll shows. It had everything and it sparkled. Showers, bedrooms, offices and games rooms, a huge rehearsal room that held even our monstrous set, smaller rooms for separate dance rehearsals, the works. It wasn't big enough. Not for their part of the stage, but for their egos. Had we hired every aircraft hangar in Europe, Kevin Dorsey and the band's monumental sense of self-importance would still be parked on the runways. Musically they were pretty good, but as people they were, to a man, very much out of tune. Eat Your Hearts Out were catering the rehearsals, and the food was as usual amazing. By amazing I mean three or four choices of good restaurant quality dishes for lunch, a buffet spread fit for a Byzantine court with massive bowls of fruit, cereal bars, nuts, yogurts, cakes, salads, oceans of dips, groaning cheeseboards, cold meat platters and, if you wanted it, a partridge in a pear tree. The band however, didn't like the meal times, despite continually changing their schedule and so making it hard to keep up. Kevin super-bass rumbled that there was a problem, and they needed a meal just as they finished rehearsal. I investigated and found they were taking food back to the hotel, by the suitcase load, and complaining that it was cold by the time it got there. Not only was this against the spirit of the arrangement with them, it had not insubstantial cost implications. They had each received one hundred and fifty dollars per day from Jeffré for the seven days in the UK, for incidental expenses and per diems for food before they left LA, money for their evening burgers, shakes, fried chicken and all the other shit that Americans eat. Dorsal also had fifteen thousand dollars as a general expense float. Their hotel and breakfast was paid, they were staying in suites at the Intercontinental, and they were nickel and diming production for extra food. Astonishing.

Often they would roll up for rehearsal hours late, because they had been out drinking the night before. Our thirty person gospel choir, Alexandra Burke and Pixie Lott were kept waiting all morning while these bozos nursed their sore heads and tried to blame the transport department for their non-arrival to rehearsals. If Ron Weisner had any hair he would have torn it all out. "Man, I warned you about this band," he would repeat, but we could do little, as Jeffré had hired them, through the Parojim of course, and they were six thousand miles away and relieved not to have to deal with them anymore.

Kevin and Jabba the Hutt went out of their way to create problems where there were none. They couldn't do the schedule, which called for them to finish rehearsing on Wednesday evening, travel to Cardiff and be ready to rehearse Thursday lunchtime. A standard touring schedule. "There's no time for the boys to sleep," they chorused. No time to hit the town for one last session more like, but I had to get these evil tossers on that stage, so I suggested a tour bus for their poor little heads. They grumbled that might work. They decided they didn't have enough drinking buddies around them, so they drafted in a third or fourth, I lost count, guitar technician from Austria, and demanded nine hundred pounds in cash for his per diem, brought to them at the rehearsal space immediately, almost immediately, well, tomorrow because they had finished early for the day. I refused and told them to take it from their fifteen thousand dollar float if there was any left. Spawn of Evil Semblance did not like this one bit, and began to threaten me with all manner of violent retribution, which I would have taken seriously if I thought he could move, professionally or in combat, faster than at slug speed. Nevertheless I stayed away from the rehearsal space after that, in case he got me by projectile vomiting deadly acid or something.

* * *

Finally the deal with QuickDraw is completed. Michael Henry had been persuading Sara Giles that *Michael Forever* was a sure bet. On QuickDraw's side, Sara needed reassurance that her investment was secured against something tangible. The money wanted proof where the makers could offer only promise. Squaring this circle is done by a process known as due diligence, where the investors check the veracity of what is being presented to them. It took weeks, but was still comparatively very quick. For QuickDraw the investment appeared a safe one, as there was a large amount of income on the way; a sponsorship deal, the Facebook live stream, and hopefully even some ticket sales. Sara had declined a major participation earlier in the gestation of the project, because her specialism is gap financing, providing the last bit of money. It's usually a more secure, less risky investment than being in first.

I imagine a robust, battle-axe of a woman, picking one pearl off a string around her neck and tossing it to Chris and Michael, who gratefully run off to the sweetshop.

The conclusion of the deal means the BEPs get their two million bucks and we can all finally stop stalling their managers, lawyers, agents and florists. GLE get some cash in the bank too, to pay hotels, airlines, ground transport companies, staging, lighting, rigging and outside broadcasters, venue caterers and a myriad other suppliers, big and small, who all want at least some if not all of their money up front.

"What happened to settlement of account in thirty days?" wailed Chris.

GLE's track record so far, of not paying anyone on the agreed date, and no track record at all prior to May of this year – that's what.

Paul King has found a merchandising outfit that can design, print and distribute all the merchandising. They can also do the commemorative souvenir brochure. They'll do it all at their own risk and split the revenues 60:40 in our favour. With just over two weeks to go, it's a great offer, but Chris thinks the percentage is too high. I don't want to negotiate with them, I want to kiss their feet in thanks and send them on their way, which is what I do. Within days we have a mock-up of the brochure, and it's good, or at least better than it could have been. We also have the hats, spangly gloves, t-shirts and coffee mugs, all the stuff the Parojim were supposed to be doing and failing on, ready to go and on the website. The Facebook streaming guys will run parallel ads and links to the site, as well as time-limited special offers, which will maximise the merchandising and create a total viewing and purchasing opportunity for fans. It's a brilliant and grown up way to present live-to-air in the twenty first century and we are the tip of the trailblazing spear.

Borkowski and his Manchester cyber-team have the Facebook page under control at last, but both the cyber troopers and the mainstream media need stories to run, to keep us in the news. Beyoncé has filmed a performance of *I Wanna Be Where*

You Are in New York, tacking it onto the end of her show. She has put a lot of effort into it, with a retro seventies wardrobe, a Frank Gatson choreographed routine, and wearing a huge seventies era Michael Jackson afro wig. One of the Parojim was responsible for the filming, and they've done a very good job. It looks great and lifts everyone's spirits. This performance is news and will get us a two page spread in the Daily Mirror, but only if they get a picture of Ms Knowles in the wig. Juliette runs around LA trying to get clearance, but nobody in Beyoncé's organisation is going to take responsibility and give us permission, the Parojim have lost the photographer who was at the shoot, and Beyoncé herself is on holiday and unavailable. I ask the Parojim to download some still frames from the video, but they send unusable stuff of B with her mouth open or with ugly lighting shadow across her face – none of which looks bad in a moving sequence but sucks as a still of one of the world's most beautiful women. So I ask again, and again, until in the end I lose patience and get them to send a high resolution copy of the entire piece. This takes a day to upload and the same time to download this end, and in the meantime Borkowski's hand maidens are getting desperate as the Mirror deadline looms. If they don't get the picture, they'll run a negative story, they chorus, so I spend an evening in a London edit suite pulling down some stills from the High Definition copy of the piece. I get half a dozen really nice pictures, but it is a painstakingly slow process, inching through the video frame by frame, then regrading and painting out blemishes and irregularities (not on Beyoncé, she has none, ever, but in the background). I email the stills off to a hand maiden at six am, with a dire warning that they are not cleared and there will be hell to pay if she was to use them regardless. What I meant of course, was 'use them!', read between the lines, publish anyway. But I'd covered my arse too well for her to notice the instruction.

* * *

I finish writing the biogs of the creative principals for the brochure. By now Kevin Dorsey and his band of butt-fucks has pissed me off so much this is what I write:

> As a vocalist, musician, producer, writer, vocal arranger and voice-over talent, Kevin has worked with top artists and some of the most record breaking projects in the entertainment industry. The worlds of music, film, TV and theatre have all been blessed with Kevin's huge talent. His credits include The Colour Purple, Forest Gump, Spiderman, The Fantastic Four, The Lion King, Men In Black, Austin Powers, Law and Order, The Cosby Show, Family Guy, American Idol, Michael Jackson, Aretha Franklin, Garth Brooks, Celine Dion, Stevie Wonder, Bette Midler, Sting, Luther Vandross, Sammy Davis Jr., Frank Sinatra, Barbra Streisand, Gene Kelly, Ella Fitzgerald, Ray Charles, to name just a few.

Substitute the word "ego" for "talent", "worked with" for "sung some backing stuff for" and you will see the irony to which Kev the Dorsal was blind.

I organise a huge pre-production meeting. It's a good way of everyone to meet in one room, a happening that can be surprisingly rare on an event this size and in a venue a big as Cardiff Millennium. It's supposed to be a talk through of the film as it's going to happen. All heads of department attend, everyone puts in their tuppence-worth, and all go away with a clear idea of what they need to achieve and how their methodology will impact on others. That's the theory. I get everyone to introduce themselves and invite Ron to talk us through the show. Ron says what he has been saying for weeks:

So and so does their number, which could be this or that, then this artist comes on, followed by this artist and so on. What he describes is not a show, it's a wish list of maybes, and it's nowhere near enough for anyone to work with. Music, microphones, lighting styles and vitally show duration are all missing details. I had called this meeting to flush out the lack of preparation in Ron's team, but I had scared out a big empty pot of nothing instead. This was not going to be fixed easily, and I could see worried looks from sound, show production and TV, supercilious lip licking delight in the misfortune of others from Dorsey and Co, and blank stares from Ron's show team. To be fair to Ron, he was trying to build a show around huge uncertainties, themselves a consequence of the delay with the Black Eyed Peas, and trying to keep artist feathers unruffled, despite the lack of anything concrete to tell them.

What I wanted to know however, was who was doing what, who was singing what, how long were they doing it for, how were they getting on and off and what did the stage look like. Ron had from the start intended to present a show full of the kind of visual gags MJ himself used in his live tours and TV work. Ne-Yo's *Billie Jean* was to be an exact replica of Steve Barron's music video, lamp-post, suitcase, light-up paving stones and all. Jamie Foxx's *Rock With You* was going to use a ring of laser light, and so on. Production Petes told us the laser ring needed a circular target to be brought onto the stage, accurately positioned to catch the laser beam, and taken off after the number. He thought it would take no more than a minute. I pointedly suggested his stage crew would be fucking about with the thing for at least five minutes ("Ten!" chipped in Mallet) and in the meantime what did we present to the worldwide live TV audience? The Petes promised to think again, and although mollified, I was also aware I was chipping away at Ron's vision for the show.

There had been a string of famous and not so famous performers climbing the three floors to our Soho office. JLS, Leona Lewis, Pixie Lott and most of the other UK acts had come into Ron World to discuss and plan their contribution. Songs and sets, position and props, frock and frills; all laid out on Ron's master plan, enshrined on two peg boards with different coloured Post-It notes denoting the progress from thought to locked down performance. The last was indicated by fuchsia pink, and there were precious few of those.

Choice of song and place in running order was Ron's province, although his gruff New York charm ensured no-one felt coerced into anything. The big set piece ideas were his too; recreating the video for *Billie Jean,* putting Leona on a crane arm for *Scream,* pairing JLS with the Jacksons for *Don't Stop...* He also trusted the artists to figure out their own performances, guiding yes, but never imposing.

The staff enjoyed these visits, and the office juniors fussed around the artists so they could tell their mates down the pub that they had given Leona Lewis a diet Coke, and that like the Coke she was nice and bubbly.

One artist who would never be seen in the office, nor on the stage in Cardiff, was Janet Jackson. Her support for the project had always been seen as crucial, and Jeffré still believed she would come on board. Janet was still appearing in emails as a 'maybe', and this was causing Ron some concern. He had spoken to her on a number of occasions, and late one night in his very swanky Intercontinental hotel room he played me a message from her she had left on his voicemail. Janet was polite, friendly yet adamant that she was not going to take part in *Michael Forever*. She thanked Ron for reaching out to her, for offering the opportunity, but said:

"I just can't do it Ron, not at this time. It's not right for me. I wish you the best with it, but it's not for me."

I however, had more mundane things to worry about than whether Janet was in (according to Jeffré and Chris) or out (as per Ron's voicemail), or whether Pixie Lott wore yellow or blue; I needed to address the issue of who was lighting the show, and with a director on board I finally got the answer.

Of the very few names suggested as suitable, we were incredibly lucky to find Bobby Dickinson available. He has lit every major show you can think of, has enough Emmy awards to use as pieces in a chess game with himself, and is absolutely ideal for the job, with an equal understanding of the needs of a live show and those of TV. His price for him and his team is not unreasonable either, and he is quickly hired. This immediately upsets HaSH and his peck of Petes, all of whom thought they were lighting the show. I reminded them of my conversations in April, but they went off in a huff with their noses put out, and it needed soothing words from Chris to get them back on board. The Petes you see, although totally lacking experience in lighting for TV, were very capable and efficient event production managers. We needed them to put the bloody thing up and take it down afterwards. What they needed to put up, we could now finally decide on, and it certainly wasn't what they had drawn or what they were now building, nor was it what Cardiff stadium had signed off on. The topsy turvy world of *Michael Forever*, where key creatives become involved late in the day while construction managers are in place from the start, is finally being turned the right way up, but it's taking needless truckloads of cash to do so.

There were two areas of huge concern: the stage and the lighting rig. HaSH and Co had designed and built the fedora hat out of truss. The huge circular screen hung in the middle of the hat, and did not look much like the hat band it was supposed to be. A second, flat screen was suspended inside the big circular one, positioned to drop down in front of the band. All this steel weighed so much there was very little loading capacity remaining for the lighting. For TV, the back lights were insufficient, and the front spot baskets at the wrong angle and too far away. Bobby Dickinson immediately requested more lighting, more washes, more poke, more oomph, but the rig could not support the extra weight without some major redesigning. The solution to Ron's laser was to put the target up in the rig and fly it in for the number – perfect, a twenty second drop into the correct position that could easily be covered by Jamie chatting to the audience. Unfortunately the additional weight of motors and target had pushed the weight to the max. Something had to come off for Bobby to get his lights in, and the whole thing had to be re-specified and resubmitted to Millennium stadium, Cardiff Council, the Fire Brigade and for all I know the Prince of Wales too.

From the bunker, Chris screams that he wants his fucking glove and he wants his fucking hat, and who the fuck is Bobby Dickinson to start fucking about with the fucking set design. Bloody hell mate: Do you want a bit of world class telly or not? Do you want to finally make an A list, award winning, stunning piece of work, or is all this heat unnerving you to the point you're hankering for the days of documentaries about Maria Callas?

I ignore Chris and tell HaSH to do whatever Bobby wants. HaSH tells me the show lighting design is perfectly adequate.

"For a supermarket opening maybe, but not for world class TV presentation," was my retort, shorthand for some serious questions about exactly how many 3D TV concerts HaSH's people had lit, how they understood the challenges of lighting for that and 2D, getting the key light balance correct, at the right angle, and intensity, and so on and so on. Stick to the first aid kit HaSH, and stay the fuck out of my way. I moved on to the issues with the stage.

Step one was easy, to get the band out of a two foot deep pit (why were they in it in the first place?) in the centre of the "palm" and onto a two foot high riser in the same position. This would stop them looking ridiculous on stage; like little munchkins in their very own playpen and cut off at the knees. Off stage, because of their antics, they remained looking ridiculous to the end.

Step two was harder, to deliver a stage front that the singers could sing from, the audience could get close to, and DDD^M could film from. Our original sculpted, organic spangly glove surface had morphed into a plywood glove-shaped cut-out with massive, one foot square light boxes inset into it in a vaguely random pattern. Blocky fingers sitting on a quickform scaffold platform, no centre line, no stage front, and the artists about half a mile from the audience. I re-drew the thing, giving as much of a clean edge to the front as possible. The end result looked like a hand where all the fingers had been broken and laid out at impossible angles, a road kill hand with the light boxes as tyre tracks. It was horrible, it still lacked a clear centre, but at least there was a front edge, and enough room for the thirty person choir to fit on it. I also insisted on three big screens running along the back of the stage.

A couple of weeks back, in consultation with Paul "Kingy" King, I had instructed the north stand restricted seats be taken off sale, saving hundreds of thousands in production costs and simplifying the load in so the Petes actually had a chance to get the show up in time for the Saturday night. This meant there was no longer an audience there as background, and instead three screens, called Andy 1, 2 and 3 were put in. The issue of no audience in the foreground, now a possible reality brought on by the poor ticket sales, was not one any number or size of screen could solve.

I convene a second big meeting, at which I run through the schedule. I get Kevin the Dorsal to agree in public that, with the tour bus in place and a revised rehearsal schedule I have negotiated with Ron, he and the band can actually bring themselves to be ready for a Thursday afternoon rehearsal on stage in Cardiff. That was the earliest HaSH could give us stage access. Prior to that the place would be a building site. Then Ron drops his bombshell, that there will be a full dress rehearsal on the Saturday morning, the day of the show. Mallet and I look at each other in horror. This was not in the plan. Thursday tech rehearsal, Friday staggered rehearsal and a Saturday morning tidy up of stuff which needed doing again was the plan. People were going to finish at midnight or later on the Friday. Starting a dress run through on Saturday morning at eight am, creating a sixteen hour plus day that would not be over until that midnight, was madness. Everyone would be tired, everyone would make mistakes, everything would overrun, meals would be missed, and instead of hitting showtime fresh and ready, the performers and crew alike would be well below their best. Ron takes me aside and tells me the full dress on Saturday was Mallet's idea. Mallet tells me he's not too bothered and whatever Ron wants is fine. I don't think a full dress on the Saturday is fine at all, especially as the important missing information, how long the show is going to be, is unfortunately in the hands of Dorsal Kevin and the Wank Fucks.

"Weeelll, it's kinda hard to tell, 'cause, you know, the boys start to play and they have a good time sooo, I don't reeeeaaallly know…" If they play as slowly as Kevin speaks we'll be there for a week.

* * *

The Black Eyed Peas are on board. Two million dollars, less the UK withholding tax every foreigner has deducted at source, are paid directly by Sara Giles' QuickDraw fund into a bank account Michael Henry is happy with. Immediately the workload increases as every department is bombarded with demands for what Will-He-Wants. The Peas camp also want details on ticket sales, TV deals done and being done, show schedules, names, addresses and telephone numbers of all the other performers and Ron's inside leg measurement too. They also want half a million dollars for flights, hotels, per diems and God knows what else. Suddenly everyone's workload has doubled. But we are here to serve.

With the BEPs confirmed, Ron has finally come up with a running order. Chris had from the start insisted on an interval, an unusual thing in a pop concert but there we were – those tens of thousands of fans needed an opportunity to buy T-shirts and mugs and beer and hot dogs, although no GLE slice of the stadium food and beverage revenue had been negotiated, so the benefit was the venue's not ours. It meant a long show would be even longer. Using the running time of the recorded versions of the songs, we looked, at one point, to be over five hours in length. This was a problem for the venue, for the cinemas taking the live feed, for the TV recording, for everyone really. It also created the possibility that the last hour or so would be played to an empty hall, because many in the audience would not stay past midnight. We had to get Ron to shorten the show he had spent weeks painstakingly negotiating with the artists. To add to his woes, HaSH had unilaterally decided not to put the screens on the flown speaker stacks, depriving Ron's screen director of two vital surfaces, and told him he couldn't have his toaster platforms (a fast moving elevator platform that "pops" artists onto the stage. The term "toaster" comes from the speed of the pop up, not because the device burns the artist to a crisp). In addition, the boom arm Ron wanted to use to fly Leona Lewis over the audience had been sourced from a plant hire depot in Cardiff. It was slow, jerky and usually deployed to clean windows. What Ron had in mind was a bespoke designed, beautifully engineered arm built into the set. Our one was going to have its bright blue body camouflaged by black drapes, and wasn't actually going to reach the audience.

  These were small issues when placed alongside the Saturday morning destruction derby I knew the rehearsal would become. Just killing this rehearsal would not help anyone. I had to beef up Ron's painfully inexperienced stage team with some hard core, so Ron would be backed up by some heavyweight guys and could relax away from insisting on the rehearsal. During the show DDD^M would be confined to the truck, a mobile TV gallery from where he directs the cameras. He needs a set of eyes and ears on the stage to make sure the right stuff goes in front of the right cameras at the right time. Artist control is in the capable hands of Carol Brock, who does this on every show you can think of and has a runner with a radio, bodily attached to each artist, and a mental plot board in her head positioning each in make-up, or wardrobe, or giving a media interview, or eating in the artist restaurant and chill room, or crapping on the artist bog. She knows when to call them up to stage to microphone central and then to the access hatch so they can emerge, smiling, buzzing, wardrobed, miked, made up, fed, watered and de-shat, to give the performance of which they are worthy. Getting them on, kicking them up the stairs and into the light, is the job of the floor manager, with stage managers to send on and take off the kit that goes with them. All this needs split second timing, because two minutes of nothing in a live show is not a big deal to the audience in the hall, but the same two minutes on TV is a channel-changing, audience-losing age. So Mallet's floor manager is a key role. Again we are lucky, as Garrry (who spells his name with more 'r's than is strictly necessary), one of the best, is available. I need to insert him into the stage team without upsetting Ron. I run through Ron's team with Garrry on the phone. There is a silence as he hears the names, but fortunately he still takes the job, just requests his two guys come with him.

Ron gives the impression of a miserable old goat, but I spy a grumpy bear underneath that just needs a cuddle now and again. We sit down at a meeting – Ron, Chris and I, to try and resolve some of these Ron-issues, make them non-issues if you like. We agree to aim for a four hour show plus the twenty minute break. A couple of numbers get cut, but the projected running time is still over target once you add applause and resets. Ron has put the interval to good use, by getting Christina to open part two, and put the Peas at the head of the show so their truckloads of kit can be built and tested beforehand, and then thrown off in seconds after their fifteen minute set. He's positioned the follow on artist on the thumb thrust, giving the stage crew time for the de-rig of the centre. So far so good. Next I vigorously blame HaSH for nixing the speaker screens without asking. Chris says he knew nothing about it and feigns anger, but I check and find it was a decision made weeks ago to save money and that Chris was aware of it. It must be hot in that bunker. Next I get a promise from Ron that he'll lose the boom arm if it's crap. I warn that the thing will chew rehearsal time, but Ron is adamant and won't give way. I move on to the main course, the full rehearsal on Saturday morning. After an age of arguing, I get an agreement it will be a part rehearsal for artists who want to do some more prep, and a tidy up of entrances and exits, but during the debate

I begin to grasp that Ron needs the rehearsal for his inexperienced team. He looks tired and battered. He has been dealing with the fallout from the antics of the Parojim, the uncertainties about the songs available to the artists, about the lack of clarity in everything, the mess with airline tickets and the dust from the fan hate as it wafts under the noses of the talent. He tells me he is on the phone daily, hourly, trying to keep his end of the show on the road. I wonder why he doesn't quit, walk away from this mess, and then it hits me. For reasons different to mine, Ron needs this show as much as I do. Ron is doing it for closure with Michael. He is paying his own tribute to an artist he was close to, and nothing is going to stop him. This understanding validates the event for me more than anything else, especially when Ron tells me he has phoned John Branca, told him to stop being an arsehole, to release the rights he has and do a deal with Chris. Branca however, is about to do something quite different. Given the strain Ron is facing, and the fact we've just hauled him over the coals, added to his misery and beaten him up some more, I hold back from telling him about Garrry.

More grief, more trouble with the flights, more nonsense streams across my virtual desk. HaSH continues to spit nails at Bobby Dickinson for putting more lights into the rig, foolishly and again arguing that the existing design is adequate for the job. Ron is in uproar because his stage team is not trusted and who the fuck is Garrry? (He knows perfectly well who Garrry is, he's worked with him a dozen times and each time Garrry has pulled Ron's nuts out of the production fire.) Ron's stage team are sulking. Paul King is putting posters up in Welsh chip shops and Jeffré is becoming hysterical. Not only does Heavy D have to have two first class tickets, presumably because he is so heavy he cannot fit in one seat, but his groomer has to come with him. Groomer? What the fuck is a groomer? Is it some child-seeking advance party, lollipops in one hand and handcuffs in another? Or is it a long suffering servant with super-sized Q tips he uses to clean the fat folds that make up ninety per cent of Heavy D? Whatever it is, it's just cost us another ten thousand dollars in hotels and airfare. Jeffré also wants airline tickets and hotels for twelve of his bestest friends and La Toya needs more rehearsal time on top of the month she's already had. Well at least Jeffré has finally committed his artist to the show. For days prior he had been trying to have the whole thing cancelled and pulled back to the US for a 2012 presentation. Chris talked him down, mainly by showing him the length of the line of lawyers that would come after him, Jeffré being a partner in GLE after all, but these antics just add to the sense of unreality. Katherine Jackson won't commit to when she is coming, or from where, the Jacksons want more managers and entourage and – get this – two wardrobe people each from LA, everyone is screaming at everyone else, and the mayhem rolls us along and flings us, gasping for breath, into the last two weeks before the show.

Everyone is asking me about ticket sales. I say I don't know, but I am on the distribution list for the daily sales figures, and they are appalling. We are selling sometimes in excess of a dozen a day, but never more than twenty. At this rate we might just fill the stadium in nine years' time. I quietly shelve my grandiose plans for the VIP enclosure, the tented village, the twenty identical Winnebagoes each with a picket fence and some garden furniture, and make friends with a local Cardiff promoter who puts together packages for the rugby. He proposes drinks and nibbles at a local hotel, a T-shirt, a poster, and two tickets, all for fifty quid on top of the face value. It's low rent, it's cheap but it can shift some tickets, so like a whore scoring tricks down an alley and letting go of the dreams of royal clients on yachts in Monaco, I do the deal and split the premium 60:40.

Why aren't we selling? The answer lies in the uncertainty about the event. Nobody will spend money on something that might be cancelled, and although that was never going to happen unless the investors pulled out, headlines the likes of "TROUBLED CONCERT IN CLASH WITH FANS" would presage articles and web posts listing the latest woes on top of every glitch that had gone before. Here's one from early September, posted online before nearly half the stadium was taken off sale, before Cee-Lo tweeted he had "heard" it was off, before a lot more shit got piled on the pile.

> *Michael Jackson fans are furious over reports that promoters of the Michael Forever tribute concert in Wales have slashed ticket prices and offered two-for-one deals in order to combat slow ticket sales for the event. Fans in a Facebook group called Fans Against Michael Forever Tribute posted a link to the promotion, noting that the discount would not apply to tickets already purchased for the October 8th show.*
>
> *In addition to feeling ripped off by this new ticket promotion, fans were also angered by the clarification that Beyoncé's involvement will be limited to a pre-taped segment rather than a live performance via satellite, as previously promised.*
>
> *This is only the latest setback for the Michael Forever Tribute. The show has been denied authorization by the singer's estate, rejected by his siblings Janet, Tito and Jermaine, and was forced to drop Kiss as a headliner when organizers were criticized for condoning bassist Gene Simmons' inflammatory comments about the King of Pop's alleged child molestation. Last month, a coalition of 35 Michael Jackson fan clubs from around the world came together to call for the cancellation of the show, which is set to include performances by Christina Aguilera, Smokey Robinson and Cee Lo Green.*

Would you spend a hundred quid on two tickets, plus go through all the fuff of getting to Wales, if you thought the show would be scrapped? Of course not – nobody would, and nobody did. Quietly the capacity at the venue is reduced down to 45,000 by taking the upper tiers off sale. This is not announced anywhere, and I only find out the day before the show. But by then I have enough on my plate without worrying about the tickets.

The Black Eyed Peas pull out. They were supposed to do two nights in Vegas and then fly to London, but have cancelled their second Vegas show and, I presume, told their managers to get them out of *Michael Forever*. A joint press release has to be agreed. I suggest one:

'The members of the Peas, thrown together once more for two Vegas shows, have been forcefully reminded how much they hate each other, which no amount of individual hotel rooms, separate Mercedes Vaneos and bunches of lilies can assuage. They cannot bear to be in the same building at the same time so will not be appearing together in Cardiff. They are going their own separate ways, the band is splitting up and Will-I-Am will not appear in Cardiff for reasons that are nothing to do with us. Will-I-am has become Will-I-ain't.

It's not what goes out.

I struggle to take seriously someone who has come into adulthood with a play name most people leave behind on their primary school (second grade) exercise books. Like Nicky with two 'k's and hearts for the dots or Pete with a smiley fat Pac-man for the middle 'e', it's something one should grow out of. I also never liked the idea of the Peas in the show. It didn't fit, made our show a Black Eyed Peas plus support event, and caused huge production problems and vast expense. I didn't think they were worth two million bucks either. As I-Am-To-Discover, I was wrong on all counts. Andy-I-am-an-idiot (Well-I-Am-Mis-took) for not seeing the bigger picture.

On the plus side, it means the running time of the show is within our four hour window. It means we have enough video tape and satellite time to deliver the whole thing live and keep a record of not just the line cut but all the individual cameras too. I ask if Stevie Wonder will now be drafted in to replace the Peas. He would be a popular choice and add gravitas to the bill, but, tacked on to the end of a conversation about getting the refund of the Peas fees to us and not QuickDraw, I get an evasive "maybe".

What's not evasive is the meltdown of Chris' longest-serving Bristol elf. She has come to the end of her tether, and I spend an hour with her on the phone as she tearfully recounts the final dissolution of her loyalty to and respect for Chris. She tells me he is doing awful things, lying to suppliers, funnelling money around, acting bizarrely, being rude. She tells me she has been completely side-lined, that she no longer knows what's going on, she takes countless calls from irate fans and disgruntled customers (this because GLE is registered at the Bristol office and the Bristol phone number is on the public record). She tells me that the vital secondary use licence is only now being applied for, that she is being made to do things she really doesn't want to do, and that she is going to walk out.

"Andy, you have no idea of the things he is doing. I can't bear it. I've told him he has to stop, it has to stop. It's just awful"

I have known her for as long as I have known Chris. They have known each other for even longer, twenty, twenty five years or more. There was once undoubtedly a romantic bond too, either real or imagined, requited or not, but when married with their very close working relationship, it created a solid partnership of fierce protection from her and trust and reliance from him. Now this closeness was being rent asunder by the huge pressure piled on every hour as the tiny clouds seeded months before fast developed into hurricanes thundering towards the show, and Chris twisted and turned ever harder and faster to try and avoid them.

It's a sorry state of affairs and I know exactly how she feels. I tell her what The Better has been telling me, that she's there to do a job and not there to worry about how Chris is doing his. I say we need her, the project needs her, and I tell her to reconsider. Gradually the tears stop, but the resolve remains. She tells me she will go out and eat much cake, come back and hand in her notice. I sit back and wonder why, feeling at times exactly the same way, I have coaxed her not to run out of the door. I come to the conclusion that it was the best thing for the show, the least bad option, better than having to replace her at short notice, better than losing momentum and continuity in those areas she was covering. It probably was best for her too, to leave properly, give notice, and not dump Chris in the lurch even as he appeared to be doing exactly that to her.

* * *

The Estate announces that Katherine and the children are to receive thirty five million dollars. Apparently and in the words of the estate, catalogue exploitation has been better than forecast, so money is available now that wasn't available before. This cannot be a retort to Chris' hundred thousand dollar trust fund. It's also impossible to imagine the payment having anything to do with the estate's desire to have Katherine endorse the Cirque du Soleil show by going to Canada, with the children, for the premier on October 2. It's just happenstance of course, or is it? But wait, the trial is in full swing! Michael's murderer is about to get his comeuppance! Surely a circus show is grossly inappropriate at this time of justice seeking by the fans? Nah, seems not. It seems the inappropriateness attaches just to *Michael Forever*. This move by the estate does however, cause havoc with the travel plans for the family. Katherine, the kids and their security team now need tickets from Los Angeles or Montreal to Germany or the UK. Nobody knows which, and the indecision begins to worry Jeffré, who is fast to see conspiracy in every twist and turn, and the money paid to her by the Estate as an attempt to buy Katherine off, away from *Michael Forever*.

Meanwhile, in the London office, Dawn, Purple and a host of assistants beaver away, heads down, calm, conscientious and paid weekly.

CHAPTER 8.
JERROLD LAPURNEE
Once You Get The Beat Inside Your Feet
There Ain't No Way To Stop You Movin' Good

It's hot. Autumn has begun and the lacklustre English summer has given way to an Indian heat wave, which is making London warmer than Calcutta. It's also Saturday October 1, one week to go, and although I've picked a sunny spot in a park to sunbathe, the mobile is on and ready. Soon enough, it rings. Purple is on the phone, beside herself with concern. Jerold Lapurnee, one of Christina's dancers, has been stopped at Heathrow and denied entry into the UK, because as a Cuban he requires a visa, which he does not have.

"He never told me he was Cuban and needed a visa," she wails.

"When you were organizing the work permit for him, did you get a copy of his passport?" I ask.

"Yes."

"Does it say "Cuban" on it?"

"Er, yes."

"Well there you go. Whom have you spoken to?"

"I've talked to immigration, but they say he needs a visa and he can't come in."

I tell her to give me the number for immigration and I punch it into my iPhone. Then I call her back to get the number again because what I punched in seems to have disappeared when I disconnected her call. She gives me the number again, and this time I write it down along the edge of the newspaper that I am still to start reading. Then I dial. I find myself speaking to a firm but friendly lady who informs me that the electronic work permit scheme does not obviate the need for a visa from those countries that need visas, and that sadly, Mr Lapurnee, a Cuban national, cannot enter the UK. She further tells me that Mr Lapurnee would have been well aware of his circumstances as he was in the country back in April, on a work visa that has now lapsed. So there cannot be the excuse of ignorance.

The imminent exclusion of Jerold presents me with several issues, each greater than the absence of one dancer from Christina's retinue of eight. Christina has been, throughout this project, the most easy-going, professional and undemanding person within our firmament of talent. Despite many early mutterings to the contrary, how she is a world of pain, how she is flaky and unreasonable, how she always wants tons of stuff, Christina has asked only for four dancers from the USA, four from the UK, some tattered flags like in the *Dirty Diana* video, a wind machine and some dance bars. All of this was requested in good time, detailed with visual references, and all of it was a pleasure to provide. There were no outlandish dressing room requests, none of the anticipated demands for biscuits made from ground fairy wings, sofas covered in woven frogs tongues, fruit bowls held by children under five who had not, at any point in their young lives, been in contact with detergent yet were clean and smelling of Madagascan vanilla – none of the usual diva bollocks. Just some dancers and a few props.

Christina had signed first and resolutely stayed signed throughout the trials and uncertainty of August, and the maelstrom of hate in September. Now she was here, in London, ready to rehearse. Minus one dancer – not a big deal with one week to go, as he can be easily replaced from the massive pool of talent available in London. And besides, she has already hired four locals, so one more won't be hard to find.

Unfortunately however, Mr Lapurnee was not just a dancer, he was also the boyfriend of the choreographer, artistic director, and all round rock of support to Christina (that's one person, not three). If I failed to deliver his Cuban to him, the Rock could quickly and in seconds explain to Christina what a bunch of fuckwits we were and get her on the plane and back to New York. She would depart not in a huff, but from a huge concern at what else would fail and the impact of those failures on her performance. So the issues were clear: Keep the Rock happy equals keep Christina happy equals our one last of the moment star gets out on that stage. I explained all this to the immigration officer, not the bit about the boyfriend, but pretty much everything else, and she said she would talk to her line manager.

Purple rings again, worrying about what to do with the car, the driver and The Rock of Christina. I tell her immigration are reviewing the case and the car should wait. She says the Rock, arrived on the same flight, is beside himself with worry, and fretting in the way that only gay American dancers can fret. I sensed what Purple was going through, and even my mascara started to run – and I wasn't wearing any. I talk to the Rock of Christina and calm him down, tell him everything will be okay, and he should go to his hotel. He wants to stay, sitting in the car in a Heathrow multi-storey, and wait for Jerrold. How touching. Eventually, calm immigration lady rings back.

"We have reviewed the case of Jerrold Lapurnee and we have taken your comments into consideration. As he appears not to present any danger to the UK, nor is he a flight or asylum risk, we have, in this instance, allowed him temporary entry into the country. You are responsible for ensuring he leaves when his work permit expires, which is October 10. We will NOT allow him in again without the proper documentation, and this is a one-time concession for this occasion only."

I am beside myself with delight. Thank fuck for that. I profusely thank the lady for her kindness and wisdom and offer her tickets to the concert, which she politely declines as they could be seen as a bribe. I ring Purple and tell her the good news. I ring the Rock and tell him he can stop crying. I take my expensive earphones out and lay back in the sun. Five minutes later Purple rings again.

"What about Estephez Perez? He's one of Frank Gatson's Dance Jam dancers and is coming in tomorrow from New York."

"Is he a US national?"

"No."

"Is he from the EU?"

"No, he's Dominican."

"A monk?"

"No – he's from the Dominican Republic. He needs a visa too."

"Is he Frank Gatson's boyfriend?"

"I don't think so."

"Okay."

I should now point out that although Jerrold Lapurnee is a made up name, and he is here representing all the support talent on the show, the above events did actually take place. I have the tan lines from my headphones to prove it. The Dominican however, never came, and I doubt anyone noticed, not even Frank Gatson.

Garrry the Floor Manager has arrived from America, and

we go straight into a meeting with Ron and his team. The purpose is to pin down the on and offs and exact requirements for each number. So far the information has been drip fed by Ron, in a vague and imprecise way, and I want it all pinned down. I tell the meeting to forget about the Peas. They ain't coming. Will-I-Am-not-doing-this-show. I learn that Ron's choice of Floor Manager is no more than a seat filler co-ordinator at awards shows, and not a particularly good one at that. We assign him a broom and he goes off to sulk. Garrry, having done this forever, quickly has his feet under the desk, and is talking detail with Ron; they are re-doing a Pea-less running order, the props lists are being rationalised, microphone requirements, wardrobe times, ons and off – everything is at last being written down in a cogent and clear way. I leave them to it and move on to my next crisis.

Jabba the Hutt continues to snipe. He has decided there is some piece of his own kit that he has rented to production, about which nobody on either side of the Atlantic knew about, authorised, or was aware of. What this could possibly be, as everything the band wanted and needed has been provided, I can but guess. An in-line spite meter perhaps. A noise reduction filter running on pure evil, who knows, but he has decided he wants paying for it. Now. Five thousand dollars. So he shuts down the show music website, a private on line resource for the sharing of music files by whichever department needed access. He does this by the simple expedient of changing the password, sits back, and waits.

The TV music PA is first on the phone, saying she can no longer access the site, which she needs to do if she is to continue working, preparing camera cue cards, breaking down the concert so that she can tell the director what's coming up, musically, bar by bar. Next up, Jennifer Hudson's people, waiting to receive the tracks laid down by our gospel choir so she can familiarise herself with what they've done and rehearse her performance, complain they've been given a website address but they can't log on. It takes the best part of the day to trace the problem back to fat-boy, who announces he won't reinstate access until he is paid for his musical shitbox or whatever it is. It takes another day for the pig to be satisfied the money has reached his account. Five grand extorted from GLE, just like that. It's easy for governments to state they won't negotiate with terrorists or hostage takers, but when the hostage is a show just five days away, even Bruce Willis would get the bad guys their pizzas.

Unfortunately, the delay has meant hat Jennifer Hudson did not receive the choir tracks until it was too late for her to work with them. She regretfully tells Ron she has no choice but to pull out. She's not ready, the song is a complex one, and she feels she would not be able to do justice to Michael's music or her performance. I don't for one moment think that Dorsal Kevin's sidekick Sack of Hate ever gave his actions a single thought. The contempt he continually expressed, for the show, for his employers, for Ron, for the memory of Michael, was never hidden by humility, nor mitigated by any degree of professionalism. I had never known anything like it, in over thirty years in the business. The guy was, quite simply, a very nasty piece of work. Kevin's support for him meant he in turn could appear not to be; a good musician/bad musician routine that stupidly I allowed to annoy me.

CHAPTER 9.
MICHAEL (JACKSON)
And who gave you the right to shake my family tree?

I met Michael Jackson once. I say met, but really I mean that I was in the presence of Michael Jackson once. It was in the nineties and I was in LA on business and trying to catch up with friend and director Wayne Isham. Our schedules were tight, so I came down to Culver City Studios where Wayne was shooting the video for *You are Not Alone*, the one where Michael and Lisa Marie get naked. I arrived early evening to find Wayne worrying about time. He was way behind schedule, and Michael was in his trailer having his make-up done, as he had been for the last four hours. We grab some coffee from craft service and chew the cud a while and eventually Michael appears, surrounded by retinue and under a black umbrella. He is to perform the master vocal, on his own, either in the temple set or against green screen – I can't remember. Wayne is concerned how many takes he's going to get, telling me he's generally got about one and a half before Michael goes back in for make-up. He's got three cameras on the set, the director of photography Daniel Pearl on one, his operator on another and there is a spare which so far has not been operated to Wayne's satisfaction. He asks me to shoot the spare. I'm honoured and, despite Daniel's protestations, I jump on the camera. I get the camera department junior as a focus puller, so I widen out the zoom as much as I can and move in as close as I can to keep the profile loose close-up that Wayne has asked for without giving the focus puller too much to do.

Michael steps up onto his mark, looks down and sort of

draws himself into his core. Someone shouts for playback, we're away, and I'm shooting a close up of Michael Jackson on a sound stage in Culver City. OM-Effing-G! The transformation from skinny, nervous artist to amazing performer is instant (Michael's, not mine). He explodes into his vocal, his moves razor sharp, his delivery incredibly powerful. Part of me is mesmerised, another part fights to keep the camera steady. Suddenly, consummate entertainer that he is, Michael finds my camera. He spin turns towards me and delivers a line staring right into the lens, his gaze laser focused. I almost fall over, such is the voltage in the look, but my professionalism holds as I hold onto the pan bar as Michael's eyes bore down the lens, through the eyepiece and down into my soul. Wow! Everything is slow motion until, line delivered, Michael snaps back to the main camera in front of him. I've seen this kind of power before, where the singer's love of performance is returned by the camera's love for the artist. Jon Bon Jovi has it, so does Michael Flatley. Michael Hutchence had it – but I've never seen it so strong as that balmy July evening in Los Angeles.

A moment of context for this video. Michael had suddenly and without warning married Elvis' daughter Lisa Marie. This followed the first child abuse allegations which ended with Michael paying off the family. In his "is he isn't he" book, *The Final Years of Michael Jackson,* author Ian Halperin explains the union as an attempt by the Scientologists to recruit Michael by using their ardent acolyte Lisa Marie. It's a theory that makes more sense than any other. Michael certainly works hard to be sexy in the almost buff with a curvy, glistening Lisa Marie. But the scenes lack chemistry and just felt wrong, because seeing Michael in a steamy sexual context didn't seem right. Michael Jackson is above sexuality. His power as a performer was so great, so pure, that to define it in terms of sex is to belittle it, to drag it down to an earthy level when it actually belongs in a plane far above that of a bit of bump and grind. His sweet, virginal girlfriend in *Thriller* is much more fitting, because the interplay is matey, not sexy. This is part of Michael's universal appeal, why his fans are men and women alike. He is to sex what nectar is to fish and chips – a world away and a world above.

Anyway, my second biggest thrill that day was to put my British NatWest bank card into a Culver City Studios ATM, the one by the gate, and get dollars back. Forgive me even mentioning this, but in 1995 this was a very, very big deal.

* * *

I arrive in Cardiff on Wednesday, October 5th, in the afternoon. A runner meets me at the gate and I am walked along the car park under the stadium, through an unmarked steel door and into a goods lift that groans and grumbles up to Level 3. I ask about the lift, and I'm told we are in luck because caterers were using it when we got to it, so it was available. Otherwise we would be detouring to a staircase some hundred metres further on. Eventually I end up in the massive production office, usually the press room for rugby matches and as such the only place with broadband. I stand in line, get photographed, and am issued with a pass and three paper wristbands of different colours. I lose the wristbands within eight minutes and demand something a bit more permanent. I am met with blank stares. So much for Access All Areas passes.

I regretfully wish I had stayed in the accreditation meeting at the stadium back in May, instead of just poking my head around the door and saying hi and well done and please don't do anything silly like at the Olympics where everyone had a washboard on their fronts. At the time I considered the dreary contract meeting next door a greater priority.

I remind the pass team that today it's me arriving and twenty others, but tomorrow and Friday it's hundreds of people at a time and their system will collapse. They promise to look into it, but I can tell that the head of Accreditation Control, Mrs HaSH in charge of passes, who looks like Mr HaSH but with glasses, couldn't hate me more if she tried. Shame. Another friendship stillborn, another dinner party invitation torn up before it's even written. No hard hat goulash for me, in that Norwich portacabin. I go off to find Dawn, get briefed on TV progress, go through the TV budget which is holding where it more or less should, and then I go out on the floor for the first time.

It is a litter of flight cases, pallets half loaded with truss and stage, racks of lights, of cranes and scissor lifts beeping and flashing as they trundle around the stadium bowl. As usual the construction crew and riggers have spread themselves over the entire available area. It looks like a giant child has thrown the contents of their toy box all over the floor. The rig is complete, and sits like a space ship about five feet off the raised deck that will become the stage. Both are absolutely huge. A hundred men and women are swarming all over it; hanging lights, running cable, testing motors. Other teams are working around the stadium, blocking off the level two corridors with drape, rigging the lighting and sound control tower, flying the delay stacks. It is a busy, exciting, humming place and at the centre sits an old Winnebago, and in it sits a very tired and grubby Pete, who is controlling all this activity, making it all happen, at the right time, and more or less on schedule.

I have my push bike, so I can get around the massive

space of the stadium very quickly. The journey from the production office, where all departments – a hundred people in all – sit at serried rows of desks, to the TV truck compound is about a seven minute walk. It takes me about forty seconds, especially if I'm trying to ram Dorsal at speed on the way. A couple of times he lashes out a scaly, ectoplasm covered alien appendage, but I'm way too fast for him. Soon the bike serves as my pass, because my golden, purple and green wristbands have long disappeared in a multi-coloured paper-mâché mush down the plug hole of my hotel shower, but every security guard at every station recognises the cycling lunatic with iPhone earpieces flapping in the wind as he whizzes by.

* * *

I spend most of Thursday rushing around forwarding requests for payment to Chris' Bristol office, where they sit until Chris authorises them. The nervousness amongst the suppliers is palpable, and I try to speak to everyone, to reassure them, to remind them of the magnitude of the Facebook stream and how popular it will be.

But like everyone, I am unclear as to why there appears to be a shortage of cash. The financing deal with QuickDraw delivered three million quid to GLE. The money paid to the Black eyed Peas, another million ($2m less withholding tax) was, at Chris' insistence, paid back to GLE also. The majority of the artists were paid, and most suppliers had had at least something on account. There should have been enough money to get to the end of the show, yet the Bristol office was stalling.

I find Kim of Eat your Hearts Out. The catering is as good as its location poor – two rooms underneath the old Cardiff Arms Park with a narrow passageway between them. One is laid out with trestle tables and chairs, about a hundred places in all. The second room holds the lavish buffet and servery for the hot meals. Queuing for the food can take an age. Right at the start I had insisted on a rolling meal provision, so people could break when they could and still be fed. EYHO have ignored this and offer two hour windows for breakfast, lunch and dinner. I ask around and everyone is happy, with the quality, quantity and accessibility of the catering. I sit down with Kim, remind her of our conversations, and point out that although her system has been working well until now, it will fall apart once we are at full strength and rehearsing. Her mealtimes are going to have to fit in with the work schedule and not the other way around. Page one of the Film Catering Guide. No such chapter in How to Cater a Rock 'n' Roll Show. Kim says she cannot continue until she gets twenty five grand in cash. I tell her I'll see what I can do and pass the "request" to Bristol. So the day continues, a thousand questions, a hundred answers.

I've found a great spot to work. Outside the press office are the press tables where reporters sit and watch the match. They have worktops in front of the seats, so are ideal for lunch. I can see all the activity around the whole stadium, my mobile works, and I have internet. This is where I base myself, retreating inside only when Doreen Spunkbucket tests the PA systems, which does not seem to be very often. He's probably too busy thinking up new ways to blackmail the show. The stage is ready at half past two, just half an hour late across a five day hell schedule with no leeway anywhere. Well done production Pete, a man who has turned out to be a diamond. His stage design was pulled apart and his lighting design was consigned to the bin – both at the last minute, yet he has delivered the setting for the show on time, with good humour and good grace.

Leona Lewis has decided she will have every effect possible for her two numbers. Ballerinas dancing, live string sections, ballerinas flying, boom arms swinging, more dancers who are not ballerinas dancing differently. All of them wardrobed up to the hilt, tutus and tuxedos and ball gowns, all on the show's dollar. In contrast, Smokey Robinson and Gladys Knight have asked for a microphone. Granted the request was for one each, so even there the need for self-fulfillment was a little out of control.

As a result of Leona's excess, most of Thursday afternoon is taken up by rehearsing the flying ballerina and the damned boom arm, which, as expected, looked crap, took too long and cost two hours of rehearsal time. Mallet tells me I have to get rid of it. I tell him it will be gone, but possibly not until Saturday. I know this because I've gone up on stage after about ninety minutes of gutter cleaning, window wiping moves and Ron held up his hand, stared at me and said, "This will work". I took that to mean he was not ready to give up on it. Yet. Ron then completely takes the wind out of my sails by introducing me to Gladys Knight, and I stammer like a schoolboy as I remember hundreds (well, maybe dozens) of teen disco snogs to *Help Me Make It Through the Night*.

Breaking the spell and the memory of a time when young women wanted to snog me, I go to look for Pete, because the centre screen which drops down in front of the band for Beyoncé's performance and a couple of others is taking about half a day to descend. We have a long conversation about fast motors and slow motors and I beg him to fix it. He does, but not until the following day.

More trouble, more running around. I do radio

interviews for local stations and TV interviews for BBC Wales. I smile, enunciate properly and talk fluently about the wonderful line up and the fantastic set and the excellent rehearsals and how brilliant it's all going to be. I am blessed with my bike, for without it my feet would be rubbed down to my ankles by now.

Alien Fucking Ant Farm. What a bunch! Reading their publicity notes I learn the name of the band comes from their idea that the earth is in fact an ant farm, we are the ants, and some big aliens have us in a glass box in their alien kitchen. Why this theory has not caught on I can but wonder, as it seems so obvious. The only way to get them on and off the stage is to preset the drums on a platform and bring it up to stage height on a forklift for their performance. The drummer is not happy about this, presumably because it's not something that should ever happen on an ant farm, and the manager makes sure everyone knows about the concerns. Ron calls me up on stage and gets me to deal with the manager. I try diplomacy and tact. Then I tell him if the drummer isn't on the drum kit in ten minutes they can fuck off back to the alien kitchen from which they came. It does the trick.

Next I fight off Heavy D's manager, who dogs me like a bad smell, demanding per diems for his artist. The guy's getting a shedload of money to bolster La Toya's performance and he wants per diems as well? No fucking way. The classier acts, Christina, Jamie, Gladys – all of them in fact, do not make such outlandish requests. I tell him it's not in the contract so he's not getting any. He whines and moans and keeps popping up all day.

Then, in the afternoon, comes the much awaited Estate response to our existence, the roar of a very angry, very powerful bear, and it's a doozie, as they say in America.

Some of Michael's songs are published by Warner Chappell under licence from a company set up by Michael, MiJac Music, and now therefore part of the estate. Warner Chappell, no doubt at the estate's urging ("you're the publisher, you sue 'em") has filed for an injunction to stop the show, claiming breach of copyright and passing off if it goes ahead. Chris and Michael Henry have been in court for two days and end up giving personal undertakings not to knowingly infringe Warner Chappell's rights. A full hearing is scheduled for a few months down the line, but the compromise that prevented the judge from pulling the plug on the whole thing was that there would be no live-to-air transmission.

Chris rings me to tell me as I sit in my favourite spot, and I feel the colour draining from my face and a sick feeling growing in my stomach. He outlines what has just gone on at the High Court in London, the judge's ruling, and how Warner Chappell's action benefits us in the long term.

I cannot speak. Silent screams of "We're fucked, we are so fucked" reverberate around my head while nausea builds from my gut. I feel cold, clammy. All this work, all this effort, all this money, all wasted. Yet I hear nothing from Chris to indicate he shares my fear and concern. Is he blocking it? Does he not get it? Or does he just not care? Chris' muddling style, his blasé approach to music rights, his focus on doing the legal thing rather than the correct thing, exploiting loopholes instead of talent, has finally done for us all. I want to cry.

Then I pull myself together. I remind myself I have been hired to do a job of work, that pushing shit uphill is my forte, and that productions a la Hunt are always like this. I tell him that pulling the live TX is going to worry a lot of crew and suppliers, let alone the artists, and the demands for tranches of money will increase as the revenue streams dry up one by one. We had already lost the Sky mega-deal, there were no takers for the 3D, the promised sponsor had failed to show up, and now the major, major and vital Facebook stream was no more. I knew Chris was again down to his last few hundred grand and I told him I had to know how he intended to honour the outstanding payments. He told me the ticket revenues had improved, and we had sold around twenty thousand. The ticket money would be available in the week after the show. He told me there was half a million quid of VAT coming at the end of the month, so in total there was enough to pay everything outstanding. I believed him. I then told him he had to issue a statement to the crew, because they needed to know what was happening. I said I'd write it for him but it had to come from him. Here it is:

> To the TV crew from Chris Hunt
> Ladies and Gentlemen,
> *I want to thank you for your amazing efforts on this very difficult and stressful production. The reasons for the nature of this show are many, but all stem from the huge challenges of a multi-artist show of this size, and the fact that this is a tribute to Michael Jackson, the world's finest entertainer but also a man and an industry driven by complexities and conflicts.*
> We have achieved what until now has been impossible for anyone to achieve, and have put on stage a remarkable and spectacular show. We have all battled last minute changes, and issues, and challenges, but we have all pulled through with remarkable professionalism and talent. While you have been dealing with challenges of time and resources, I have been facing off legal challenges from one of the rights' holders of some of the songs, who is refusing permission to use their copyrightable property. One concession I have had to make to them has been to undertake not to broadcast this show live-to-air. So there will be no live-to-air t/x on Saturday.
> This however, is not more than an unfortunate delay in delivering this

> to TV screens around the world, and Sky will air an edited show next weekend. On a positive note, ticket sales are strong in the last days, so we are expecting the middle tiers and floor/lower tier areas to be sold out.
> Once again I thank you for your tremendous work in getting this show together
> Chris Hunt
> Producer and Event Director

It was a partial success, in that nobody upped sticks and went home. I think it was less the letter and more the professionalism of everyone involved, that made them stay to see it through. Understandably however, the rate of demands for payment rocketed. I got as many paid as I could. Kim from catering went to the bank with the production runner, ripped the twenty five grand cash from him as soon as he turned from the counter, and disappeared into various food wholesalers to buy the massive quantities needed to serve over two thousand meals that day.

The day before the show proceeds reasonably smoothly. A camera mount provider refuses to leave London until he gets his invoice paid in full. A lighting supplier at the venue threatens to call up their trucks, load up and head back to London unless the balance on his invoice is paid immediately. I pass these demands back to the Bristol office. Both are paid and I cheer myself that a potential head on collision on the M4 between two disgruntled *Michael Forever* suppliers, heading in opposite directions, has been avoided. There are many more that now queue along the aisle leading to my stadium seat and I prioritise all of them as super urgent. The two outside broadcast companies, providing the 2D and 3D facilities, are also getting increasingly nervous about payment. I make Chris go to talk to them, to reassure them, to stop them driving away, and he does so.

On stage, rehearsals proceed slowly. Robert Dickinson is working miracles at the lighting console, but the front of house audio sounds awful. It's so bad that two investors, who have turned up early to "see how things are going" tell me they think the sound is very indistinct – muffled yet very bassy. I assure them it's a factor of the stadium being empty. Once it fills up with people, the sound will soften and the bass seem less vigorous. I know I'm bullshitting, as I have thought the same as they, but I cannot say:

"Well, actually an oversized maggot has put himself in charge of the front of house sound, and, because the band and the musical director both support him being there, I can do little about it. Our HaSH, who is an ex-sound engineer, has told me exactly what you have just said, at least five times, and I have had to say the same thing to him."

And just as I don't say all that to the investors, rehearsals on stage stop, because the subject of our discussion has decided he is off to lunch, and has switched the audio off, not only at the front of house, but the on stage monitoring as well. Microphones die, guitars become silent, keyboards deathly quiet. I plead work elsewhere, politely excuse myself, leaving them sitting in the lower tier, surrounded by empty seats, pointing and discussing and watching as their money is burnt to ash.

Late in the afternoon I manage to get away for a couple of hours and cycle back to the St David's Hotel, which is about three miles from the venue. It's the only five star hotel in Cardiff, a rating it gets by being the best in the city, which it is, rather than being on a par with five star hotels elsewhere, which it isn't. It's tired, rusting and a little smelly under the arms. The "sofa" in the living room of my suite consists of two single divan beds pushed together at right angles. The door to the balcony doesn't open, which is probably a good thing, as the Indian summer has turned into a Welsh autumn and there is a gale blowing across Cardiff Bay. Breakfast has been uniformly poor. Scrambled eggs done in a microwave and cooked to seven deaths – so hard you could construct walls with them. Disgusting sausages made of rusk and fat and little else; bacon so shrivelled and dry it's better used to exfoliate; thin, nasty coffee and cheap orange juice. It's just above awful and it's where all the artists are staying. The alternative was a privately owned ex-mental home of a hotel perched on a hill above Newport, some twenty miles way. A huge, rambling and very quirky red dragon festooned monolith called The Celtic Manor, it was too far and too weird, even for the artists, although the breakfasts were a little better. I should have put the band in there though, as I'm sure Doris the Bottom Feeder would have enjoyed the dragons.

    I get a quick swim and head back for the evening rehearsal. It goes well and Garrry gets it done by a quarter after midnight, forty five minutes later than planned because of Leona Lewis and her fucking boom arm. Honestly, she looks petrified as the thing jerks and stutters above the pit in front of the stage. She cannot even stand on it let alone deliver a meaningful vocal, and I know it's time to act. Ron is reassuring her, and Leona's blonde and very pretty manager stands close by. I wait until they come off the stage and take the manager by the arm.

    "If Leona is on that jib arm tomorrow, I'll cut the song from the TV show. It's unfilmable, looks awful, and is not doing her or anyone else any favours."

"But Ron says it will be okay," she pouts.

"Suit yourself," I reply, and leave her to scurry after Leona and think of something else. Sorry Ron, but the thing was crap and you were blind to it.

The call time is 8:45 for the nine am rehearsals. I tell Garrry these have to be done by noon. Doors are at six pm, so a noon stop to all work will give us six hours to clean up and get focussed for the show. I also tell this to Ron, and he feigns not to hear me.

CHAPTER 10.
SARA GILES
SHOWDAY

And she promised me forever
And a day We'd live as one

I am beset by a sense of unreal wonder that we have reached the morning of the show day. Since April, this ship called *Michael Forever* has taken torpedo after torpedo, hit after hit and yet, miraculously, it is still afloat, still limping towards the end of its journey. Its crew is close to mutiny, the majority of its cargo is lost. The captain, like Captain Ahab before him, pursues his aim with a relentless vigour. And I? I am not Ishmael, narrator and innocent abroad, as much as I'd like to be. I am in this up to the tips of my top head hair. I am like Starbuck, the loyal first mate, loaded with misgivings, wracked with doubt, yet bound by duty to support Ahab in his quest. I am also full of crappy coffee. It is six am, I am wide awake, and we have the whale in sight. (Yes, Starbucks was named after this character from Moby Dick. The founders had considered the name of the ship too, but rejected it as too weird: Pequad Grande mochachino anyone?)

I cycle to the venue. Already a few punters are milling around outside, trying to get a peek at what lies within. The stadium, built with lottery money, is a bit see-through, a bit transparent, as any publicly funded building should be. This is especially so from the public footpath that runs alongside the river side of the building. We have put up some drapes, but there are still holes here and there. Inside, everyone looks fresh, rested. There are some smiles, although not many. I find it hard to recognise anyone, as Millennium has a rule that everybody out on the floor must wear a high visibility jacket. I can no longer spot the promoter in his leather jacket, the box office manager in her Chanel suit, or the chief rigger in his shorts, black singlet and tattoos. Everyone looks the same. A health and safety requirement has levelled us all to the garb of road workers. HaSH must be proud!

Rehearsals kick off on time, but within minutes Dorsal and the Whale are moaning about something, and it all grinds to a halt. I begin to have serious concerns that these two jokers will sabotage the show. I have a detailed discussion with our TV sound guys and they tell me that Doreen has the wherewithal to interrupt the feed to the TV whilst keeping the mix going to the stage and the house. I consider this a serious weakness and a likely target, so I make some contingency plans. On a walkabout of the many nooks and crannies within the stadium, I spied two police cells, complete with concrete slab bench, steel urinal and two inch thick steel doors with one of those slidey things over the small, grilled window. This I figured was the perfect place to dump Jabba so he could do no harm to the show. I had a chat with our head of security, and she said she would get some big chaps together who could easily whisk fat-boy from the mixing desk out in the stadium, back through some doors immediately behind, into a goods lift and on into the cells. Any members of the public in the vicinity would be unlikely to see this, as they would be watching the show. If we jumped him during or immediately after the interval, neither Kevin nor the band would be able to do anything about it, even if they noticed his absence, which, given his input so far, would be surprising. As for the sound, that would only improve. Paul McCartney's favourite sound engineer was our crew chief. He had spent the last three days in the stadium with his head in his hands, listening helplessly as good 'ole Sluggy had contrived to mix the worst concert audio since Hendrix set fire to his guitar.

One thing missing from my plan was a hood to slip over his head, but I found some over-sized cushions in the Eat your Hearts Out designed artist chill room and quickly snagged a cover. It was a bit bright, with some fetching and bold squirly patterns, very trendy and of the moment but in that way that you knew it would soon date. Pretty tho'; bold but not overbearing, much like Kim. Gay fabric moment done, I figured it would do the trick for the lift. The material was quite thick, so the bastard may well suffocate, but I dismissed that concern, reasoning that any harm he came to was totally self-inflicted by being such a tosser. While I had been structuring my plan, someone had sourced some bluebell-flavoured yoghurt or whatever it was the band were demanding, and rehearsals restarted.

Diversity came off the stage, sweating with the exertion of cartwheeling and jumping and flying and generally jigging about to a ten minute MJ medley. The dance troupe winners of *Britain's Got the X Factor Talent* had been due to open for MJ at the O2, so their participation was fitting. Their choreographer and dance captain Ashley, a giant of a man, complains about the slippery state of the floor surface, and of the Perspex tops to the light panels. He has put his foot through three in rehearsal, and is concerned about injury when they perform again without holding back. Wow – so they were holding back during that display of energy and power? God help the light panels tonight! I look for Pete, to tell him to reinforce the stage with concrete, but see him on stage already with a work crew adding support to the panels. We talk about a sticky dance compound which can be applied on to the stage to help traction. In the end Pete pours Coca Cola all over the floor, which does the trick.

The morning scoots by. I find myself the designated evacuation officer at a ten minute meeting to discuss bomb threats, fires and major crowd disturbances. The stadium will come to me for a decision, asking to suspend the show in the event of an occurrence serious enough to warrant one – a fight say, or a fire in a part of the building. They'll come to me to tell me of their decision for a show stop, if there's a bomb threat or major fire or building collapse or a full scale riot. In this instance the place is evacuated and the show is not restarted. I wonder whether Michael Henry covered that in his insurance negotiations. Lunchtime comes and goes but the rehearsals have not stopped, so Kim's two hour window for lunch, twelve until two, has allowed only those not directly involved in rehearsing to eat. I sense trouble brewing, so I head over to catering to make sure that lunch stays open. It's harder to get around by bike now. We are just a few hours from "doors", when the audience is allowed in, and so barriers and security have blocked my well-worn pathways in numerous places. Eventually I find a way through, but find my way to catering barred by a security guard, who tells me lunch is over and I cannot come in. It's always a fine line this, between somebody doing their job diligently, yet in so doing getting in the way of the bigger picture. I cannot bring myself to say, "Do you know who I am?" – as that's the most wanky thing a person in authority can say to a subordinate doing their job, so I say nothing, speed dial the head of security and pass him the phone.

Once in, I find Kim more stressed than I have ever seen

her. I remind her of our catering plan, different to the one she has put in place. She promises to do what she can, tells me she has already served four hundred lunches, and gives me another two hundred meal tickets, demanding a thousand pounds for them. I cycle back to production control and hand the tickets over to one of the TV production managers, telling her to deal with it. I then get over to stage and ask Garrry why we are still rehearsing at twenty past two, only to see Leona Lewis struggling to climb into the window cleaning jib. For fuck's sake! My phone rings for the hundredth time that day, and I see it's director David Mallet. I ignore the call – I know he's going to complain about the jib arm. I thought I had fixed it but I plainly hadn't. I wish Ron would let go of this idea; the execution is appalling and it's costing huge amounts of time. He seems, however, to be grimly hanging onto it as a talisman for the showmanship MJ used to deliver, without seeing that it does nothing for Leona's performance or the show. Let it go Ron.

Dawn is on the phone. Bobby Dickinson has told her that unless he gets a hot meal, on a plate and at a table, at the end of rehearsal, he will switch off the lights and go home, so there will be no show tonight. I tell her it's sorted and please can she get a thousand pounds to Kim in the next five minutes and tell Bobby he'll get his lasagne.

Next I head over to the media village, a massive plastic sided marquee put up in one of the car parks. Here, Mark Borkowski and his ever-growing band of hand maidens are masterminding the press coverage. For weeks now the FB page has been a well of positivity, the only thing visible when you visit the page are postings by *Michael Forever*, full of facts, gossip, preparations for the show and so on. You need to dig deep into the comments on each post to find Andre Salinas and his band of merry mud slingers, and even there they are outnumbered by positive notes from fans, arguing the rights and wrongs, supporting the show. I find the Facebook commandos in a corner hunched over a laptop. I congratulate them on their work.

Now, on show day, the media circus is in full swing. The tent is full of photographers, camera crews, journalists. I've been asked to do a radio interview, but it turns out they want Chris, so I head back out. As I do, I get a call telling me that Katherine has arrived in Cardiff and is on her way to the hotel. Talk about cutting it fine. I mention this bit of news to one of the acolytes, and instantly the already frenetic pace in the tent picks up a few gears. News crews grab their video cameras and rush out. Assistants point hand satellite dishes into the sky, searching for an uplink signal, photographers unsling their longest lenses and the reporters lick the end of well-licked pencils. Just as they do a stunningly beautiful and achingly slim young woman approaches me and asks where she can find some more brochures. I instinctively and instantly turn on my smarmy charm to full power, take her by the arm and personally escort her to the subterranean dungeon which merchandising have made their home. I dream of a well-licked pencil for at least an hour.

In an age of a moment it's gone three pm. The hall is silent apart from cohorts of stewards being briefed by their superiors. The concession stands are opening up, and the cleaners make their last patrols. In the middle of the floor some last minute camera positions are going up. Dawn stands next to the activity looking worried. The riggers are using eight by four foot quick-form truss, and they've orientated the long bit towards the stage. The Mojo barrier is two foot wide, and security want a stretcher width either side of the camera platform. So a sixteen foot wide motorway is being constructed in the middle of the hall, pushing the audience still further away from the stage.

"Who the fuck is building a motorway across the floor?" I ask rhetorically, knowing full well that it's DDD^M trying to find a better position for his cameras, having now at last seen something of a rehearsal that was lit and on a stage clear of workmen.

"It's David, he's moving three cameras," says Dawn, looking anxiously at her watch.

"Don't worry, you've ages yet. Besides, it's more fun when he wants to move the cameras during the show," I console her. At that point David appears and tells us he's saving us money by using one camera fewer. I tell him the width of barrier he is creating is stupid. He tells me the riggers are stupid for not putting the platforms cross-ways, like he told them to, and which they now start to do. Later, the riggers tell Dawn that Mallet had insisted the platform went in length-ways, and Dawn passes that on to me. I tell her that, after more than twenty years on and off with David, I already knew that. Bless 'im!

I find Jeffré and Chris and voice my concerns about the Slug Doreen. They tell me not to worry and expressly forbid me from having him snatched from the mixing desk and thrown into a cell. I show them the cushion cover but they are not swayed. I point out the bold patterns, the vibrant colours, but they stay adamant. On their heads be it. They do however want to divert my quick reaction squad and task them with keeping the Jackson Brothers' manager out of the building. Apparently he and a Japanese video crew are expected any moment now. They are going to use *Michael Forever*, the unique and exclusive family tribute to MJ, to launch another, no doubt equally exclusive and unique, tribute in Tokyo. Ah these jolly Jackson japers! What with KISS launching their cruise ship show, the Jacksons relaunching their career, and our stage full of *X Factor* finalists getting a much needed career boost, it would appear the world of music has taken Chris on a very expensive and fancy ride!

I cycle back to the hotel, dump the bike, have a quick shower, get my suit on and head back in one of the shuttle vans. The three mile journey takes an age. Because of the concert, main roads are closed, traffic diverted and we're sitting in a tailback inching towards the stadium. While I fret I sort out yet another issue by phone. The enterprising young team we have hired to find three or four hundred willing, attractive and excitable fans that we can put right up in front of the stage have reported a minor hiccup, in that Paul King has at the last minute flooded the colleges and universities with free tickets. Of the three hundred we need, around thirty team captains were being paid, shown some dance moves for some of the numbers, and rehearsed the day before. They would each then teach their team of ten the moves, and the result would be a mini flash-mob at certain points during the show. Finding the two hundred and seventy team members however, was proving quite difficult as many had taken up Paul's offer of free tickets, and therefore were able to see the concert without having to turn up two hours beforehand.

My solution is to talk to our excellent security company. I ask them to fill the golden circle and front of stage areas by letting people in from the back. The security coordinator goes off to talk to the stadium and get some coordinating done, because the venue stewards will have to help make this happen.

Eventually we make it through the barrier, past the fans wondering who is behind the blacked out windows (relax girls, nobody famous), and I walk onto the stadium floor with just two hours to go to showtime. I sense the closeness of the moment, yet still believe something could – at any moment – pop out of the woodwork and scupper the show. So much has happened, so much has gone wrong, that my doubts remain as to whether anyone is actually going to sing a note. Finding Chris I congratulate him on what he has achieved, tell him nobody else on the planet could have done what he has done. I believe my words to be true, but believe also the promise could still die. There could be a sniper out there right now, zeroed in, a bullet ready to hit the off button even as we reach for the starter switch.

My maudlin worries are cut off by a call from the venue catering. They need another thirteen grand to cater for additional boxes Michael Henry has ordered for the investors. I find Chris again, who again finds a credit card that still works, and I get down to the Millennium Stadium catering office to give them the money. Then a call from a Borkowski hand maiden. Another TV interview needs doing, and now. I head over to the media tent, find the earnest young reporter and his cameraman, and lead him away from the mayhem to a spot outside the stadium, up some steps and onto the concourse. The cameraman is happy with the background, sticks a lapel mike on me and I wax lyrical for a few minutes about the line-up, the challenges and how exciting it is for everyone to have reached this moment where finally there will be a worthy tribute to MJ. For a moment I think to hang onto him and the TV crew, so they can document the imminent catastrophe that will grind everything to a halt. I am getting more and more convinced this is about to happen, but I decide against dragging BBC Wales into my own private hell.

Coming back down the stairs I meet a petite, sharp looking woman in jeans, smoking three cigarettes at once, accompanied by about half a dozen various women and boys, and carrying VIP invitations. I ask if I can help, as they all look a bit lost, and she shows me the invites, which are for box 211. Having been here for what feels like a year I know exactly where this is. I'm pleased that I sorted out the additional catering, because this was one of the extra boxes, and the woman before me looks like she needs a bit of feeding up. There are so few calories in nicotine after all. Before directing her up two levels and to the other side of the stadium, along a complicated route path involving goods lifts, catering areas and police cells, I ask her name.

"Sara Giles," she says. I smile, introduce myself and offer to personally escort her to her corporate box, on the way pointing out the finer features of the stadium, and the show in it that she now completely owns. I apologise profusely for the lack of red carpet along her route and offer the frog tongue sofa instead. All she asks for is a dozen programmes all signed by the Jacksons, the principal performers, and Katherine. I tell her I'll see what I can do, but refrain from pointing out that at present, the last signature is impossible to get because Katherine is not here.

Dropping our saviour and main investor at her destination, I head down to the main artist entrance, grabbing a walkie-talkie on the way. I am to cue Garrry, who will cue the wonderful opening title video sequence I have designed to play on the screens. This is forty seconds long, and ends with a flash of white which Bobby Dickinson picks up on with a blast of white light into the audience to start the show. Then a city backdrop comes up, and Ne-Yo opens with *Billie Jean*.

Except none of this is going to happen until Katherine Jackson and the kids are in their seats. Quite where she is now nobody knows. We know she went to Montreal, we know she decided at the last minute not to go to the premiere of the Cirque show. We know she then flew to Hamburg and we know she reached Heathrow at some point yesterday. The transport department however, seem completely unable to locate Katherine, or the minibus she is in, and we are but 35 minutes from showtime. The spacious foyer, steps leading up to the player tunnel and doors either side to the dressing room areas, is crammed with people. There is a welcome desk, where increasingly stressed lovelies get the artists checked in. Wardrobe and make-up people mill around, ready to grab their charges and drag them to prep rooms carved with Kim's billowing drapes into chapels of transformation. Dancers, choreographers, managers and entourages all contribute to the station concourse feel. Chris is there too, anxiously looking at his watch. Jeffré's lawyer arrives, two very scantily clad nieces on his arm and he grins his shit eating, Californian-dentistry-designed grin from ear to ear. He asks me where his box is. I look at the nieces and tell him they are right there. The nieces giggle.

Jeffré is as Jeffré, nowhere to be seen. I ask Chris and he tells me he thinks he's in with La Toya. Garrry comes on the radio, asking for an update. I say I don't have one and stand by. He tells me Mallet is seriously concerned about the lack of people in front of the stage. I tell him security are working on it, pulling punters from the General Admission area on the floor and feeding them into the Golden Circle, for which hardly anyone has bought tickets. They are also taking people from the Golden Circle and getting them right up to the stage, but this process can only get up to speed once the punters are in the hall.

Just as I finish speaking a black minibus pulls up in the covered driveway outside and Katherine Jackson steps out. At the same moment, a portacabin on the other side of the roadway disgorges a dozen ballerinas, white tutus sparkling in the spill light of Harrison Funk's flashgun as he photographs the family. The surreal moment passes; the ballerinas make their way down towards the stage access and don't sow yet more confusion into an already over-crowded lobby. The children file into the mayhem; Paris looking beautiful, Prince looking normal, and Blanket staring blankly.

Suddenly and as if from nowhere, Ron's flight coordinator barges through the melee and greets Katherine and the children like a long lost friend, then guides them away. Chris manages to push his way to Katherine's side and exchange words as the bundle of Michael Jackson DNA heads towards the dressing room area. It's three minutes to showtime. I hold up my radio.

"She's going to say hello to the brothers before going upstairs," Chris shouts. "Five minutes!"

I tell Garrry it's going to be at least fifteen minutes, pass the radio to Chris, who is determined to stick close to Katherine, and tell him to tell Garrry when he wants to go. Then I head over to merchandising, grab some programmes and try to find Carol, the floor manager in charge of artists, so she can get as many signed by as many as possible. I also try to understand what the hell was going on between Ron's entourage and the Jackson family. Why did Katherine and the kids latch on to Ron's flight co-ordinator as if she was saving them from drowning? I give up and put it down to either the machinations surrounding them all for the last fifty years, or the fact they wanted to be sure to have their plane tickets home.

As I head towards Level Five and the President's Lounge, I hear the roar of the crowd as the house goes black. Seconds now, and my worst premonitions and harbingers of further disaster will be banished forever. I'm half way up some deserted stairs when I feel the tremble of the opening thunderclap I carefully put together, what feels like years ago, onto the head of the opening sequence. It's not just a library thunderclap you see, but an eighteen track audio construction of thunder, gunshots, cannon, explosions and car crashes. It is a perfect, seven second sonic metaphor for my time on *Michael Forever*.

By the time I find The Better, my kids and their friends, the opening bars of *Billie Jean* have kicked us off, and Ne-Yo is halfway through the first verse. Tears stream down my face as I look at this vast auditorium, fifty thousand people screaming with delight, the biggest lighting and screen rig ever installed in the stadium sparkling and flashing, the massive stage glowing, the show, my show, *Michael Forever*, finally getting under way.

The rest of the evening is a blur. I spend most of my time on the VIP level, moving between the boxes with the investors, the press and the President's Lounge, where the food is excellent and the chef has plainly listened to what I said back at the tasting. Sara Giles keeps asking for her signed programmes, but in a goldfish kind of way where each request is presented as a new one. Perhaps I am too insignificant, too far removed from her firmament of Indian cotton magnates and Ukrainian champagne dealers, the guys that put the money into QuickDraw, the hedge fund she controls, so she can take it out again and give it to us to stage this show. Then I realise that's more about my sensitivity than her lack of it, and I berate myself for stereotyping her. She has after all, stepped in at the last minute, funded us when nobody else would, saved the day and made those dark times in August morph into the powerful show in front of us on the stage. Everything around us is down to her faith in the product we are creating and her ability to find big bundles of cash.

Each time she asks me, politely, for some signed programmes for her kids, I smile and say "of course". Sara is the sort of person who, in a restaurant, makes her request of every waiter and waitress that passes her by, and then considers the seven extra forks, five more wine glasses and four plates of the same dessert as an excellent return on her investment. It shows a quiet and dogged determination and is probably what makes her a very successful financing producer.

I however, decide to give up on her request for now, see what Carol has managed to achieve at the end of the show and, if Sara is still in the building and not dead of lung cancer, give her the fucking programmes.

Just after the Beyoncé video, which goes down a storm with the audience, I am collared by PR hand maiden-in-chief who is desperate from some stills of Beyoncé doing the number. The Mail on Sunday will run a double page on the show if they get pictures of Ms Knowles in her afro wig. Both she and I have completely forgotten we went through all this a month ago, and I run around like an electrically charged lunatic for twenty minutes trying to figure out how I'm going to get the pictures.

Each time I turn a corner I bump into Mark Borkowski himself, who asks me for the Beyoncé stills. I assure him I'm getting them, run off to another part of the stadium, only to come across him once more. I begin to think there's more than one of him. That would explain how he straddles the world of media communication so successfully. The tape of Beyoncé's performance is with the video screens director, so I descend under the stage into the massive dungeon like space beneath it. It's full of quick change dressing rooms, lighting and PA racks, runners with radios and a nervous Christina Aguilera plus entourage doing a last minute warm up. I find the screen guy but he doesn't have the tape, telling me it was played on to the screens from the TV truck.

I run to the truck, cursing my knees and the fact I left my bike at the hotel. I mount the rickety metal steps and open the door really carefully and slowly, knowing from experience that anyone barging in is likely to receive a barrage of abuse from the control desk. I ask the head technician if we can get some stills off the tape, but he tells me they can do nothing until the interval because they are not configured for sport, where instant replays come out of a special box, but music, where everything is set to record. I say I'll come back, and leave as quietly as I came in.

Alex the Iron Grip paces outside the President's Lounge, looking more worried than I have ever seen him. I am relieved to have found him, for on my travels I have seen every TV screen in the public concourses showing the line output of the TV truck. I tell Alex to shut them down, straight away, because standing under virtually every TV is a member of the public pointing a smart-phone at the screen. I remember in one of our hundreds of discussions we thought putting the line cut up would be a good idea, but that was before Chris and Michael Henry gave personal undertakings to the High Court, under pain of imprisonment, that there would be no live transmission. Given that many of these punters would be uploading the images directly to YouTube, and with my brain too tired and emotional to clearly calculate through the rights issues, I thought it best to keep the two GLE bosses out of clink for now. Thinking about it now, I realise there was probably no breach because the TV pictures had no sound on them. Any audio on a YouTube upload would have come from the house PA, muffled, indistinct, and too far out of synchronisation with the images to have created a sync right.

That done, Alex tells me the stadium want to present a Welsh Wooden Spoon of Wonder to Katherine Jackson. From the serious look on his face, and the fact he is flanked by two older but still burly gentlemen in navy blazers, each sporting a sporting crest over the chest pocket, I begin to doubt that he is having a laugh.

"Let me introduce David Jones, the president of the Welsh Rugby Union, and Daffyd Jones, Chairman of Cardiff Millennium Stadium," says Alex, and I shake hands, make polite small talk about how wonderful the show is and I hope they are enjoying it, whilst all the time wondering how they breathe, given how bashed in their noses are. Like bulldogs I suppose. As one of them embarks on a long speech about the history of the Welsh Wooden Spoon of Wonder, I can only surmise that it's some kind of totemic item once used for removing coal dust rings off the sides of miners' baths, or for stirring trouble outside the gates of Chester during Michaelmas, but it proves to be none of these things, but a way to eat leek soup. Anyway, they tell me how honoured they would be for

Katherine to accept it. Two problems stand in the way of this however, the first is the whereabouts of Katherine, and the second the location of the spoon. I am assured minions have been despatched to find the thing, and could I get Katherine to come to the Presidents Lounge at half time (yes, they said half time) for the presentation. I promise to do my best if Alex gets the orange segments. The two pillars of Welsh rugby stare blankly at me for a few seconds until Alex rescues me with a small laugh. I trot off to find Katherine but bump into Chris. He tells me he is up to speed on the Welsh Wooden Spoon of Wonder, so I immediately cross it off my "to do" list.

Christina Aguilera closes part one of the show, and as she does so I suddenly remember the Beyoncé stills I pulled off the video weeks ago. I text the head hand maiden immediately telling her to check her emails and head out to the trucks to see how the recordings, both sound and vision, are getting on. In the 2D truck, Mallet is on form and enjoying himself. The 3D looks absolutely amazing, drum kits and dancers floating in front of my eyes as if I'm standing on stage with them. The audio truck is managing to curb and repair the worst acts of incompetence of the albino lizard Semblance. Our post-production producer is doing a sterling job, but she desperately needs a paper edit to know what to throw out straight away, and not waste time and money transferring and transporting to London for Monday morning. I grab her running order, draw red lines through the Rod Temperton stuff and tell her the rest will depend on performance. Having already seen Alien Ant Farm I cross out *PYT*, which was absolutely awful, worst even than if performed by a tone deaf primary school class. She also tells me we are under by twenty minutes on what was expected. I point out that Sky's 190 minutes of programme might be achievable without too much sacrifice after all, tell everybody they are doing a great job, and head back up to the VIP area.

Passing through the main concourse I have to battle though lines of men and women queuing for pints of watery lager, served in thin plastic beakers so flimsy they collapse under the pressure of the customer's hand as they try to pick up the six they bought in one hit. Then more queues, lining up to buy some kind of pink, rusk-, fat- and salt-filled torpedo slammed between two pieces of baked cotton wool, which they wolf down with yellow and red sauce that dribbles down the front of their national rugby shirts, the colours of the sauces blending with the colours of the team. Is that why red and yellow are the colours of Wales? If so, what does the green represent? Who knows? Who cares? I then push though lines of more men and women queuing for the toilets, where they evacuate the beer and the hot dogs they've just wolfed down, sometimes still wolfing as they enter the conveniences, before queuing up to buy more. If a process ever cried out for streamlining, this was it. A system of hoses springs to mind, one attachment from beer pump to mouth, another from urinary tract to toilet. Pop a coin or credit card operated meter somewhere within arm's reach, and the punter can stay in their seat all evening without getting in my way as I journey around the stadium. The pipes would have to be laid properly of course, neatly bundled together and not left snaking around the floor and causing a trip hazard. Liquidizing the hot dogs would allow them to be sent down the same pipes. I'm pleased to see the *Michael Forever* logo up on the TVs. Alex was not diverted enough by spoons to forget my request.

By the time I get back to the VIP level, the Welsh

Wooden Spoon of Wonder has been safely presented to Katherine, and one cannot but wonder what she made of it. Or with it. Part two, the second half as the rugby players would have it, has started. I watch some of it from the Millennium Stadium box. It still looks fantastic. The huge screens add so much power, have so much presence, that they light up the stadium almost as much as the hundreds of lights in the rig above.

The stage is massive, and on it as I watch is the amazing Yolanda Adams, delivering the most gutsy, super strong rendition of *Earth Song* I have ever heard. Backed by our thirty-strong gospel choir, the choirmaster in front of them dances and pummels and punches and writhes, his every move amplified on the screens, Yolanda's every perfect, sustained note is sent screaming, tearing through the air by the PA. Earlier JLS and the Jacksons, duetting *Can't Stop 'Til You Get Enough* asked the audience if they could feel Michael's spirit in the house tonight, and the audience screamed back "Yes!". It was true, you could. But now, as Yolanda took *Earth Song* to an incredible climax, that spirit, that strength of Michael Jackson's genius was not just felt in the room, but embraced, remembered and enjoyed. At least by me. The crowd loved it, the VIPs loved it, and even the hardened crew were softened by what they had heard and seen; Yolanda Adams had delivered the performance of the night. Thank you Ron, for fighting past Chris' ignorant arrogance to get her onto the show. It is a magical moment, and a truly world class performance. The tears are in my eyes again; this was everything I had hoped for, this was one of those never to be repeated events, this was Michael and right now he was forever.

CHAPTER 11.
ANDY PICHETA

Things come and they come and then they go
And where they go nobody knows

It always amazes me how fast an arena empties – not just of people, but of the energy, emotion and power that filled it just a few short minutes before. The ambience and the magic just evaporate away. The de-rig crew are already tearing into the lighting rig, which has dropped to a working height. The venue floor is ankle deep in discarded plastic cups and burger and hot dog wrappers, the harsh house lighting bathes everything in a vaguely green, bright uniform wash, an entire spectrum away from Bobby D's beams and swirls in two hundred and fifty-six colours. Lines of cleaners, highly visible in bright yellow jackets, make their way along the stands, a mini tsunami of rubbish piling before them as they go. The cherry pickers and scissor lifts bleep across the floor, orange hazard lights flashing. I walk briskly across this scene of almost devastation, heading for the artist area first and TV truck second. Someone thrusts a party invitation into my hand, and I tell them to make sure The Better gets three more for her and my kids. Heavy D's manager asks me for per diem, and I laugh. Purple emails me a demand from Dorsal Semen for two thousand dollars, per diem for the band so they aren't in any danger of losing any weight on the way back to Los Angeles. I respond to that one straight away:

Fuck 'em. Tell them Jennifer Hudson has the per diems.
Sent from my iPhone.

I bump in to Jeffré, who cuts off my congratulations with

a curt demand for the whereabouts of Chris and five grand for La Toya's per diem. Fucking hell, there's just no shame to these people; they'll keep sucking on the per diem teat until there is no teat left. On to the TV truck, where I sign off on the running order for the Sky Arts version of the show. An edit suite called Preditors in London, experienced in 2D and 3D post-production, will start making this assembly tonight. This means there will be something for me to look at and start fine tuning by Monday lunchtime. The post-production supervisor, Holly, raises a concern that the paper edit, the list of songs we are going to put into the programme, looks like it might be about forty minutes short of the four hours Sky Arts wants. I remind her that by the time applause, bumpers (the short ident stings that go either side of a commercial break) and end credits have been put in we should be okay. She says she's already allowed for all that extra time. I move on, leaving instructions for her to get hold of all the documentary material that has been filmed over the last few days, figuring that if we need to pad, we can throw in a load of Fearne Cotton interviewing and high fiving stars, and some flight cases being wheeled around. And there we were, just days ago, worrying about an over-long show!

She makes notes and barks, in the nicest possible way, at the truck crew, about the labelling of tapes and shipping instructions, and all the other detail that is so vital if you want to avoid sitting in an edit suite swearing blind there should be a close up shot of the guitarist for that one bar of music where he goes "da-lan-dan-dan-a-lan dan-dan", whilst assistants and runners and tape ops run around like lunatics trying to locate one tape out of fifty, and you begin to seriously consider going through all seventy five hours of rushes to find it. I swear inwardly that I will hire Holly on every shoot I do from now on; she's calm, efficient, good-humoured and first class. She's also very attractive, in an English rose, minor public school way and even DDD^M is reduced from wily fox to simpering puppy whenever she is near.

I don't find Chris on my travels but I do find his senior financial elf who, with five grand in his satchel, is seriously worrying about getting mugged. I remind him he has been constantly mugged since he started working on *Michael Forever* and relieve him of the cash, promising I'll make sure it gets to where it needs to get to. I sign for it and stuff the envelope containing two hundred and fifty twenty pound notes down my trousers. As I head off to find a car to take me to the Oceana nightclub, which we have booked for our after show party, I look like a porn star because five grand is fairly bulky. Once there I freak out my son Rob by giving him the money and telling him to look after it. He's a serious seventeen, so stands rooted to the spot. Other sons would wave over the nearest drug dealer. I'm proud that he is more mature than I have ever been.

Gin-hazed, raucous flashes of memory are all that remain of that night: Drunken Welsh tarts and even drunker crew; a leery Paul King salivating oral pre-cum over anything in a skirt; Purple gyrating on the dance floor whilst simultaneously downing eight G&Ts at a time; slurry congratulations and enough back patting to fill many back packs. I spot a heavily guarded empty square of sofas held on reserve in case the Jacksons turn up and burn the last hours of my authority on insisting I sit there.

As I do I think: Fucking hell, we've made it! I finally find Chris and tell him he has the balls of ten bullocks, which of course is nonsense, because bullocks have no bollocks. I tell him he's pulled off something amazing and unique, yet deep inside I have uneasiness that it is a fucked thing, a Ripley-gone-wrong from *Alien Resurrection,* and that it was only the last minute cash injection from Sara Giles' fund that got us here at all. Just as I have that thought Chris tells me he's been avoiding Giles since the end of the show. I'm too pissed to see it as anything more than keeping investors at arm's length whilst partying a little of their money away.

Back at the hotel, at a very respectable two am, and the parties continue. Christina has commandeered the ground floor terrace, where she sits surrounded by acolytes and patio heaters, both giving off equal quantities of warmth. Jamie Foxx and Smokey Robinson are at the bar, swapping tour war stories. JLS and Leona Lewis sit in the lounge area laughing and drinking. Pixie Lott, Fearne Cotton and Craig David are having some food, talking quietly and earnestly in a banquette. I'm tired, a little drunk, and with nothing to say to any of them I head up to my suite which, despite the demands of Ne-Yo, Heavy D and a cohort of others, I have managed to hang on to. I ponder that I build the Rolls Royces, put them on the road and make them purr; I have no experiences or common ground to share with those who ride in them.

* * *

It's Monday afternoon and I'm at Preditors in a two-hundred-and-fifty-year-old terraced house on Newman Street. Who knows what centuries of debauchery took place here? Right now however, it's about as un-debauched as a space can be. What was once the front parlour is now the reception area: Tastefully stripped oak floors, a warm coloured leather sofa and a coffee table groaning under bowls of fruit, vases of flowers, and periodicals about post-production. I meet Reg, who reminds me we have met before, in a disused church in St John's Wood that housed an early video edit suite. Simon West and I did all our editing there, back in the day of Mel and Kim and Rick Astley and one inch analogue video tape. We would come in the evening, because the hourly rate was cheaper, and our editor, whose father had worked with David Lean, would shake out the keyboard before commencing work. Godley and Cream had been in during the day, and the amount of coke residue in between the keys was enough to keep us going through the night. But that was then and this is now. Three editors have been working round the clock to create Sky's 190 minute version of the show, and they are about half way there.

We have all the 2D rushes, the recordings of each camera's output, but none of the 3D material. This is annoying as the really great crane positions, and the best dolly tracks positioned nearest the stage, had 3D cameras mounted on them. The head of the 3D truck, one of the best in the world and operating out of Holland, had agreed, just before the show, with Chris, that he would not pack up and leave when the live-to-air transmissions were pulled, but hold on to the 3D camera tapes until he was paid. This magnanimous gesture meant however, that as we waited for the ticket revenues to come in, we had no 3D camera material to use in the 2D Sky show, and no time to wait for their eventual arrival. We ploughed on, inserting shots over the very safe and quite dull line cut, to make every number as exciting and dramatic as possible. The performers had charged through their songs, and we faced the running time problem Holly had highlighted earlier. She and the editor asked me to look again at Alien Ant Farm's rendition of *PYT*. They said they had spent some time on it and thought it looked okay. It was dreadful. No amount of fast editing can disguise a crap performance. An overweight sweating Alien Ant stomped around the stage hitting every note but the right one, trying some moves in the same way old, fat Steven Segal tries some moves, and you think, as the audience to both: Sit down in a comfy chair, have some Horlicks, and give it up gracefully.

I tell them to use more 'B' roll, the backstage stuff of a happy Fearne Cotton being friends with absolutely everyone, and that *PYT* is out and stays out, because to put it in would not be the sort of tribute anyone would want, to anybody. Then I ring Chris to chase up the payments to the 3D truck so we can get our hands on some of the footage we need.

"We won't get the ticket money, at least not from WorldPay, because Sara Giles has sequestered the GLE bank account, and we can't get to the money. So the 3D truck won't be paid for a while. You'll have to work with what you have."

This time, with this latest in a long line of body blows to *Michael Forever*, I don't feel sick, just tired and fed up of the struggle up a hill of treacle this job has been from day one. I resolve I will do my duty, deliver the two versions to Sky whatever it takes, and walk away. Together with the money for the 3D truck and hundreds of other suppliers, my fee has been locked up by QuickDraw. But I concentrate on the job at hand, choosing to ignore the wider predicament I am now in. I don't have time to ponder why Sara has acted in this way.

"We'll need to pay this post house before they release the tapes, and we'll need the audio as well. Are you going to be able to make these payments, or am I just wasting my time here?"

Chris is conciliatory, patient. He repeats what I have heard a number of times before, assures me he is diverting ticket money from other agencies to Iambic, reminding me of the importance of the delivery to Sky.

I just want it over with. I can see the end of my involvement once the two versions of the programme are delivered to Sky. Not far now. It's not just a loyalty to Chris that drives me, it's twenty eight years in the business, of doing everything necessary to get a film finished and delivered to client. I don't care what it takes, I don't care about the blood spilt on the way, all I care about is that it's the best possible film we could have made and that I am not found wanting in its creation. Am I a fucking dinosaur?

When we sat in the board room at Sky's Isleworth headquarters, way back in August, and when Chris read out his list of artists (despite our knowledge at the time that several on that list were most definitely going to be elsewhere, otherwise engaged, or able to be anywhere but at Cardiff Millennium), the Sky execs got terribly excited, spiralling and ramping up their delight for the project so much that for a moment I thought they might rename Sky One *'Michael Jackson'*. The mutual adoration and back slapping continued for the entire meeting. Chris mentioned a price of two million quid, and still the execs virtually moonwalked with joy. We parted smiling, cheering almost at our good fortune and theirs. I even gave the life size Homer Simpson, sitting with his life sized family on a life sized sofa in reception, watching a real TV pumping out what would soon become *The Michael Jackson Channel*, a friendly pat on the shoulder. We were buddies now, sleek programming racehorses in the same stable, eating Rupert Murdoch's hay like it was the only hay in town.

This early euphoria soon dissipated. Head of Programmes needed to clear the acquisition with Head of

Channel, who was on holiday in Tuscany. Head of Compliance needed signed artist contracts and Head of Legal needed to talk to Head of Television before progressing the deal. All of them needed Head of Scheduling to run the numbers past Head of Comeuppance, who was also on holiday, also in Tuscany. By the time Head of Channel got back to his desk, Head of Programmes was on holiday, not in Tuscany, and Head of Legal was off on maternity leave. Somewhere between Isleworth and Tuscany the price Sky was willing to pay dropped down to seventy thousand pounds. Chris never confided that to me, but he did repeat and repeat his desperate need for a UK TV showing of the concert, on any channel, at any price. Had Sky pulled out, our multi-million pound, showcase tribute to Michael Jackson may have had its world TV premiere on Bid Up TV or The Shopping Channel, or any channel that had a blanket music licence in place with the MCPS.

You might recall the existence of Blanket Secondary Licences, PSMPLAs and that Iambic had one which had expired. Chris had re-applied to the MPCS, and been assured it would be granted at their September monthly board meeting. That board meeting came and went without Iambic's licence being renewed. A second reassurance about a second board meeting, at the end of September, also came to nothing. The October monthly meeting also passed without the vital paper being released. Chris began to wonder whether someone at the MCPS had made a link between Iambic Media Limited, of 89 Whiteladies Road, Bristol, and Global Live Events LLP, registered at the same address. Did Warner Chappell have a representative on the MCPS board? Possibly, and by early October the publishing giant had made their attitude to GLE very clear. It would not therefore, be way beyond the realms of reality for the MCPS to have a good idea why Iambic was so keen to get a secondary licence, and for them to be nervous in granting it and, by doing so, upsetting Warner Chappell – one of their biggest members.

Even once the prized secondary licence landed in his pocket, Chris needed a UK transmission of the programme, under a broadcaster's primary blanket agreement, for the secondary rights to be triggered. No primary use, no secondary use. Now you could argue that selling a thirteen million pound production to Sky TV for seventy grand was not really any kind of primary use at all, but such a view would question what the primary use would then actually be, and whether Chris had the rights to such a use. This was the issue for Warner Chappell, used by their lawyers to get the injunction against any live-to-air transmission. Fortunately for Chris, the issues were complex enough to require a full hearing, which meant the show could actually go ahead and be recorded (of course it could have gone ahead regardless, as live performance rights are automatically covered by payments to the Performing Rights Society. The legality of recording it however, would then be resolved in court).

Regardless of the rights questions, my job as media producer was to produce some media. By the middle of the week following the concert we had Sky's long version more or less edited. For speed and ease, the editing had been done with low resolution pictures and the rough audio mix from the night. Now the programme had to be finished. The edit was automatically rebuilt with high resolution images, and the sweetened audio was prepared separately and elsewhere for matching up to the picture. Once built, the pictures needed grading – changing the contrast and colours to make everything look vibrant and crisp.

For a brisk and exciting thirty six hours our major female act occupied much of my time, as Christina left Cardiff less than happy with her performance of *Dirty Diana*. Her music producer and agents were sent, on demand, a copy of both her songs, and while *Smile* was smiled on, *Dirty Diana* was not. Had anyone asked me prior to uploading the tracks for Christina to view I would have told them to hang fire until the edited versions were ready. The line cut was very dreary, missed most of the complex dancer action in *Dirty Diana*, was ungraded and with crappy live audio, so it looked and sounded shit. It's a big leap of faith for an artist to see something rubbish, and yet trust it's going to be great when completed – especially when there's no previous working relationship to help the judgment along. I spent a day re-cutting *Dirty Diana*, and Christina was enamoured enough with the result to agree to sweeten both her tracks, and the final audio was repaired and no doubt re-voiced by her in New York. I needed to turn the *Dirty Diana* thing around because we desperately needed the five minutes in the show; we had used every frame of Fearne, of backstage antics, of dancer warm ups and artist interviews and we only just made it to time.

Finally, on the Thursday the programme was ready, on two tapes, to be delivered to Sky. I had turned it around in record time, a feat only made possible by the dedication and skills of everyone at the post-production house and the calm fearlessness of the redoubtable Holly. But, before delivering the tape we had to enter the mysterious and magical world of Professor Harding, a snake oil salesman and low rent conjurer, who had magicked up a quite spectacular circularity of problem and solution, one that vortexes tons of TV cash into his stuttering coffers, and one that was to throw a sparkling spanner into my delivery schedule.

A few years previously, Professor Harding had lobbied the government for a solution to the problem of his epileptic patients bursting into fits whilst watching TV. The government had listened, and made it law for all TV programmes to comply with a set of standards he, Professor Harding, had drawn up. To ensure compliance, Harding invented a box that analysed television pictures for epilepticity. Ofcom, the broadcasting regulator, then made it compulsory for every programme to be tested by this box. Harding owned the box. Exceptions were made for news programmes, imported programmes and feature films. In these cases, Ofcom demanded an announcement be made, warning viewers that the upcoming programming contained flashing images.

Editors hated this encumbrance. The box appeared arbitrary in its findings, it was protected by patent and no third parties were allowed to create software that would resolve the picture issues without the need for expensive testing and retesting, and it was expensive.

* * *

Part One of the long Sky version came back with over sixteen hundred fails from the Harding box. One thousand, six hundred occasions during the programme where something in the image was deemed epilepsy sensitive. The editors groaned and started replacing shots, toning down the grade, doing what they could to get the pass certificate without which Sky would not accept delivery of the programme. A day later, and the tape was tested again, at six hundred quid per go, only to come back with two hundred and fifty fails, many of which were new, unidentified in the previous pass. Meanwhile, part two was sent off. This did better, but still required over a thousand fixes. Over half of these were in Christina's fast cut, dramatically lit performance of *Dirty Diana*. Too dramatic and too fast for the Harding box, an absolute arbiter of visual style, applying criteria to pictures that had nothing to do with the creative process of film making. What a bastard!

I spend hours on the phone with Head of Acceptance at Sky, arguing that *Michael Forever* is an acquisition for them (and therefore exempt from Harding), and a gutsy, dramatic music show. Surely, instead of wasting all this time and money and editing the programme to make it worse, they could make the announcement – give the verbal warning about flashing images? In fact I'll do it for them, build it into the title sequence and each beginning of part bumper. Serious, sombre:

"The following film contains flashing lights, strobing effects and fast edits. It needs to do so to make Christina look good, and present a much better film than you will otherwise see. So forgive me for narrowing your viewing choices if you are prone to fits. Coronation Street is available on another channel. Or you could watch and re-watch the Royal Wedding press conference, where Will and Kate drown in camera flash. Now that really will get you going, and probably blow up any Harding box it's put through."

No, no and no, comes the answer. I play my final card:

"I won't be able to make delivery tomorrow."

"That's okay, have another week."

Somewhere within the *Michael Forever* communications grid, a creaky, leaky thing at the best of times, Sky's decision to delay the broadcast of the long version, on minority channel Sky Arts, was lost in transit, and not relayed to the coal face. Head of Biscuits tells me Chris knew days ago. I ask about the

Sky One sixty minute version, which DDD^M is to start editing next week, ready for an October 21 transmission, just eleven days away, Trafalgar Day and my birthday. She tells me that's nothing to do with her, it's Sky One, and I must talk to Head of Oneness. I get the same response: No Harding Pass, no acceptance, breach of contract, big slaps on wrists all round. I warn DDD^M and he tells me not to worry, he has tricks up his sleeve to fool the box. Good-oh. I leave the edit suite around nine that night feeling I've survived another day, solved the Harding thing (kind of), and taken a step closer to completing my duty and finally getting out of Dodge.

  Half an hour later, and the issues with Sky and Harding and the re-edits all fall to second place. QuickDraw and Sara Giles, not content with seizing the ticket money, have come after the film. They've found Preditors and their lawyers have contacted one of the editor partners, breathing fire and warning of dire consequences if any materials are released to Iambic. QuickDraw owns the film, they say. Iambic has no right to exploit it, and they want everything locked in a cupboard and for it to stay there. Emails fly between the post house, QuickDraw's legal eagles Wiggin LLP (yes, Wiggin, like Muggin and Friggin) and Chris, who is apoplectic with anger. I just see it as another, further, additional fucking hurdle put up between me and the exit from this terrible thing. I WILL deliver to Sky, and I don't care HOW I do it. But I need the editors to stay on side. I phone them, talk to them, explain that just because a lawyer says something doesn't make it the law. Judges and court cases and judgements make things the law and so far there haven't been any. Right now Wiggin is demanding action, against the interests of Iambic the client, on the basis of their legal opinion. I have a different opinion, as does Chris, and so far we have not been proved wrong. I send the editor an email:

Reg, ignore this cunt, I'll deal with him in the am

Erudite, concise and a fine distillation of my position. I stop only to curse Harding and his box for the delay they caused. Had it not been for his stupid box and his stupid expert postulations listened to at the highest levels of government the tapes would have been in Sky's reception by now, signed for and delivered. As it was, Part One was at Preditors and Part Two at the Harding facility (the larger facilities leased boxes from Harding, smaller one like the one we were using couldn't afford the tens of thousands a year that the Prof demands). The audio has yet to be released because Red TRX, who recorded the show sound, has not been paid. The edit house has not been paid. A sound editor has not been paid. Chris asks me for a mission critical list of people needing money. It's plain I am not on that list, neither is the lovely Holly, nor Dawn who has put in an extra week, nor any number of runners, young people starting out in the business desperate for cash, nor car service companies, travel agents, lighting companies, camera houses, hotels, caterers, riggers, set designers, drape providers, make-up artists, dancers, costumers, security providers; the names go on and on and on, each a provider of services, labour or equipment, not from the goodness of their heart but as their way of making a living. The runners I feel for especially, and I use some of the five grand I liberated at the stadium to pay a few of them. The rest goes on keeping the job and me afloat.

I give Chris the list of people who can prevent delivery by hanging on to tapes. He pays them. The edit house agrees to release what we need. The sound drives arrive and the audio is laid back onto the masters.

A worry filled day follows as all the elements are put together and copies made. Wiggin continue to threaten everybody, repeating demands for the work to cease. I am certain they will send the boys in, combat boots and cargo pants, to grab the tapes and stop me in my tracks. Every time the entry buzzer goes I prepare to do battle with whatever QuickDraw forces come through the door. Charming, nice telly people come and go, giving worried glances at the tense, pacing madman who won't leave the reception area and who stares at them, challenging them to do anything, say anything, come anywhere near the machine room where copies are being run and audio tracks laid onto masters. Finally the tapes are ready to go.

I nervously check the outside of the house, looking up and down Newman Street. Even now, an attempt at physically securing the materials could be made by the opposition. It's what I'd do. Burst in, hard and fast and noisy, grab the tapes and let the lawyers argue the toss. But the coast is clear. I stuff the tapes into two Tesco bags, put two bananas on the top, load up the offered swanky branded post house carrier bag with yachting magazines and a Yellow Pages, and step out of the door. This is the critical time, when they know exactly where the tapes are, in the open and vulnerable, when a move has most chance of success. The Tesco bag decoy will buy only seconds. Nothing happens. A taxi cruises past. I check the driver, to make sure this is not a clever trick to get the tapes, but he's fat, disinterested and with the air of resigned misery that marks him as a genuine London cabbie. Waving the Yellow Pages I get him to stop.

"Isleworth please, Sky TV."

I settle back in my seat, check behind for a car either haring up the road after me or pulling out of a parking space to follow but again, nothing. Ha! Wiggin wigged out. Forty minutes later the tapes are at Gatehouse 1 and I walk down to Osterley tube station, happily clutching a delivery note signed by Head of Tape Traffic.

* * *

A few days in Scotland follow, during which the plaintive pleas and desperate demands for payment ramp up. Dozens a day want to know when they are to receive their money. I forward them to Chris and his financial elf. Chris is embattled, assaulted on all sides by creditors, by QuickDraw, by Warner Chappell. Of Jeffré, there is no sign and Paul King has disappeared. I can see the whole crumbling edifice is falling apart, masonry crashing to the ground, columns collapsing, water bursting through walls. The rent on Shaftsbury Avenue is overdue, the tax man is unpaid. Chris is trying to divert ticket revenues to Iambic instead of GLE, which is about to go into administration. He's hoping for a VAT reclaim, but even he admits it's nowhere near enough to get everyone paid. Where the money is coming from I have no idea. The whole thing has become even uglier, even more upsetting. I hire a voice over artist, and direct him by phone to deliver the stings, announcements and other bits and pieces we need to make the one hour version. I feel really, really uncomfortable doing so, as I suspect he will not be paid for his work. I'm near tears yet again, on the verge of quitting, but still I persevere. Fool. Instead of resigning I urge Chris and Michael Henry to come clean with the array of people they owe money to. I even write the letter for them, leaving blanks for them to fill in.

MICHAEL FOREVER THE TRIBUTE CONCERT October 19th 2011
Dear All,

We apologise for the lack of information and confusion over outstanding payments. I assure you this is not borne out of any reason other than a daily, sometimes hourly, changing situation. I understand you all need to know what is going on, so I'm laying out the facts as they stand.

The financing of this concert and its filming comes from numerous small investors, together with bridge funding from a hedge fund [SARA GILES]. The latter has a charge over the main GLE account into which WorldPay has deposited ticket revenue from our direct sales. This amounts to £…

On Friday, [SARA GILES] acted to debenture the account and denied us access to it. This was done just as the WorldPay revenues hit the account. We immediately issued to her a list of payments that were scheduled to be made from this account to meet contractual obligations to artists and suppliers. To date she has chosen not to make these payments.

Over the weekend and on Monday, we acted to assign the rights to the show, and the right to receive further ticket monies, to Iambic Entertainment. It is Iambic that already owns the media rights to the show. This assignment is now complete and Ticketmaster, together with other agencies, are due to make payments into the Iambic account tomorrow and Friday. This will amount to £… Assuming broadcast critical payments can be made from this account in time for Sky's transmission this weekend and next Thursday, Sky will pay £… by… We expect to finalise a US TV deal for around $3 million. This will happen by……… At the beginning of November, Iambic will receive a VAT rebate, already agreed and signed off by HMRC of £……

We are in advanced negotiations to release Michael Forever theatrically as a 3D and 2D motion picture. This will attract film funding in the order of £………..

All these revenues will ensure that everyone is paid eventually, but they all depend on those who have licenced or assigned rights to continue to grant *them under their contract terms. To assuage the understandable anger and concern, we ask you to levy late payment charges on outstanding amounts of 1% per month from the date of the concert.*

Yours faithfully
Chris Hunt and Michael Henry
Partners, Global Live Events LLP

Needless to say, they didn't send it out, so the concern and confusion continues to increase. They argue that to send such a letter would tip their hand to Sara Giles. Much later I learn that on the show day, October 8, as I was going round everybody reassuring them that everything would be okay, Chris and Michael were resigning as partners from Global Live Events. That too would account for their reluctance to come clean to those that made the show and film.

The assurances however, keep rolling in. Chris tells me he has nearly completed the process of transferring the ownership of film into Iambic, where it will be safe from QuickDraw. He tells me there's a $30 million deal on the table, from a major US player.

Meanwhile the one hour Sky version moves along. Mallet is digitising his material at Onsite, the edit suite he has used since I've known him. He expects to start editing on Monday, and be finished by October 21. I'm cheered this date is not after the thing is supposed to go out, and talk to Head of Oneness again to clear a fast turnaround once they get the tape. She tells me the broadcast of the one hour version is being put back a week.

* * *

My son has become an avid American football fan. Back in September at a hotel meeting, I learned that the Chicago

Bears were due to stay at the Intercontinental in London for their Wembley NFL game against the Tampa Bay Lobsters on October 22, to which I had tickets. As GLE had spent over one hundred and fifty grand with the hotel I figured I was due another big discount, so I asked for a room. Last time they gave me a suite. This time there were no such promises, because my suite would be full of quarterbacks, and they offered only a small discount on the room. Still, it put my son in the same building as his footballing heroes so I figured it was worth it. I checked in on the Friday night and gave a credit card at the desk.

Earlier in the day I was at Preditors. QuickDraw's lawyers had not persuaded them to hang on to everything so I loaded up all the tapes they still had, copies of the masters, the audio and anything else I could lay my hands on. I signed for it all, bundled it into a big box and threw that into the back of a taxi, which I directed to the Intercontinental. There I stored it with the concierge. Not even Wiggin, with all their digging, will find it there. An Iambic elf is dispatching a courier van from Bristol to collect the box.

All this cloak and dagger is necessary because, like the giant alien spaceships in *Independence Day*, when they locate the president at Area 51, Wiggin has found Onsite, Mallet's edit suite, and are heading over there, at least electronically. David had finished editing, and booked the grade, a specialist process that enhances the pictures and has the power to solve Harding problems, to start Saturday morning at yet another facility. Sara Giles' storm-troopers unleashed an impressive email barrage which had Mallet's facility manager, a thin, once-young man called Tony, in a complete panic. The poor guy was being threatened with all manner of legal pain if he let so much as a single frame of film out of the building. From the other side first I, and then Chris, were pointing out, vigorously, that we were the client, not Wiggin or QuickDraw or Sara Giles, and they were seriously fucking up the post schedule, and jeopardising the delivery to Sky as a result. Tony had taken legal advice, and his lawyers told him to do nothing.

Unfortunately nothing, in this case, was not a neutral position, because it was exactly what Sara's Whigs wanted. The emails fly but Tony is not budging, so I hatch a plan to construct an alternative one hour version down in Bristol. Everything I need is in the box at the Intercontinental, and will soon be winging its way down the M4.

Eventually, and with undertakings from the grading house that he'll get them back into Onsite and they'll go nowhere else, Tony relents and releases the tapes so Mallet can grade. Unfortunately, this doesn't happen until late Saturday evening, so the grading cannot start until Monday. I make plans to go to Bristol and start to build another one hour version on the same day, as I have no confidence that Tony will release the tapes to Iambic at all. He's just too scared of the Wiggers, too worried to let go of his only leverage with Iambic.

For the rest of the weekend I enjoy my birthday, encourage my son to stalk some NFL players around the hotel, and lay some more smoke to cover what I'm about to do next week.

> FROM: Andy Picheta Friday 21 October 2011 14:36
> Today is my last day on Michael Forever. You've all been amazing and it's been an honour to work with you. Except you Doreen, you're a wanker.
> Bye

I send it to everyone, and get a few back saying nice

things, a few LOLs. I also get this one:

> FROM: Doris Slugfuck
>
> Ha!
>
> That's really funny. When I saw you in London and Cardiff you didn't say anything to my face. You were riding your bike around the arena like a retard!
>
> In fact when I came up to your face you said nothing. Even when I called you a "Bitch" in front of my whole crew...You did nothing. Like I said...You talk hard on the phone, but in person your (sic) a used tampon!
>
> Like right now, you and GLOBAL LIVE are hiding from people that you owe money to! That's what you guys do best is hide! Like some in the closet homosexuals! Anytime your (more sic) in the LA area please look me up. I would love to show you how we do it in america. You fucking idiot.
>
> Kill yourself....Twice...No one would give a shit.

See! I told you he was lovely! And he sent it to everybody! What a wanker! Fun with Dorsal aside (although he was and remains right about the money), the email saying goodbye was quite a cliff-top moment for me. I had delivered the long version to Sky, and I would do the same with the one hour film, mine or Mallet's, it didn't matter, and when I had done that, I would complete my duty to Chris and be able to walk away. Limp, wounded, bruised, battered and emotionally drained, back to Scotland, where I could hide, switch the phone off, ignore the emails, and finally get some peace. I was hired to do a job of work and, despite the shambolic, devious and underhand behaviour of my friend and employer, I had succeeded in my task. But I felt not elated at having pulled off the near impossible, but dirty, abused and ultimately guilty that I had drawn hundreds of people into something they were now regretting. The freelance world is tough, for suppliers and crew alike, and to work and not get paid is just wrong, ugly, and upsetting. Chris' inability to be straight with these people, just like his inability to be straight with the fans, was not a new character trait. But *Michael Forever* was several times bigger than anything else he had ever done, and so the evasions and deceit had been bigger too.

But first to Bristol, where there is no decent hotel, and three days of editing and finishing at an edit suite still willing to work with Iambic. I have to go on. The film has taken on a life of its own. It's bigger than my fear, bigger than my loyalty, bigger than anything else. On the Monday morning Mallet rings to tell me he needs another day and a half to get the show through Harding. He asks me where I am, and I lie, hating myself for it. I tell him Sky need the tape before the coming Friday, and he assures me he will have finished in good time. He tells me my goodbye email was silly. Sorry dad. We talk about the likelihood of Tony releasing the tape to Sky, and Mallet feigns ignorance of any legal shenanigans.

"My dear boy, I'm just doing my job, but I doubt Tony will release anything until he is paid."

But Chris can't pay him the sixteen grand or so that is still outstanding, because the coffers are completely empty. He cannot pay the rent to his Chinese landlord of Shaftsbury Avenue either, nor can he pay any of the two or three million quid he owes to the UK film and event production industry. The gravity of the situation permeates the Bristol Iambic office, creating a somewhat tense and unhappy atmosphere, but also an unreal one, the false-calm eye of a raging storm. Chris' most senior elf is gone, as she promised. Her workspace, overlooking Whiteladies Road, is as she left it. Needing a computer, I and the remaining elf finally crack the password, which turns out to be the name of her dog. Chris makes a weak attempt at humour, something about the end of the need for political correctness now the elf is gone, but it's obvious the feeling is that the Russians are at the Brandenburg Gate and it's only a matter of time. Can he really be so dismissive over the end of a twenty five year relationship? Then he disappears into his office and sets about getting some money out of his wife's trust fund.

It takes me a day to edit the long version down to an hour, including some music edits in Yolanda Adam's amazing performance of which I am very proud (completely seamless, I guarantee not even she would spot them!). It takes the Bristol facility three more days to finish the piece. I'm fortunate that I'm working from copies of the delivered master, so it's all Harding compliant and properly graded. I chop the show down, using audience shots from unused songs to cover the cuts. Quite why it takes three days to online the thing I have no idea, but I've experienced post-production Bristol style before, and it's never as fast and as slick as in the capital. This is not a unique thing, I've posted stuff all over the place and found the same differences in attitude, skill and approach: Los Angeles is great, Minneapolis less so, Paris is okay, Marseilles is a struggle. But at least the bouillabaisse is better there than in Bristol.

I have no choice but to hang around and wait for the tape. I avoid the office, avoid the depressing post house up the road. I spend my time in pubs and coffee bars, using my own money for a crappy hotel and a train back to London, a flight up to Scotland. My iPhone gets pushed email after email; from the ground transport company owed eighty thousand, from an LA based travel agent owed two hundred thousand dollars, from the lovely guys with the 3D truck, owed over a third of a million pounds, from runners owed just several hundred – but to them as important as the bigger sums to the bigger people. Car crash after car crash after car crash.

Talking to Chris, which I do less and less, I try to gain an understanding of how this could have gone so terribly, awfully wrong. With some thinking time now that I'm at the last hours of my involvement with this thing, I try to work out why Sara Giles, the biggest investor, has jumped on the ticket money, locked it away and is after the film. Chris tells me it's because she wants to sell the project short, make a fire sale to Universal that would raise enough money to get her investors out, but shaft every creditor and a pile of other people who put money in. Yes, but why?

"Because she got nervous. When the Peas pulled out, the sponsor pulled out, and ten million dollars of revenue went up in smoke, followed by another twenty or thirty from the Facebook feed".

This last, huge sum was lost because of the Warner Chappell injunction against any live broadcast. Chris describes it, Peas pulling out, the injunction, and QuickDraw's action, as a perfect storm raging against *Michael Forever*. He has more to say about Sara Giles too, his one-time saviour and 'all round nice person'.

"When the shit hit the fan, and I got the Peas refund QuickDraw had paid directly to the agent back into GLE, she went completely hostile. She told me to pay the money back, breach any agreement I had to, to make the thing work. Little did she know I would choose to breach the agreement with her"

Eventually I leave Bristol, without the tape which the local facility has still not managed to release to me, and head back to Paddington on the train. Chris assures me I can go, that I've completed my mission, but it doesn't feel like that. The failure runs deep, has done for months, and I take a lot of it with me on the journey north.

It turned out that my efforts in Bristol were not needed after all, surplus to requirements, as Tony did release the Mallet master to Sky. This was in return for a binding instruction from Chris for Sky to pay Tony directly out of the proceeds. Like everyone else, he remains unpaid.

* * *

It took me about a week and a half to even begin to emerge from the shock of it all. During those first ten days, I moped around the hotel, chopped some wood, talked to some guests. I couldn't sleep, couldn't focus. News kept filtering up from England. News that Sky had pulled both broadcasts. News of Chris and Michael Henry walking away from Global Live Events, a process started on October 8th, the day of the show. News that GLE was going in to administration.

Creditors and investors were being divided up by Chris between GLE and Iambic. This division seemed completely arbitrary, no rhyme or reason behind it. The film, the major asset, now belonged to Iambic, so that was where any revenues would go, and any payments hopefully come from. Michael Henry's favoured investors were assured a return from Iambic, as were TV suppliers and anyone else Chris felt was worthy of paying. Many suppliers to the show were left in the cold, as creditors to GLE, where there was little money. An LA based travel agent, owed two hundred thousand dollars, desperately tried to secure at least some payment, but she was ignored. Finally she revoked the Jacksons' plane tickets home, so they had to make their own way back. As promised, the agent told of her misfortune to TMZ, who ran the story. Good for her!

Cee Lo Green wasn't paid, Yolanda Adams wasn't paid. Nobody was paid, except those that had a chance of shutting Chris down, or those smart enough, like Doreen and the band, to get paid up front.

* * *

My stay at the Intercontinental comes back to haunt me when the hotel puts forty thousand pounds of charges on my American Express card. Apparently they did the same to Chris, Ron Weisner and Harrison Funk. I alert the AmEx fraud team. Chris did actually give them his card to underwrite the bill, but we – employees of GLE – certainly did not. I checked and rechecked my deal memo: Nowhere was there a clause making me liable for London hotel charges! Nowhere did I agree to pay for extra cotton buds ordered by Heavy D, who sadly died on the plane journey back to LA. Of Jeffré, of the Parojim there was no sign. Paul King had not been seen since show day. I ask Chris for assistance with Amex and the Intercontinental. I need proof I was employed by GLE and acting on their behalf to make this go away, but Chris is unable to help: he too has been hit by the Intercontinental and told them he is nothing to do with GLE. Chris refers me to Michael, who also cannot do anything, as he has resigned from GLE. Thanks guys.

Everyone had gone to ground, leaving just Chris with his ginger head still sticking up above the parapet, still shooting at everyone – defiant, unremorseful, dogged. What once seemed magnificent now appeared daft. What once was a fierce determination to get through was now reinforcing his inability to see reality. A man that once appeared clever and resourceful is now nothing but a hustler playing a sad shell game where there are no Peas. The snail had reached the ark, and burned it to the ground.

* * *

Cirque du Soleil presents *The Michael Jackson Immortal World Tour*. It's a huge success, and sells out around the world. Backed by the estate, backed by Katherine Jackson, the Jackson children, the Jackson brothers – including Jermaine – the show, the spin off album and no doubt soon the DVD sell, and will sell, in the millions. It's a perfect exploitation: it feels right, it's done right and the fans and customers flock to it, cheering a sleek, well designed supercar flying round the entertainment track powered by the music of Michael Jackson. By contrast *Michael Forever*, built on deception, driven by hubris yet powered by the same fuel, lies broken in the ditch. I've tried to tell, from my perspective, how it got there, and why *Michael Forever* became no Ferrari, but an unwanted DeLorean.

The last part of this sorry tale, about what happens to the smouldering remains, is still unfolding. Central to that process, is the move from stadium to courtroom.

CHAPTER 12
THE WIGS OF WIGGIN

Through my joy and my sorrow
In the promise of another tomorrow

The Chancery Division building in London is squeaky new. A wall of sheet glass reflects the aged Portman stone of the Victorian Royal Courts of Justice next door. Rotating glass doors, engraved with rampant lions and unicorns and crowned griffons, arranged into the logo of The Law, swish me into a marbled foyer, spacious, clean, and dominated by a wall sized eighteenth century mural of the Pool of London, with modern buildings superimposed on it. All this, the wall suggests, this trade, this industry, this business, this progress, is possible because we have The Law.

Further access is barred by airport style security scanners and X-Ray machines, and I check the area for signs of Chris or Michael Henry. It would not do to bump into either of them now I am, in their eyes, of the Dark Side.

The queues of well-dressed men and women, uniform dark grey or black, are dotted with people in brighter clothes; summer dresses and wedding frocks, louder suits and brown brogues: Clients and witnesses all garbed for a great event beyond their ken, being borne to it through security on a sea of lawyers.

Within the throng bob younger, slighter frames. Mostly boys but a few girls too, they wear sharp, shiny, three piece suits, the kind with two pocket flaps per side. Their hair is neatly strimmed, their tattoos of permanent loyalty to Millwall, or West Ham, carefully hidden. Like their cousins and terrace mates at Billingsgate or Smithfield, these lads push trucks of produce around a market. Fish, meat or justice, it all needs trundling around by smart barrow boys in pointy shoes. A crate of apples, or a crate of damning emails, it matters not to those who move the stuff about. The vast numbers of boxes, each containing dozens of lever arch files, are delivered to court each morning, in penta-plicate (is that right, for five copies?), through their own security channel and on to one of the twenty bright courtrooms.

I am here at The High Court because I have had a Damascene conversion. The stories that trickled north to Scotland over the last few months had layered a stink over Chris' behaviour that even I could not ignore, so I have headed south, with a bottle of Febreeze in my hand and no idea how I was going to use it. But I soon found out.

* * *

A month previously, Iambic was facing bankruptcy. Sara Giles and QuickDraw were suing Chris and Michael Henry for taking the Peas refund, for taking the agent's ticket money and for transferring the ownership of the film into Iambic. Back in January, QuickDraw had gone to court and for speed filed for an interim judgment. These are fast tracked through the system, and there had been an interim hearing in February at which the judge found Chris and Michael had acted dishonestly and improperly. As the injunction was an interim one however, the two men were able to take the matter to full trial, for a full hearing and summary judgment. So Sara, QuickDraw and their legal team had to do it all again, present their case again, spend time in court again, because the Defendants believed the first judge was wrong. In the meantime Chris and Iambic were barred from exploiting the film. Not that they had much to exploit anyway, as all the songs published by Warner Chappell were banned from use as part of an earlier interim hearing brought by the publishing giant three days before the concert. This matter too was due for full trial. Sara wanted the film back in GLE. She argued she would do a better job than Chris of marketing the film, but more pertinently that it didn't belong to Iambic, but GLE. And everything in GLE belonged to her, under the terms of the loan she made in September.

I meet Dawn in a café in Camden. She tells me she went to the interim hearings, heard the evidence put up by Wiggin. She tells me the whole thing is fucked. I sense also that she doesn't trust me, sees me as Chris' man. We promise to keep in touch, but I know the bond between us, forged in the intense flame of *Michael Forever*, is no more.

While I have been skulking up in Scotland, hiding from the fallout, Chris has continued to twist and turn to avoid the forces gathering against him. From friendship, from respect, and from concern at seeing him in such huge trouble, I decide I must do something to stop his headlong rush to oblivion. There is self-interest too, because at this moment I believe that if Iambic goes to the wall there will be little chance of anyone getting paid. With over half my fee, and all my profit on the job, still owing, I know I have to do something. Quite a few of the unpaid individual crew have looked to Dawn for leadership in this, and she has made some noise on their behalf, enough for Chris to say of her that she has gone over to the Dark Side. True to form, anyone who disagrees with him, who questions his actions or motives, who doesn't accept the Chris world view, is side-lined and ignored. He does seem to do it more to women 'tho.

I don't believe that Dawn can help me in any way, nor

that she would have the inclination to do so if she could. I belatedly do what I should have done months and months ago. I ring Sara Giles.

It took her a couple of days to respond, and we arrange to meet in a Shepherd's Bush pub. I'm nervous, she arrives late. Fuck me it's like a first date. We sit outside under large umbrellas with SAGRES emblazoned on them. This is so close to SAGILES, her moniker, that I fear her reach whilst admiring her power. I mean, if she can get her name on the umbrella in the pub, albeit misspelt, what else can she do? The rain pours around us, and Sara smokes eleven cigarettes. She tells me her lawyers counselled against this meeting, and says it was Ron, dear old Ron, who pointed out she had nothing to lose by agreeing to see me. Thanks Ron, you wise old fish.

The scale of the mountain I am to climb is revealed early on. Some time ago, when ranting about Sara, Chris told me she had accused him of threatening her kids. It was presented to me as a marker of her paranoia, of her unreasonable and on the edge, character.

"As if I could ever, would ever, do such a thing" he finished.

She told me, quite calmly, that during late October she received a phone call during which the English male voice made it quite clear if she didn't stop her attempts to secure the film and get back the ticket money diverted away from GLÉ, her children and family would regret it.

"That's a financial threat, not one of violence" I interjected.

"No, he said that my children were beautiful and if I wanted them to stay that way I must stop."

Then she said she thought the caller was me, which is one

of the reasons she was very unsure about this meeting. I was stunned. I'd threatened Wiggin you see, used the 'C' word even. Apparently this made me chief suspect as Chris' number one thug. A big mountain indeed.

I learn it was she that got the Sky broadcast pulled, by appealing directly to James Murdoch. She argues, persuasively, that selling *Michael Forever* to Sky for seventy grand was short sighted and an almost criminal devaluing of the product. All the potential of DVDs, PayTV, Facebook stream style Video on Demand and cinema screenings would have been rendered almost worthless. As soon as it was broadcast by Sky the film would be all over the web, universally accessible everywhere. Why would anyone pay to see something they would get for free on YouTube? She gives the rights issues little credence, pointing out that if the whole thing had been negotiated properly, cleared professionally, there would have been no need for the Sky deal. She appears a woman of integrity, of passion for the film with a belief and vision for what it should be. She is ready to bang on doors and do the deals that Jeffré and Chris shied away from.

For the rest of the meeting Sara trotted out four month's worth of investigation, of digging, of trying to understand, like all of us, where the money had gone. She found links with Michael Henry and Paul King that went back to a solicitors called Thurloe and Lyndhurst, an investment company called Thurloe Place, and Paul King's dodgy South African hangover cure operation, the one that he went to prison over. This was once registered at the same building in, you guessed it, Thurloe Place. She found links between David Bailey, the lead early investor in the project, and Social Media Limited, which for a short time tried unsuccessfully to stem the web-tide of hate, and Social Events Limited (the successor to Tix-Me, who were in administration at the time of the concert, despite hiding the fact) and Stadium Events Limited, which was Paul King's outfit. All of these companies netted tens, hundreds of thousands of pounds. She tells me Paul King trousered a ton of cash on his way out of the back door of the stadium. Now that's taking ownership! Yet nothing she says makes me see my old friend as corrupt.

"Chris may have been grossly, hugely and stupidly negligent", I said, "but I don't believe he is a crook. I think he has been taken for a massive and very expensive ride"

"He's in this up to his neck", Sara replied, with the strength of a wounded tigress refusing to give way "and the longer you support him, the worse it gets. Every week that goes by adds hundreds of thousands to QuickDraw's penalties, and tens of thousands to the legal bill. Chris and Michael have sacked their lawyers and are now defending themselves, and refusing to give way. This thing is heading for trial and if it gets there, the costs just ramp up and you and the other creditors move further away from the money. Get him to stop, get him to see he's going to lose, and you can help yourself and everybody else."

"I'll accept naïve, foolish and too trusting of those around him; I've always thought his faith in Jeffré was misplaced, but ultimately he was just trying to do the right thing, only in the wrong way. You can't hang him out to dry, because if not for him there would be no film to fight over."

"I'm not going to let go of the wrongdoing. He and Michel Henry tried to fuck me over. Not only did they lie, cheat and defraud me and QuickDraw, but they have made it very personal, attacking my character, claiming I act bizarrely because I work late into the night, suggesting I'm irrational, trying to make me out as some kind of mad woman. Since early October, when they took the Peas money, they have seen me as their enemy. All they had to do was come to me and say 'Sara, we've fucked up, can you help us?' I would have worked with them, we would have found a way forward. Instead they put the film into Iambic, redesigned the truth to suit their actions, and labelled me the bad guy for challenging them. Look, they tar everyone with their brush, believe everyone is as crooked as they. Chris insists I told him to breach any agreement he had to, he heard what he expected to hear himself say. I said 'reach', not breach. My advice was inclusive, supportive, yet he took it as an instruction for hostile action. They have even demanded my phone records to prove I was using my mobile on one day in all of this that I told them I was unreachable."

"Were you?"

"My grandmother was ill, rushed to hospital. I was on the phone to my kids reassuring them, telling them what was going on. They need to make this about me because they don't have a leg to stand on. They had no right to take the Black Eyed Peas refund, nor the ticket money from Tix-Me. To claim that the film belongs to Iambic is just laughable. What they are doing is plain wrong."

"But the film is fucked anyway. Nearly half of the songs are with Warner Chappell, so Chris can't use them, and he's cobbled together some abortion of a mess with what remains. This he says he can't sell because of your injunction."

"Chris is unknown in the world of feature film. He has no track record with major distributors. I've talked to Warner Chappell and I've put feelers out to the Estate. I think they'll talk to me, but they will not work with Chris, and nothing can happen until the court case is resolved. Everybody wants some certainty, nobody wants Chris involved. Andy, I want to do what is right – ensure that Michael's children are empowered, help them use *Michael Forever* as a platform to build a tribute that they can be proud of. I want the endorsement and support of the Estate, Warner Chappell and the MJ Community and I want to make something worthwhile. I believe that Chris' non-Warner Chappell version is an insult to everyone, the family, the fans, the crew, the artists, the MJ Community and Michael. Do you believe Chris' half concert is a fair reflection of your work? Stop him and Michael taking this all the way, stop the waste of millions of pounds that could be paying you all."

"I've got to be able to offer him something. I understand he cannot be seen to win in any way, but can you offer some honour in his surrender?"

"Why should I? He's trying to destroy me. This court case is costing everyone hundreds of thousands of pounds and is not in anyone's interests. He has defamed me, lied to me and blamed me for the whole thing."

"You'll offer him a lifeline because you're not like him"

Sara reaches for another seven fags, lighting one from the smouldering stub of the other. I fetch another two pints of beer (I've always admired a bird who drinks pints). I return outside, under the SAGRES umbrella.

"Fuck. Why did I agree to this meeting? Okay. I'm not doing anything for Michael Henry, because he's a snake, and I hate Jeffré, who has stood in my way when I tried to reach out to Katherine, blocked the door, but, you know, if Chris backs off, after a period of time, once he understands he is drowning, well…I'll not ruin him."

I do love a mission, and this one could just satisfy both protagonists. If I can get Chris to drop his fight against Sara about who owns the film, then maybe I can get Sara on side, she can run with the project, make some money, and everybody will win. But I know none of this can happen if Chris is going to behave in the stubborn and arrogant way he always has. I need a new Chris, a humble and contrite Chris, and the impending loss of Iambic, the company he built from scratch over twenty years ago, could just refocus his centre and reveal a more inclusive, understanding person.

To avoid administration or bankruptcy, Chis has asked the creditors of Iambic for a Company Voluntary Arrangement. This is a step less severe than administration, where the operation of a company is taken away from its directors. The CVA involves all the creditors voting on Chris' proposal of how he will repay us. Seventy five per cent, by value of debt, need to agree. We meet in a serviced conference facility near Paddington station.

There is a small crowd outside the room where the meeting is to be held. In a corner seating area, Chris and two elves are in discussion with some suits. At the other side of the space, Dawn is chatting to a small group; a few grips, a couple of editors, Holly and the chap who runs the 3D truck. On the list of creditors he is right at the top, with over one fifth of the total owed to his company. I scan the paperwork. Chris seems to be owed, one way or another, about a third. The thirty five grand he owes me seems small beer, in the totality of what's outstanding, but a vote is a vote.

We file in, followed by Chris and his suits, who sit at the table facing us. There are around thirty people in the room, facing the two accountants and Chris, who sits slightly away from the table. He is fatter than when I saw him last, back in October. His close wired, bushy hair is more grey than ginger, and his face is beetroot red, as if he is permanently embarrassed. As I am soon to see, so he should be.

The meeting kicks off with the administrator giving a long and detailed account of the process of the CVA and what it means. Most pertinently, he reiterates that a 'yes' vote means the company will continue trading under the sole control of the directors (Chris) and under standard credit terms. So everything will stay as it ever was, and our collective debt will be kicked into touch for fifteen months. Hmm. Then he covers Chris' proposal, as to why we, the creditors, should leave him alone for those fifteen months, to carry on as if nothing has happened, as if he didn't owe the film industry two million quid. He also tells us there are creditors who have not been contacted, creditors who have amounts outstanding different to those listed, and there's Wiggin, representing Sara, who have written to him, the administrator, explaining why Chris' proposal does not stack up.

For Chris has given us two options, helpfully labelled in the documentation as Case A and Case B. He has done this to get round the minor detail of QuickDraw and Sara's impending court case against him, already looking good for her with the preliminary judgment and due for a full hearing soon.

In Case A, Chris retains the film rights and makes a new film, using the concert (those bits outside of the control of Warner Chappell) and splicing in previously unseen home movie footage of Michael. This he will sell worldwide for forty two million dollars. If he doesn't get the CVA, he will have to concentrate on other projects, and make the film in another way.

I'm immediately bridling now at the suggestion the film I spent so much of myself on is worthless without a bit of home video of MJ chucked in. Six months of work, a host of artists, the efforts of industry A listers like Ron and Mallet and Bobby D and everyone else who worked on this show; all their hard graft is meaningless until attached to some shots of what, exactly, that will enhance and propel the narrative? Michael barbequing? La Toya kicking a football? Some Jackson family fun day where they torture a youthful looking Ron Weisner?

In Case B, QuickDraw regain the rights to the film they claim they always had, and go on to exploit the film through GLE which they now control. To do this they pay Iambic two and a half million bucks, because Chris tells them to. The administrator in the audience representing GLE, and the young lawyer representing QuickDraw, are quick to point out that there is no evidence of such a debt to Iambic, so such a payment is as unlikely as Iambic getting the film. Chris appears to ignore them, on the grounds that Michael Henry disagrees. Here's what he says:

"The outcomes are not certain and you should hold in your head what is the better outcome for the creditors. The central issue is which is the better outcome for creditors, so certainty in cases A or B is not the key issue. In answer to a letter received at eight am this morning from the GLE administrator, who you need to remember was appointed by QuickDraw, there has been a rebuttal by Michael Henry who has disagreed with every single point as a point of law. The key thing is that if Iambic is not successful at trial, does it have a claim of 2.5 million dollars against GLE? This is getting a bit into the legals of the case and don't want to be here all day, but essentially by definition either there was a production or there wasn't. If there wasn't a production then Iambic wins; if there was, which as far as lawyers tell me is the case, then the debt stands. The contention of Wiggin and GLE is that if there was no production there can be no debt. Now this requires a degree of doublethink, and you have go backwards through this; if there was no production, we win, if there was a production, the debt stands. You cannot have no production and no debt, it's not one of the options"

Surprisingly, the meeting does not explode into rapturous applause at Chris' masterly enunciation of why he is right. Nobody dances in the aisles, reams of A4 paper are not joyously thrown from the windows, no open topped Lincoln purrs ready downstairs for the tickertape parade. Instead, there is a confused silence. I'm certain many in the room are wondering whether this no production thing means they actually imagined they were employed on *Michael Forever*, which actually never happened. Or perhaps everyone is just stunned at the bullshit. Chris continues:

"I would hardly expect a bunch of people whom I am fighting in court to come along here and agree with every word I say. Their main task is to obstruct Iambic at every point. I don't give the words of Wiggin much credence. Incidentally the debt of Iambic to GLE is outweighed by a couple of hundred thousand by the debt of GLE to Iambic, and that can be confirmed"

Oh good. Chris asks to stop there, but the chair of the meeting, a man who earlier told us he's not a lawyer, merely an accountant, suggests, with a touch of edge in his voice, that people may want some further clarification. He too perhaps is worried that there may not have been a production, he has not actually been hired, and there is no CVA. I swear I see him pinch himself. Sorry mate, it is all real.

Somebody asks about the trial date. Dawn suggests the CVA request should wait until after the trial, as the options will then be much clearer. Chris comes back that in the meantime any creditor could wind up the company, in which case we, the creditors, would get nothing.

"If that's what you want, then fine"

Another worried soul brings up the issue of the other trial, not the one with QuickDraw, but the one with Warner Chappell. The injunction that stopped the live transmission needs resolution in a full hearing. Chris is adamant they'll owe him a shedload of money. The meeting is not so sure. One of the editors asks about the new film, and the home movie footage, and Chris tells us it's amazing and will make a great film.

"Who owns the unseen footage?" I ask, already knowing the answer and remembering being told about Jeffré's week in Michael's house immediately after his death. Did he find it then? Did he resolutely sit on the porch, shotgun in hand, defending the memory? Or did he have a little mooch around in between shifts of guard duty, of standing to? Did he peek here and glance there? Did he sneak a shufti in the drawers, a look in the cupboards? I would. I wonder what he found.

"Jeffré Phillips" says Chris

Before I can ask Chris whether he might, yet again, be confusing possession with ownership; how he intended to get a product out there without the Michael Jackson Estate shooting him down once more, Dawn leaps in:

"You talk about this perfect storm arriving on your doorstep as if it could not be foreseen. I assume it was years or months in the planning. Can you pin point a time you started putting the plans together?

"It was talked about a year prior. It was begun to be put together in April. If the question is did we have the rights, then yes we consider we did."

"Did you have, as I'd expect, meeting, communications, contracts, six months in advance before starting to action and spend. Could these documents be shown? I'd like to see them.

"They are not here. It's hard to answer the question given the terms you've asked it in."

"Would you like me to rephrase it?"

"I'll answer the question in terms of what happened. This is to do with music copyright, the agreement to use a particular song in a concert, either live or broadcast live or recorded. And there are different rights attached to these uses. Whether a song can be used or not depends on what the song is. Songs were decided [on] two weeks before the concert and were changing up until that point."

"I don't believe that"

"Well actually they were changing until three days before, but they were largely locked in two weeks before. We had one author tell us he didn't want his material used, but as for the injunction, the live broadcast would have been done under existing blanket rights that were available."

"That wasn't my question"

"But that's the point that matters"

"What matters is someone, like yourself, working in the business for many years, who understands the great complexities of music clearance, especially with an artist such as Michael Jackson, would have seen that the responsible course of action was to have cleared the necessary rights well in advance, rather than be surprised when the inevitable injunction appears in a perfect storm two days before the show".

If only she knew how desirable yet unattainable that was. Dawn gets some 'here here's' and Chris responds harshly, as if he cannot believe the crass stupidity of this woman:

"You have it all exactly backwards" he barks, forgetting that a few minutes ago he was suggesting that was the only way to look at things, and shows me and the assembled creditors there has been not one iota of change in his position, attitude or approach since the day he came to believe he and Jeffré were going to take the world of MJ by storm.

Others follow. A grip jumps Chris about an invoice Iambic claim never to have seen, and there is some debate about how so much confusion existed and exists still about who was supplying Iambic and who was supplying GLE. Dawn gets much of the blame for this from Chris, but as a comeback for the kicking she has just administered it's weak, and a little pathetic to blame someone doing their utmost to keep things going, for an accounting mess in Bristol.

I finally get a word in about this new film idea, which has wound me up about than anything else:

"The artists have contracted with GLE for their performances to be in a concert film called *Michael Forever*. How are you going to get them to agree to be in your new film?"

"I'm sure they'll do a deal. The process is nearly complete"

"Good luck with that one" I think, but don't say so. Maybe I should have.

The meeting then votes on a motion from Visions, the 2D television facilities suppliers and second behind the 3D truck with the amount outstanding. They haven't had time to evaluate the proposals put forward by Chris, so want to adjourn the meeting for a fortnight. By God, he's got off the hook again.

I have looked in vain for the new Chris at this meeting, but there was no sign of him. I don't know how I'm going to get him to give up defending his position against Sara when he won't even countenance the notion that he has been even slightly wrong anywhere down the line. Nevertheless I do my best. I go back to Sara, who despite second thoughts keeps her word from the first meeting. Reluctantly she confirms that if Chris backs away now, accepts the interim judgment, stops insisting on his day in court, she will do a deal with him. I send him this:

Dearest Chris,
I write as your friend, and I hope you will take my words on board. At the creditors' meeting in London on April 5th you presented true to form, arrogantly, defiantly and aggressively refusing to accept not just any point of view other than your own, but the very notion that you have acted in any way other than with due propriety. I had hoped to see some humility, some contriteness at the string of broken promises, some sense of you reaching out to a room of people you have at best taken for granted, and at worst lied to, yet whose help you now need to keep Iambic alive. You were unable to do any of this, and as a result I must act in my own interests, which coincide with the interests of all the creditors owed money, whether by Iambic or GLE. In summary, my position, a Plan C if you like, is this:
The only chance we have of getting paid is if the film of the concert is properly exploited. This exploitation can only happen properly with the approval of the estate, the continued support of the Jackson family, and a full and successful rapprochement with the fans. Such a film would succeed spectacularly. Anyone making such a film would be duty bound to pay the people who worked on and supplied to the concert, and honour bound to create a royalty pool to compensate for the long wait for our money.
You on the other hand, are proposing to edit a film around those limited

rights you can acquire, add some footage of Michael Jackson that would automatically exclude exploitation in the US, and create a product that would do nothing to assuage the fury of the fans towards Michael Forever. Such a film would fail just as the concert failed, and for the same reasons.

Too much has happened for the estate to open the door to you. Too much mistrust exists for you to persuade the performers to grant the required additional licences. There are just too many secrets, obfuscations and part truths for anyone to believe anything good of Michael Forever. The thing is poisoned and dead in the water.

So dear Chris, step aside. Let it go. Do the decent thing and lance the putrid boil that disfigures this project and diminishes our chances of success. With you off the picture, others better placed to create a lasting monument to Michael Jackson can move the thing forward, get some traction with the estate, make Warner Chappell go away, and get everyone paid. I have gone to great lengths to negotiate with QuickDraw an honourable withdrawal for you. You will not be hounded, you will not be destroyed. You will receive your monies owed and full and proper credit. In return, you must fully support the efforts of others, assist in every way in keeping the family and children on board with the project. Time is now of the essence. It is still possible to save Iambic at the next meeting, despite your denial and arrogance at the previous one, if everyone can see you embrace the opportunity being offered. You must resign from Michael Forever and withdraw from your action with QuickDraw, as maintaining your position in the light of the interim judgement delays the inevitable while adding £250,000 a week of lawyer fees that get paid out before we do. Your withdrawal is the only way out of this for everyone. It's taken me four long days to get this for you, but if you don't act now the tanks will roll in and you'll lose everything.

If you see this not as the act of a true friend but as a betrayal, you haven't yet got it. This is your only chance to emerge with dignity. Take it, empower yourself to do the right thing, use your relationship with the family to build on what we have, open the doors you can open, but be brave enough to let others walk through them.

I also send it to everyone else, together with an apology to them for being an abject coward until now.

Chris comes back with an 'eyes only' response, pointing out that Katherine Jackson is already talking to the estate about *Michael Forever Mark 2*, that the family hate Sara, that Sara in turn hates him, wants him bankrupted and his head on a plate. He does however, turn the offer around, twisting it one eighty degrees, writing that he'll consider up the exploitation of the film in return for a written guarantee that all claims against him and Michael Henry will be dropped.

Did I mention Michael Henry? Did Sara? She badgers me for days to get hold of this email, but Chris has put 'For your eyes only' and PRIVATE AND CONFIDENTIAL all over it, so I refuse. My argument that I'd do the same with a similar stricture from her is given short shrift, and we have the first argument of our new romance.

The Better and I head off to Vietnam on our first holiday for five years. We are able to do this because there has been a boiler fire at the hotel, which is now shut for repairs. Electricians, painters, carpet layers and heating engineers are crawling all over the place. We don't have to be there, so we're not.

Before I get on the plane I give a witness statement to Wiggin over the phone, covering everything we consider pertinent. But I don't sign it. Something in me still holds me back from turning completely from Chris. The lack of a signature causes Sara to lose further faith in my conversion.

Like most Asian cities, Saigon is wired for the 21st century. Superfast broadband and free wireless everywhere make it easy to stay in touch. The updated creditor lists for the reconvened Iambic CVA come in. There are loads more names, some of whom have languished unloved on the lists of GLE and some who have come forward only now because Iambic never initially contacted them. There is also Dragonfly Limited, new on the list and owed nine hundred and seventy thousand pounds. Wow. Who the fuck are they, and where did they come from? A quick bit of digging shows it to be a Bristol based company with a director named Christopher Hunt. Bastard.

This discovery kills off any sympathy, any remaining sense of loyalty. A hard choice, and one I was struggling with; a fifteen year friendship or doing the right thing, just became no choice at all. Like Brutus before me, I am clear that the emperor must go for the good of the empire. The bonds of camaraderie are not strong enough to resist the pull of the truth, indeed they have been rent asunder by his mendacity. He has lied by omission, evaded, schemed and plotted at the expense of honest professionals delivering his show for him. Some believe he should go to prison, that his actions were criminal. I thought that at the very least, Chris was guilty of a staggering incompetence, a terrible negligence and a complete lack of probity. The late addition of Dragonfly Ltd to Iambic's creditors, Chris stacking his hand with a few more counterfeit aces, adds a plethora of choice new descriptions. Bastard was top.

I offer Sara everything, including access to my emails. She tells me to sign my witness statement, but this proves difficult for we have left Saigon and are on the coast, in a remote hotel where the young staff smile sweetly and stare blankly at the memory stick I have presented at reception.

"I'd like to print a document from this memory stick, then I'd like you to fax it for me."

No response, apart from the smile getting a little sweeter. I'm a seasoned traveller, so I know talking louder and accenting English words into the local lingua is futile. I try mime instead, reinforced by keywords. I act out the process, inserting the stick, air typing on the imaginary keyboard, hitting 'enter' with a flourish. My performance of a piece of paper coming out of a printer is world class; I even manage the little flick at the end when the sheet clears the rollers.

"STICK. USB. OPEN FILE. DOCUMENT. PRINT." punctuates my enactment. I move on to act two.

"BRING. SIGN. FAX. SARA" This last one represented by manic smoking and fist shaking. I struggle to portray someone slim, (and I have so struggled since about 1995), but I end with a very passable interpretation of my head being nailed to the reception desk.

The girl, clearly concerned that one of the guests is having a seizure, has fetched her supervisor, whose smile is even sweeter, but whose ability to assist is just as limited. I sigh and start again, refining my presentation to include tonally accurate beeps in the 'dialling Wiggin's fax number' scene. Then I go too far: mimicking the noise of a fax machine connecting only scares them.

By now I'm tired. It's very, very hot in the wall-less reception area and I'm physically drained. I'd hate to have to do eight shows a week of this. I fall to my knees and beg:

"Pleeese, I'll do it myself. Just tell me where your printer is."

A look of an awakening crosses the face of the supervisor. She stops smiling and adopts a sparrow-sweet frown, her poppet nose wrinkling in disappointment

"Ahh. Plin-laa! Plin-laa no Wo-ka" (please don't judge, I'm not being racist. They really do talk like that. In common with other Asiatic languages, there are no poly-syllabic words in Vietnamese, so Eng-lish words are bro-ken down in speech. They are really lovely in attitude, resolutely refusing to allow their inability to help get in the way of wanting to try.)

"OK. Where might there be a printer, a plin-la, which does work?"

"No plin-la. Plin-laa" I bridle a bit at having incorrect pronunciation bossily corrected to a different incorrectness, but I let it go.

"I have to print this document. I need to sign it, then fax it to Wiggin, and I need to achieve these things today. There is a very important lady in London requiring this to happen, and if I don't succeed she will be even more disappointed in me than she is already. I can't bear that. I've spent months with my head in the sand. She has helped me see the light, look around, wake up and smell the coffee. I have to deliver"

"You like Ko-fee? You go down they"

She charmingly points to the restaurant, and smiles.

Aargh! I'll find another printer. I ask about the bike rental service, as advertised on their website and by a big sign on the reception desk, and after the requisite confusion, I'm told the bike ser-vis not wha-king. I can see two bikes just outside reception, a passable mountain bike and a Vietnamese road bike which seems ubiquitous throughout the country. It is made of a whitish metal, has a huge frame, and a charming metal dragonfly attached to the back bumper. If the Vietnamese aren't out an about on a scooter, they'll be on one of these. When I ride one, later in the holiday, I find it incredibly light and flimsy, as if the metal has been mixed with boiled rice.

But for now I am thwarted, because they won't let me have a bike, because the nearest working printer that I can access is probably twenty miles away, and because it's so searingly hot I need to get in the pool.

A few days later, at the next hotel, I finally get the damned thing signed and sent. The standard of the hotel is higher, the standard of the English is higher, the smiles are even more lovely, and the printer works.

Wiggin trawl through my emails, and so does Sara. I have a two stage security process on my Gmail account, put in place after I read an article about people getting locked out of their email accounts by hackers who demand ransoms. Every time I log on, a verification code is texted to my mobile. This number needs to be entered to get to the inbox. Sara is quite American in that she completely ignores time zone differences. I get the texts at the oddest times, when swimming, on the toilet, whilst asleep. Is she watching me? I brush away the feeling of discomfort, of someone with their hands in my underpants and not in a good way. If my emails and my statement help secure the truth, it is the right thing to do. I should have done this months ago.

Have I, am I, betraying Chris? I do feel a sense of guilt, but I remind myself that the right way is often the harder way. Or has Chris betrayed me? Has he used our friendship, relied on it to have one less person chasing him hard for the money, one less source of criticism of his actions? I've always had the view that when friends work together it should be because they'd rather that than with someone connected only on a business level. Chris I think, had the view that working with friends gains him an advantage. I was a softer touch. Not anymore.

I am still in Vietnam when the postponed Iambic CVA meets to vote. I have given my proxy to Dawn, trusting her to do the right thing. Chris has asked for fifteen months grace on what he owes. Few of us can bring ourselves to trust him for even fifteen seconds, and his request is denied.

The trial date looms closer. Nobody is given much notice of when it will start, and the process of allocating court time seems very last minute. Eventually however, it comes up on the Justice Department Chancery Division Hearings List, which the Lord Chief Justice has been most helpfully emailing me.

* * *

The courtroom is large, airy and white. Two rows of metal chairs face forward from the rear. In front of them is a row of desks. In front of these, another row of tables, with table top lecterns for the resting of papers or elbows. Beyond them, facing into the room, is the clerk's desk, and to the left a table and chair for witnesses. At each of these positions is a row of lever arch files. Five sets, each of over twenty files, labelled A1 to Z2. In there are five copies of all my emails, of my witness statement, of everything anyone has written or said or done since this whole thing started. It must have kept the barrow boys very busy. At the far end of the court from my lowly spot in the audience seating is a white wall, over five feet high, separating the courtroom floor from the elevated position for the judge, who gets a comfy looking leather executive chair, with a high back and wheels for zooming around when no one is looking. Above where the judge's head will shortly be, is a huge lion and unicorn, the Logo of The Law.

Coming in for the first time is like arriving at a church wedding. Bride or groom? I sit down directly behind Sara's side of the courtroom. Definitely bride for me. Before me, so close that if I stretch out my legs I'd be playing footsie, is the rearmost row of desks for solicitors. This runs uninterrupted to the other side. There is no physical aisle, but a yawning chasm between right and wrong. On the other side this row is empty. Chris and Michael have no solicitors. This is either for lack of money or disagreements on how to handle the case. If the legal advice was; 'you're fucked, give it up', it was not something Chris and Michael would ever accept. Both men are in the middle row, reserved for barristers and litigants in person. Only from this row of desks may one address the court. I know this from watching *Silk* and *Judge John Deed*. I also know that the defendant who represents himself has a fool for a client, a lawyers' homily that pops into my head. From episode four of *Silk*, I recall.

On my side of the court (how quickly that seems natural. I could never be over *there* now) and right in front of me, are Wiggin, two of them at present, plus two empty chairs. If this was a film set there would be names on the backs. In front of Wiggin, reclining nonchalantly, are Sara's barristers, the two Wigs of Wiggin. They appear confident, comfortable, relaxed, smiling.

A door leading into the judge's area opens. A portly clerk in a gown just like my English master wore announces:

"Court rise" and we all stand up. The judge enters, a demure looking lady with glasses and a kindly face, and bows to us. Those in the know bow back.

"Let me tell you where I am" she says, settling herself in the big chair, like a svelte Deborah Meaden talking to a room of nervous pitchers auditioning prized toilet seat cover cleaning machinery. Fortunately she does not follow with "I'm out", but tells us she hasn't read the file. The reason for Sara having not one but two Plaintiff barristers is then explained: One Wiggin Wig will cover the money, and the other the rights. For Chris and Michael are accused of three things by Sara Giles and

QuickDraw:

That by knowing deceit and false representation they misappropriated the Black Eyed Peas refund, and later the ticket receipts from Stadium Events Limited. These are the two financial actions being tried. Iambic is accused of breaching GLE's copyright in the film of *Michael Forever*, because the film belongs not to Iambic but to GLE. This is the rights dispute, and QuickDraw is fighting the case because they have a proprietary charge over the assets of GLE, and therefore a charge over the film.

Chris Hunt, Iambic and Michael Henry dispute these accusations. They argue that they had every right to the Black Eyed Peas refund, every right to the Stadium Events ticket money, and Iambic has every right to exploit the film, because it owns it. And so, with battle lines drawn, we adjourn, barely ten minutes after the judge entered.

Being near the door has its advantages, and I am quick to get out of the room and so avoid Chris and Michael. This is a tactic I have chosen over confrontation and fisticuffs, as I don't believe Her Lordship would tolerate either in her court.

The following morning there is a commotion at security. I have just gone through and am struggling back into my jacket when I hear a raised rumbustious, bumptious voice. I turn to see *Michael Forever* investor David Bailey, all eyebrows and belly, doing the 'Is it me? Did I set that off? Oh dear!' routine as yellow lights flash and sirens howl. He is escorted back out to the other side of the scanners so he can go through again and empty his pockets of all the metallic investments he has brought with him. Really! Has he never been through an airport before? With him is Gavin Breeze. I last saw these two in Cardiff the day before the show, worrying about the sound quality. Now they are in the High Court of London, no doubt come to worry about the quality of Michael Henry.

Today the QuickDraw solicitors' bench is full. In addition to the two I saw yesterday, there is a third, senior, lady and Sara, who has decided to dress in a neutral grey and tie her hair back as tightly as possible in a neat ponytail. She looks like a nun whose habit is smoking, her femininity masked. At this early stage, the beginning of the first full day of the trial, I still have only a slight grasp of the issues at hand.

I knew that at the beginning, GLE owned everything, Iambic was the production company for the films of the event, and Chris was to make the sales of the films to various broadcasters, cinema chains and so on. There was a commissioning agreement to this effect, an arrangement where GLE commissioned Iambic to record the concert. I knew this because I was hired to produce the filming, and that's how Chris explained it at our first meeting.

I also knew, because he had made no secret of it, that when relations with QuickDraw broke down, Chris moved ownership of the film into Iambic. Whether he did so legally was being tried in this courtroom. Chris' view at the time was that he had to take these actions, because he believed Sara Giles intended to seize the film and sell it fast and cheap, realising only enough money to pay back her investment fund and shaft everyone else.

Chris also instructed Social Events Limited, the company name of Tix-Me, to pay the ticket receipts they held into Iambic. He did this, he told me, to pay some 'mission critical' suppliers around the time I was desperately trying to deliver two versions of the film to Sky TV. He told me the reason for his doing so was to make delivery to Sky, activate the secondary music licence by so doing, and thereby have a film he could sell around the world. What he didn't tell me, was that he had Michael Henry sign Jeffré Phillips up as an officer of GLE, then get Jeffré to issue the instruction for the money to go to Iambic. The legality of this diversion of the ticket money was also being tried.

The Black Eyed Peas had shown an interest in taking part in the concert since mid-July. Their fee of two million dollars however, was not available, so Michael Henry, Chris, Ron, Jeffré, the Parojim and I all stalled the Peas management while Henry worked hard on completing a financing deal with Sara. As soon as this deal was done, time became of the essence, so QuickDraw paid the Peas directly to save two days on moving money first to GLE then on to the Peas. I believe the stalling, together with the increasing controversies over the show and the fan approbation, rang enough alarm bells with Will-I-Am to cause him to pull out of the deal. I also think there was a good chance they would have pulled out even if they'd been signed and paid back in July, because the mistakes over ticketing, artist signing, and the attitude towards the MJ community would have created the same odium and rattled them just the same.

Chris persuaded the Peas lawyers to return the money QuickDraw had paid back to GLE, because at the time he was seriously short of cash again. Whether this was legal or not was the third action presented to Her Honour for judgment. Grammarians amongst you will notice the lack of an 'e' in 'judgment'. That's how a judge's ruling is spelled. When we mortals take a view on something, it's a judgement.

The schedule for the trial had been agreed between both sides. A day presenting the cases, three days for presentation and cross examination of witnesses, and a day of summing up.

Each side of a legal dispute is required to disclose their evidence, witness statements and the basis for their position to the other. Each side then develops legal presentations to challenge these stated positions.

The financial wig was first up. Dapper, erudite and supremely confident, with a passing resemblance to Daniel Craig, his polite, clipped presentation was edged with steel and a little well placed contempt. Michael Henry must have argued that QuickDraw did not have any ownership of the assets of GLE, because much of the morning was taken up with explanations of the differences between standing charges, mortgages, mere charges, debentures and proprietary charges, and how these decided who owned what when they were applied to a contract.

"The terms charge and mortgage are often used *interchangeably*," Daniel Craig postulated, "which may account for the defendant's confusion" he added, helpfully. Michael Henry's pained look was the first of what would be many.

After an age of ploughing through the contract between GLE and QuickDraw, we were treated to the accepted legal test of dishonesty. This, the Bond actor told us, was not measured against the standard of honesty in the mind of the defendants, but of an ordinary honest person, sharing personal characteristics such as age and experience, and having the same motive and knowledge of the facts as the accused. Hearing this I looked to the court clerk to check if she was off immediately to find some overweight ginger people and ask them if they would have done what Chris had done. But it appeared not to be necessary at this point, for she was patrolling the room to find who had their mobile phone on. The sound system in the court was being affected by mobile phone signals, and we were warned at the start to turn them off. The interference persisted, that annoying pinging and static causing me to completely miss the differences between dishonest assistance, breach of trust and knowing receipt.

After two verbal warnings the clerk was up to find the perpetrator. Most in the court, including Her Judgness, nervously checked their pockets: All except Sara, who was too busy texting to notice. Luckily for her the clerk failed to spot this blatant disregard for courtroom protocol. Eventually Sara put her phone away and the distracting noises ceased, just in time for me to hear that acting in the perceived best interests of GLE or Iambic was not relevant, in this test of whether or not Michael Henry and Chris Hunt should be labelled deceitful.

As we break for lunch, I say we because I am completely caught up in the quiet and purposeful drama unfolding here, I can see that two planks of Chris and Michael's defence have been comprehensively challenged. For the defendants had argued that QuickDraw's charge was only over the bank account of GLE, not the assets. They also defended their actions of appropriating the Peas and ticket monies as acting in the best interests of GLE, the assets (the film) and the investors, including QuickDraw.

It's a gloriously warm late May day in London, and the city squares and streets are full of office workers enjoying an hour of sunshine before returning to their air conditioned steel towers. I return on time, to see a crush of gowns and suits waiting to pass security. Amongst them is David Bailey, this time managing to get through without incident.

Wiggins wig number two is up. He is tall, with unkempt locks of curly black hair escaping from all sides of his battered hairpiece. His gown flops around loosely, and the folds are ill defined. Where wig one was sharp, rapier pointed and precise, wig two is a blunter instrument, a little less organised. His direction of the judge, where to look in the mass of evidence, is a slightly less fluent. I can see Chris and Michael relaxing a little after the morning's clipped counter to their case.

Such thinking, confusing style with ability, is soon shown to be a mistake. I am torn in regard to wig two, in my casting for the film of this, between Alf Molina and Alan Davies. In the end I decide that the comedian should play him as a young man, growing up in the back streets of Henley-on-Thames, surviving on sorbet made from leftover champagne from the previous night's rowing. Alf Molina would appear in a post-production morph from one face to the other, fully grown, bewigged and digging deep into the constructs presented by Chris as his defence.

The barrister hones in on the script for the concert, which he argues not unreasonably, became the script of the film. He also focusses on the concert logo, the red and gold squirl of MF designed almost a year ago now by the Meerkat of Venice Beach. He hopes to pin the breach of copyright charge on Iambic's use of these two creations, which were clearly and always the property of GLE. Using the script in this way is a bit square peg and round hole, because what is clearly a big part of a film drama is less obviously so in a music concert. Surely the larger part of the script was written by Michael Jackson and the other lyricists of the songs? Alf doesn't go there however, and concentrates on the words penned for Jamie Foxx and Fearne Cotton. Then he takes the judge and us through Chris' cancellation of the commissioning agreement between GLE and Iambic, and a long preamble about the conditionality of rights passing at the moment of creation. No, I didn't understand it either, but his meaning was sure to come clear when he would, as he promised to do, discuss these matters in some detail with Mr Hunt, later in the process.

Michael Henry is next up, his legal training and background looking decidedly lacklustre when compared with the two silky performances of the barristers. He tells us he is honest, that there was no breach of trust, no dishonesty, and no gross deceit. He disagrees on the law, exclaiming that a mortgage transfers property rights where a charge does not, trying to answer the jibe about his confusion, and only reminding everyone of it. Then his first bit of evidence; an email sent by Wiggin to Tony at Onsite when they were trying to stop the work on the film. In this email Wiggin refer to a charge QuickDraw have on the materials of GLE. Not a mortgage, your worship! Not ownership, your most esteemed Governance! Case proven, m'lud, I now go free! But no, Daniel Craig quickly points out, a letter to a third party has no bearing on the nature of an agreed contract between the principals.

Chris follows his GLE ex partner onto his feet. He begins by reminding the court he is not a lawyer, but the 'poor little me' defence cuts no ice with either the judge or the barristers. Ignorance of the law, as we were all told aged five, is no excuse. Any perceived dishonesty he says, was perpetrated to protect the assets, for the benefit of all the investors including QuickDraw. Well that's okay then.

The day ends with some housekeeping, some case management. The witnesses called to appear are Sara, a senior Wiggin (possibly the one I labelled a labia) Michael Henry and Chris Hunt. The latter will cross examine the former, and the wigs will cross examine the latter. Everyone will question everyone else, and when the music stops they'll all sit down.

There's some toing and froing about the order of witness appearance, but Judy Dench (who else could it be, playing Her Judgness?) quickly and sternly tells both parties to sort it out between themselves. They do and half a day per witness is agreed upon, leaving Friday for the summing up.

As I leave I decide Sara can only be represented by a Redgrave and Michael Henry by Gary Oldman at his most slimy. As for Chris, his mix of bumbling incoherency and long winded gibbering could only be portrayed by Charles Laughton, in a very orange wig.

Another beautiful day, and Neil Gillard, Wiggin partner and Sara's head corporate lawyer takes the witness stand. Except he, like all the witnesses, sits down at a desk. This is a civil trial, not a criminal one. There is no dock, no jury, but two adversaries arguing their case in front of a judge. Why are we here? This is not the world of rock 'n' roll, of entertainment, where a group of people engaged on a creative endeavour strive for common purpose. This is adversarial argument with a most serious purpose. Something is seriously fucked in the world of pop for a failed enterprise to descend to this level of pernickety fencing of logic. There are interlopers in the House of Blues, and one of them is about to question QuickDraw's senior advocate.

Michael Henry begins by heaping praise on Neil Gillard. We hear of his fast rise to position of partner, his magna cum laude graduation from lawyer school, his intelligence, skill and experience. Then, when he thinks he has his witness all relaxed and glowing with the praise so heaped, Michael Henry jumps in for what he thinks is the kill. His argument is that because GLE paid Wiggin for the due diligence, GLE was thereby Wiggin's client, and Wiggin therefore had a duty of care to GLE which they totally and abjectly failed to cherish. What! So when you pay the other side's legal fees in a deal, their lawyers are actually your lawyers? I'm confused, and so is the judge, who tries to précis Michael Henry, is corrected by him and shows a little edge

"What is your point, Mr Henry?"

And his point is this: Wiggin relied on something Michael Henry had sent them, without confirming back to Michael Henry that they were so doing.

"How can you rely on something someone has said or written without telling them you are relying on it?" He asks rhetorically. Well to my mind, if that someone is out to deceive, you absolutely cannot, and should not. Michael Henry continues in this vein all day, and by the end of it he still is not done. The judge has spent most of her time looking at the clock, but Henry ignores this and plods on. The agreed schedule goes out of the window and everyone checks diaries for the following week. I believe he is filibustering, reducing the opposition's time with the witnesses, narrowing their window for summing up. The judge is careful, for any suggestion that the two litigants in person have failed to get the time they need to present their case could leave grounds for an appeal, and nobody wants that.

But the questioning of Neil Gillard, although boring, begins to illuminate Chris and Michael's duplicity. In August they were desperate to do a deal with Sara, who looked at the projected revenues for the concert and decided to invest. She did so on the basis of three pillars: the involvement of the Black Eyed Peas, a sponsor and a Facebook stream which promised to be huge. As she made clear when questioned on the stand by her own side, she underpinned these three absolute requirements with a plethora of conditions, security agreements, charges over everything, approved cashflows and crucially, full and comprehensive music clearance, especially of the Warner Chappell operated catalogue. Sara was also assured that the sponsorship deal needed only ink from the Peas to itself become locked down, and once in the Peas were covered by insurance for non-performance. Fuck. No wonder she was, in the American meaning of the word, pissed.

Then the Peas pulled out, as a result the sponsor walked away and finally the live to air transmission by Facebook had to be canned because of Warner Chappell's injunction. This left only the Sky UK transmission as a guaranteed screening, which at seventy grand was a little short of QuickDraw's five million pound investment. The only other revenue was from the ticket sales, and Sara had secured that money right at the start.

On the third day, Sara takes to the witness box. Michael Henry tries to impugn Sara's honesty, but manages only to show the lack of his own. The judge loses patience, asking again and again where he is going with his line of questioning about the disparity between the fifty film credits she claimed in her witness statement and the thirty he found online, about her directorship of a company back in 1993. It's poor and it's irrelevant, except to show a desperate man clutching at straws.

For the umpteenth time the judge stops him. The sun blazes through the high courtroom windows and the air conditioning has given up and gone home. We are all wilting in the warmth, and Henry is struggling to find an email in the mass of evidence.

"I'm sorry to interrupt you again Mr Henry" Her Eminence interjects for the umpteenth time, and the whole courtroom anticipates a sending down, a final, judicially invoked end to the nonsense spouted by him all day. But we are disappointed, and instead transported back to the eighteenth century, as Her Frownness continues:

"I personally find it enormously, extraordinarily hot in this courtroom. It may be just me, and I was going to encourage counsel, therefore, if they would like to take off their wigs, rather than faint to do so, and I also propose to take off my gown and I apologise for that, but I really am unbelievably hot, so I hope that you don't mind and if counsel need to do the same, please don't hesitate to do so. I think we can suffer such a degree of informality in order to stay alive. I'm sure I will be able to concentrate much better now, Mr Henry."

With the relative nakedness approved, the wigs go back into their biscuit tins and the trial continues.

From the week before the concert to the middle of October, and despite Chris taking the Peas money, Sara tried to work with him and Michael to turn the thing around. She had some serious contacts in the business, she had alternate sponsors interested, and she did everything she could to help. Chris would have none of it. For him, this was interference, and a challenge to his authority. Sara was to be kept in her box, literally. (Sara had been allocated a VIP box right on the other side of the stadium from the President's lounge, and both Chris and Michael Henry made every effort to keep her there and away from the Jackson family, the artists and the other investors. Not the proper way, in my book, to treat your most important financier).

"She told me to breach any agreement I had to" he told me and later the court. A more classic case of hearing things the way you yourself would say them is hard to find. Sara was urging Chris to <u>reach</u> agreements with his other investors, with

Jeffré, with the estate and with Warner Chappell. She was telling him to do a deal, work the way she worked, be inclusive; but what Chris heard was a spur to combat, a cry to go to war.

His battleground was ownership of the film. Once Sara decided the only way forward was to stop Chris giving the film away to Sky and so completely devaluing the product, Chris believed his only available action was to place ownership of the film into Iambic. He therefore had to retrofit this new construct into the original deals done back in the spring and summer of 2011, and in this he was aided and abetted by Michael Henry.

Henry wrote to Wiggin in September, when negotiating for the funding he so desperately needed, that GLE absolutely held all rights to the exploitation of the concert in all media. This was, after all, the entirety of the asset, the potential source of all the revenue other than ticket sales. But what was fact in September was now completely at odds with the new truth, according to which Iambic actually owned the film and not GLE. So Henry's defence was to insist that what he said in September was actually not what he said, and to rely on a statement at the bottom of his emails which stated:

This email contains no legally binding commitments or representations.

I paraphrase that as "you cannot believe a word I have written in my email". Michael Henry, clearly of the same view, asks Sara in cross examination:

"How can you possibly claim you are relying on a representation when it's expressly excluded?"

"I don't understand" she replies "Should I just say – No, sorry, you have this disclaimer so I can't move forward with this at all? I have to rely on it in order to have any kind of meaningful conversation"

His third line of defence, already mentioned, was to present a professional failure by Wiggin to spot the disclaimer as the root cause of the 'misunderstanding', and for them to foolishly suppose that the phrase 'all media' actually meant all media. Film and television were not specifically listed, so how could 'all media' include them?

"How can you rely on anything I have written, unless you confirm to me you are relying on it?" he repeatedly asked the court. At the time of course, in early September when he was desperate for the money, the film rights did rest with GLE. It was only after the concert, when Chris and Michael were fighting to get the ticket money into Iambic, that the new construct, in which Iambic had always owned the film, was created. This crucial email to Sara in September, stating that GLE owned the film, by late October had become a bit of a stumbling block in the new fiction Chris and Michael had spun. The best they could do was to argue that 'all media' does not actually mean what the whole entertainment world takes it to mean, and that the disclaimer at the bottom of the email meant the email didn't mean anything either!

The commissioning agreement, the one in which GLE hired Iambic to produce the recordings, also didn't fit the new reality, for what is the need for a commissioning document if Iambic already owns the rights? Clearly the document was an embarrassment, so Chris terminated the agreement on the grounds that there had been no live to air transmission and therefore no production existed that was commissioned by GLE. This was the point that confused us all at the CVA meeting a few weeks back. When Chris was arguing there was no production, this is what he meant. He had also applied some television custom and practice to support his position. When a producer is commissioned by a broadcaster to make a TV programme, he retains the rights to the programme outside of the uses the broadcaster wants. The fact that the broadcaster chooses not to screen the programme, (or as in this instance GLE are unable to transmit), had no bearing, Chris argued, to his right to the materials he was creating. Furthermore, the commissioning agreement also specified a programme of between ninety minutes and two hours for cinematic release. This was never made, so the agreement was null and void.

Defending himself over the taking of the ticket money, Chris tries the 'I did it for the good of the project' approach. He asks Sara how the funding gap got closed. She replies:

"...given there seem to be a lot of creditors who have not been paid to the tune of millions, I don't see why there was a shortage of money, so I believe it got closed by a lot of people who should have been paid not being paid". This was not the answer he wanted. Throughout the trial Sara was the only one who repeatedly pointed out that a lot of people were still owed a lot of money.

The thorny problem of the alleged copyright breaches remained. Chris attempted to resolve the script issues by suggesting the script was irrelevant, contributed to by the artists themselves, developed by dozens of people including himself. As for the Michael Forever logo, undisputedly the property of GLE, its use in Iambic's alternate programme bereft of Warner Chappell songs did not occur. Chris had changed the logo for a different one, slightly different colour, different words. He changed it, he argued on oath, because he didn't like the original, because the new one worked better on television. Puh-lease. If you're gonna re-badge, don't just change the colour and the words a little, change the whole fucking thing in to a tiara of spin or something. It was weak, and Alfie Molina jumped on it like a ton of bricks.

Neither Michael Henry nor Chris Hunt made good witnesses. The inconsistencies between documents, understandings and communications prior to the breakdown in relationships between QuickDraw and the defendants, and the new realities as presented by the pair since late October, were cracks that the two wigs chipped away at.

I helped a little, in a hastily scheduled chat with the wigs following one appalling lie trotted out by Chris (the one where GLE only had a right to two narrowly defined programmes of the concert and Iambic owned everything else) and offered my understanding of the two defendants. Under pressure, I told them, Chris would turn bright red, and little spots of ginger would appear on his face. Michael, I said, is prone to snapping, making an idiot of himself if repeatedly challenged. His sense of his own intellect gets affronted, I added.

A fine example of how Chris' web of deceit was built can be seen with his actions over the performer contracts. All the artists were contracted by GLE, and they licenced their performance rights in the concert for three years for exploitation in all media to GLE. Not, you notice, to Iambic. This was a potential difficulty so in late October Chris sent out letters to all the agents requesting reassignment of these licences to Iambic, but worded in a way to present this reassignment merely as a confirmation of what had been agreed, rather than a new agreement for a different company to make a different film. All but one artist ignored him. Molina asked why Mr Hunt believed he needed this 're-confirmation' and Chris responded, little flecks of bursting colour duly forming on his cheeks, that there was a failure of the production team on the day of the concert to get the artists to sign the necessary releases! So Christina Aguilera, Jamie Foxx, Gladys Knight and all the other stars, despite having signed a deal to perform, having agreed to have their performance recorded, having turned up and delivered, also should have filled in a release form normally handed to extras and passers-by caught on camera incidentally!

Never in all my years, have I heard such bollocks. He went on to blame me, Dawn, his formerly most trusted elf (the one that resigned because she could no longer bear it) and David Mallet. All of us had failed him in some way, leaving him to have to pick up the pieces with the artists and the music rights. We were the idiots, and our errors were the reasons for the inconsistencies the silks were exposing. The man by now is such a deep purple that a beetroot next to him would appear off colour.

Alf Molina keeps digging, with first Michael then Chris in the witness chair. Did GLE grant Iambic the right to make the Sky programme? Did the investors in GLE know that the most valuable assets to be created at the concert, the recordings, did not actually belong to GLE at all? Were David Bailey and the other investors aware of that when putting money in the show? Michael Henry assures us he told them, but the barrister believes none of it.

"Mr Henry, it is as plain as a pikestaff that you set out to deceive my client. Your testimony is riddled with untruths and I have a mind to ask the judge to strike your entire evidence on the grounds you are not a credible witness"

Michael Henry goes quite pale. His entire career as a lawyer is on the line. The silks are pushing hard, no doubt trying to see if I'm right and Henry will self immolate in a fit of spleen. David Bailey springs to his defence.

"I am David Bailey", he wobbles from the back of the court, "and I can vouch for everything Mr Henry is saying". Her Highness looks daggers at him. The court clerk is on her feet, about to lance him with a switched off mobile phone. Alf Molina ignores him, so the investor tries again. He is silenced by the judge and threatened with removal if he persists.

Against the onslaught from wig one Chris holds his own, at least in defence to the first charge, the misappropriation of the refund from the Black Eyed Peas. Not because his arguments are any stronger, but because QuickDraw's case is weaker. The contract was between GLE and the Peas, so when the Peas pulled out, it was not un-natural to refund the money to GLE, especially as the reason for QuickDraw paying the money was one of efficiency and speed. Unfortunately, Chris did not tell Sara the Peas had pulled out until a few days after the event, when the money was already back in GLE's account. When the Peas dropped away, the sponsor dropped too, and with them two pillars of Sara's reason for investment. Naturally she became somewhat nervous, and in that state wanted the Peas money returned safely in QuickDraw's account. But it was too late, and she became a very angry lady indeed.

My witness statement, in which I recounted a conversation with Chris about this very subject, a conversation during which he told me he was working hard to get the Peas money refunded to GLE and not Sara, was trotted out as part of the evidence. Chris disagreed.

"In fact, I disagree with much of Mr Picheta's witness statement, and I would have welcomed the opportunity to ask him about it, but you didn't call him", he tells Daniel Craig.

I offered, but Sara's team saw me as a liability. It would

have been nerve wracking, and I would have been close to hysteria and tears, but God would I have welcomed the opportunity to formally call Chris a liar to his face.

The second charge, the taking of the Stadium Events ticket revenue into Iambic after the concert, was harder to justify. Chris and Michael here relied on two parallel defences. The first was a single phone call between Sara and Michael Henry, in which he claimed she told him she would release the incoming ticket monies. The barristers asked whether Henry recalled receiving dozens of emails listing the conditions required for her to even consider risking additional sums, and whether he remembered a two hour call with Wiggin, made after the supposed call with Sara, in which they went through these requirements again. Henry however, insisted a verbal deal had been done. Using Sara's misheard assertion to 'breach any agreement' as a call to action, they breached their agreement with her that all ticket receipts were subject to a charge by QuickDraw. They tried to support this by arguing that because Sara had not acted when they took the Black Eyed Peas money, she had set a precedent which allowed them to take the ticket funds.

The other defence was a convoluted argument delivered by Michael Henry concerning events immediately after the concert. Sara was trying to work with the pair to resolve the problems they faced, and indeed was considering putting more money in to help GLE get through the latest, post show crisis. She didn't see the Sky broadcast as a priority, indeed she thought it was a mistake, but nevertheless was willing to support the project with more cash. Of course she required collateral, and given Chris' behaviour over the Peas refund was looking hard at what was being proposed. Chris and Michael trotted out a VAT return, ticket sales and, most crucially, some sales estimates from the US distributor. Sara discounted these as there was no evidence they were based on deals on the table, just guesses as to what the film might be worth. With no visible way to get her five million back, let alone anything to secure a further input of cash against, Sara decided she could not further support the project. She had no obligation to invest more, and had honoured her side of the deal. Unable to give Sara the collateral she required, and realising the QuickDraw lifeline to further funding was being withdrawn, on October 19th they took the ticket money. Michael Henry wrote an email to Jeffré, which Jeffré sent to Tix-Me as if from him, instructing them to pay the ticket receipts to Iambic. Chris then rescinded the commissioning agreement and claimed GLE had no rights in the film materials.

Sara acted immediately to seize all GLE assets. She called in her debenture over the GLE bank accounts and set about finding and getting hold of the film. She also persuaded Sky not to broadcast it. Even as she was doing this she was trying to prevail on Chris and Michael to stop fighting her and work together. A delayed Facebook stream a week or so after the show could still prove very successful, but less so if Sky broadcast the whole thing first for free. But Chris was now in a bunker deeper than ever before, and could see nothing but the red mist of hate, a filter so thick that it obscured the chance for any reconciliation.

Finally we reach the summing up. Michael's delaying tactics have failed, and the two QuickDraw barristers were able to present the entirety of their case. They even had time to cross examine David Bailey in the witness box, having agreed to accept a hastily written witness statement in support of

Henry. Bailey blusters and blathers, his voice gets more squeaky, and further belies his bulk, as Molina grills him mercilessly.

"I find it inconceivable Mr Bailey, that you and the other investors were happy for the most valuable asset from the concert to be given away to Iambic".

"It was the icing on the cake for us. We invested for the fifteen percent premium".

I doubt even he believed what he was saying.

The professionals are first to sum up. They are dismissive towards the defendants;

"We ask your ladyship to approach the evidence of Mr Henry and Mr Hunt with great caution, and invite you to disregard anything they have said unless corroborated in documents not prepared by them."

Then the killer blow:

"Should your ladyship find for the defendants in the matter of the copyright of the film, then it must follow that they were deceitful and made false representations in the email of September 3rd in which they made assurances to QuickDraw as to the assets and rights owned by GLE, in order to secure the investment". This is a very neat reversal of Chris' postulation of his position whether there was or was not a production. In either case, back at the CVA, he was telling us we would get our money. Now Sara's lawyers have just told the court, that if there was a production he nicked the film, and if there wasn't he nicked QuickDraw's money.

Michael Henry is next, presenting a summation of his defence based on his email disclaimer, his assertion that all media does not mean film and television, and in regard to a second investment by Sara, the offer of a deal is a deal.

Somewhere along the line he throws in the Oxford English Dictionary of the word 'exploit'. His daughter, a pretty girl in her twenties in court for the first time, flees the room in tears.

Finally Chris, reminding the court yet again he's not a lawyer, suggests that he and Michael Henry are either the Moriarty twins, master criminals concocting a complex conspiracy, or they are innocent producers just doing their best. In my mind they are neither, just two chancers who got in way over their heads, and messed with the wrong woman trying to get out. I found the following passage in Joseph Conrad's Edge of Darkness, about Belgian prospectors in the Congo:

> "They called themselves the El Dorado Exploring Expedition...their talk was of sordid buccaneers: It was reckless without hardihood, greedy without audacity and cruel without courage. There was not an atom of foresight or of serious intention in the whole batch of them and they did not seem aware these things were wanted for the work of the world. To tear treasure out of the bowels of the land was their desire with no moral purpose at the back of it than there is with burglars breaking into a safe"

I stand outside the courtroom, saddened and empty. What a total tragedy. The final words of the judge warned us all judgment would not be speedy. She had much to chew over, and her decision would affect not just this trial, but the Warner Chappell hearing to come, stayed until her judgment. Chris and Michael believed Warner Chappell had no case, that the judge back in October was wrong to injunct the live broadcast and that twenty million quid was coming their way in lost revenue. Will everyone get paid if that comes to pass? I very much doubt it. Even if Warner Chappell are found to have been wrong, and a damages claim by Chris against them is successful, the money will go to GLE, under the control of Sara, and QuickDraw, and not to the two men.

Chris and Michael use integrity as a tool of business, not as a way of conducting themselves in life. Even if they do get lucky, I'll be surprised to see a penny of what I'm owed, now I am firmly in the enemy camp. But I wouldn't have it any other way, and I like to think that next time, I'll act sooner.

Sara needs to be in charge of the future of *Michael Forever*, and as I deeply breathe in the clear air of honesty that at last begins to surround the project, she has my complete support in getting there. It is web posts like the one below that make me believe Sara is in with a shot. This blind faith of a committed fan makes me cry with guilt and frustration that we let her down, and fills me with humility that she still has faith. If Ms Martinez is willing to give *Michael Forever* another chance, then so, hopefully, will the Estate, Warner Chappell and all the Michael Jackson fans who rightly sensed something was off.

Vivienne Martinez: Waiting oh so patiently 2 view this on DVD!!! I'm not giving up hope :) the night was the most fabulous tribute fit 4 a King!!! So blessed 2 have been a part of it. I'll check in again in a bit and see if any progress had been made.

EPILOGUE
Every path you take you're leaving your legacy

July 2012

The Dutch company that provided the 3D TV facilities for the concert place a winding up order on Iambic Limited. Chris' company Iambic will be forcibly liquidated by the courts, it's assets seized. Unless Chris pays them, of course.

Katherine Jackson goes missing, somewhere in America. The kids appeal to their Grandmother to come home. The Jackson brothers blame the Estate for cruel and unreasonable behaviour towards her. Paris Jackson begins to assert her independence, and her aunties Janet and La Toya bear the brunt. Jeffré, like Katherine, remains invisible.

Judgment is handed down in the High Court in London. Sara Giles and QuickDraw win on all three counts. Chris Hunt and Michael Henry are dishonest and deceitful, The Law has said.
They took the money, they tried to take the film, and The Law has said they were wrong to do so. They'll also have to pay damages and probably return the ticket money they took, as well as give back the Black Eyed Peas refund. An expensive couple of weeks for Chris and Michael; I hope they thought it was worth it. They could have done a deal, but they chose a shit-fight and lost. Arseholes.

Unfortunately for those owed money by the pair, their actions have made the chance of getting paid even more remote. Millions have been added to the total by legal fees and penalties for non-payment of the QuickDraw loan. Months have gone by with the film locked away and forgotten. These things have a moment, and to recreate it, rekindle it, will be a hard road to travel.

But Sara has a plan: She wants to give the film to Prince and Paris, so they can make it into their own tribute to their father. Maybe then, the fans will accept those Cardiff performances, orchestrated by Ron Weisner, for what they are, pure tributes to the musical memory of the world's greatest pop star. Maybe the children, once used by Jeffré and Chris and Michael Henry to give credence to a malformed project built on greed, are the only ones who can wash the stench of deceit from it and turn it into something worthwhile, meaningful and pure.

Something Michael would actually support.

We'll see.

Printed in Great Britain
by Amazon